D1353021

GEORGE GREEN LIBRARY OF
SCIENCE AND ENGINEERING

BRE
Garston, Watford
WD2 7JR

Environmental site layout planning:

solar access, microclimate
and passive cooling
in urban areas

P J Littlefair, M Santamouris, S Alvarez,

A Dupagne, D Hall, J Teller, J F Coronel,

N Papanikolaou

University of Nottingham

Prices for all available
BRE publications can
be obtained from:
CRC Ltd
151 Rosebery Avenue
London EC1R 4GB
Tel   0171 505 6622
Fax 0171 505 6606
E-mail
crc@construct.emap.co.uk

BR 380
ISBN 1 86081 339 9

© Copyright BRE 2000
except illustrations as noted
First published 2000

Published by
Construction Research
Communications Ltd
by permission of
Building Research
Establishment Ltd

Applications to copy all
or any part of this
publication should be
made to:
CRC Ltd , PO Box 202
Watford WD2 7QG

Front cover illustration:
Aerial view of the Santa
Cruz district of Seville,
Spain. The photograph has
been digitally enhanced to
emphasize building edges
and vegetation.

This work has been partly
funded by the UK
Department of the
Environment, Transport
and the Regions (DETR).
Any views expressed are
not necessarily those of
the DETR.

Reports on CD

BRE material is also published quarterly on CD

Each CD contains:
● BRE reports published in the current year
(accumulating throughout the year)
● A special feature:
usually a themed compilation of BRE publications
(for example on foundations or timber decay)

The CD collection gives you the opportunity to build a
comprehensive library of BRE material at a fraction of
the cost of printed copies.
As a subscriber you also benefit from a 20% discount
on other BRE titles.

For more information contact:
CRC Customer Services on 0171 505 6622

Construction Research Communications

CRC supplies a wide range of building and
construction related information products from
BRE and other highly respected organisations.

Contact:
by post: CRC Ltd
           151 Rosebery Avenue
           London EC1R 4GB

by fax: 0171 505 6606
by phone: 0171 505 6622
by email: crc@construct.emap.co.uk

Preface

This book is the principal output of a project to develop guidance on site layout planning to improve solar access, passive cooling and microclimate. The project is jointly funded by the European Commission JOULE programme and national funding agencies including the UK Department of the Environment, Transport and the Regions. The European project is coordinated by BRE and includes the University of Athens, LEMA (University of Liege) and AICIA (University of Seville).

The main objective of this publication, and indeed of the whole project, is to produce comprehensive design guidance on urban layout to ensure good access to solar gain, daylighting and passive cooling. The aim is to enable designers to produce comfortable, energy-efficient buildings surrounded by pleasant outdoor spaces, within an urban context that minimizes energy consumption and the effects of pollution.

This book is divided into six main chapters. Chapter 1 sets the scene, outlining the importance of each of the main environmental factors affecting site layout. Chapters 2–6 then cover the urban design process, from the selection of a site for a new development down to the design and landscaping of individual buildings and the spaces around them.

Chapter 2 therefore begins by considering the environmental issues affecting site location. It will be particularly valuable for urban planners setting out environmental structure plans for their cities and towns. It will also be of value to developers who have a range of different sites from which to choose the location of a development. Chapter 3, on public open spaces, is also principally aimed at urban planners and designers of multi-building developments. It covers a range of issues on the design of groups of buildings and the external spaces they generate around them.

Chapter 4 focuses on the design of individual groups of buildings. It will be of particular interest to building designers and development control officers. A key issue, dealt with fully here, is how the new building affects the environmental quality of existing buildings nearby. Chapter 5 links in with this, showing how built form can impact the quality of the building itself and its immediate surroundings.

Finally, Chapter 6 will be of particular interest to landscape designers. It deals with the selection and design of vegetation and hard landscaping to modify microclimate in the spaces immediately surrounding buildings.

Europe covers a wide range of climate types and not all the techniques described in this book will be applicable to all of them. Section 1.13 will be especially useful here. It describes the range of climate types in Europe and the heating and cooling requirements in each, with a summary of layout strategies. The book refers to a range of prediction tools which can help evaluate the environmental impacts of buildings and groups of buildings. These are described briefly in Appendices A and B and references are given. Finally, Appendix C contains a glossary of technical terms used.

PJL

Acknowledgements

This guide was produced as part of the POLIS project coordinated by BRE and sponsored by the European Commission's JOULE programme. BRE's contribution was also funded by the UK Department of Environment, Transport and the Regions.

We would like to thank the following people who contributed to the research work on which the guide is based:

Emma Dewey, Angela Spanton and Steven Walker (BRE),

Aris Tsagrassoulis and Irene Koronaki (University of Athens),

Francisco J Sanchez and Alejandro Quijano (University of Seville), and

James Desmecht and Sleiman Azar (University of Liege).

Eric Keeble (BRE) drafted part of an earlier report on which some of this guide is based.

The following provided valuable assistance:

the Environmental Department of Seville Town Hall,

the Culture Section of the *Junta de Andalucía*,

the Spanish National Meteorological Institute, and

the residents of the Santa Cruz district of Seville who cooperated in the case study there.

Their help is gratefully acknowledged.

100601624)

About the authors

Paul J Littlefair MA PhD CEng MCIBSE

Principal Scientist, BRE Centre for Environmental Engineering, BRE, Bucknalls Lane, Garston, Watford, Hertfordshire, WD2 7JR, UK
Email: littlefairp@bre.co.uk

Matheos Santamouris

Assistant Professor, Physics Department, University of Athens, 157484 Athens, Greece
Email: msantam@atlas.uoa.gr

Servando Alvarez

Profesor Titular de Universidad, Universidad de Sevilla, Escuela Superior de Ingenieros, Camino de los Descubrimientos s/n, E-41092, Sevilla, Spain
Email:sad@tmt.us.es

Albert Dupagne

Professor, LEMA, University of Liege, chemin des Chevreuils 1, Bât. B52, B-4000 Liege, Belgium
Email: albert.dupagne@ulg.ac.be

David Hall BEng PhD CEng MRAeS CMet

Associate, BRE, Bucknalls Lane, Garston, Watford, Hertfordshire, WD2 7JR, UK
Email: halld@bre.co.uk

Jacques Teller

Research Engineer, LEMA, University of Liege, chemin des Chevreuils 1, Bât. B52,
B-4000 Liege, Belgium
Email: jacques.teller@ulg.ac.be

Juan Francisco Coronel

Engineer, Universidad de Sevilla, Escuela Superior de Ingenieros, Camino de los
Descubrimientos s/n, E-41092, Sevilla, Spain
Email:jfc@tmt.us.es

Nikolaos Papanikolaou

Formerly Physicist, University of Athens, 157484 Athens, Greece

Contents

1 Introduction

1.1 Definition of problem and energy issues

Cities are growing rapidly, and it is estimated that by 2000 over half the world's population will be living in urban areas, whereas 100 years ago only 14% did so. Today's cities are increasingly polluted and uncomfortable places to be. Industrialization, the concentrated activities of city dwellers and the rapid increase in motor traffic are the main contributors to increases in energy consumption and air pollution, and deteriorating environment and climatic quality. Urban areas without a high climatic quality use much more energy for air conditioning in summer and for heating in winter and more electricity for lighting. The urban heat island effect can cause temperature differences of up to 5–15 °C between a European city centre and its surroundings, resulting in increased demand for cooling energy (see section 1.3). In southern Europe sales of air-conditioning equipment rose by around 25–30% during the period 1985–1990[1.1.1]. Increased urban temperatures also exacerbate pollution by accelerating the production of photochemical smog; US data[1.1.2] suggest that a 10% increase in the number of polluted days may occur for each 3 °C rise in temperature.

Consequently, new developments are often planned as 'climate rejecting'- sealed, air-conditioned, deep plan, with tinted glass to cut out solar gain and daylight. Such developments may then further worsen the local microclimate; air conditioning results in extra thermal emissions to the surroundings, reflective glass (Figure 1.1.1) reflects solar heat and glare black out, and large, bulky buildings create hostile local wind effects and overshadow neighbouring buildings which depend on daylight. The result is a vicious circle of worsening exterior environment and spiralling energy costs.

There is another way, however, which aims to modulate the external climate and maximize the use of renewable energies. This strategy involves planning the layout of buildings to allow adequate access to solar heat gain and daylighting, and in warmer climates to promote passive cooling. Good urban layout design will also provide an attractive exterior environment, pleasantly sunlit and sheltered from the wind in colder latitudes, cool and shaded in hotter climates in summer, with breezes to disperse pollutants.

CEC programmes like 'Project Monitor'[1.1.3] and the European Passive Solar Handbook[1.1.4] have demonstrated the benefits of solar design in reducing energy dependence on fossil fuels and providing a benign local climate within developments. The challenge is now to adapt and widen these technologies so that they can be used within dense urban sites. Solar building design needs to come to terms with this issue, making the most of obstructed urban sites rather than using up scarce open land.

The potential benefits are immense. Of principal importance are the Europe-wide energy benefits following uptake of the climate-sensitive design. In northern Europe, passive solar gain and daylighting reduce the need for heating and lighting energy (Figure 1.1.2). UK studies of passive solar

Figure 1.1.1 Tinted glass reflects solar heat and glare

Figure 1.1.2 Passive solar housing

housing[1.1.5] suggest that improved site layout can save 5% or more in domestic energy consumption. In non-domestic buildings, the exploitation of daylight can lead to savings of 40% or more in lighting energy use[1.1.6]. In southern Europe, passive cooling becomes vitally important. Air-conditioned buildings typically consume 50% more energy than naturally ventilated buildings, and in southern Europe their maximum cooling demand coincides with times of peak general electricity consumption, resulting in utilities having to build extra power stations and increase the cost of electricity.

There are also significant potential environmental benefits (apart from reduction in carbon dioxide emissions), although these are less quantifiable in financial terms. They arise from the improved local climate in outdoor spaces, resulting in health benefits as well as extra amenity. This in turn can lead to savings in transport, as inner cities become more attractive places to live in as well as work.

This Guide is the result of three year's research work on the POLIS project, sponsored jointly by the European Commission's JOULE research programme and by national funding agencies including the UK Department of the Environment, Transport and the Regions (DETR). It forms part of a four-volume set of outputs. Two are design tools, a computer software package (Figure 1.1.3) and a set of manual aids, to assist designers and urban planners in exploring the possibilities of passive renewal of urban districts in different European contexts and climates. They are described in Appendices A1 and A2, respectively. The final volume describes case studies on making the most of renewable energy in selected real urban areas (Figure 1.1.4).

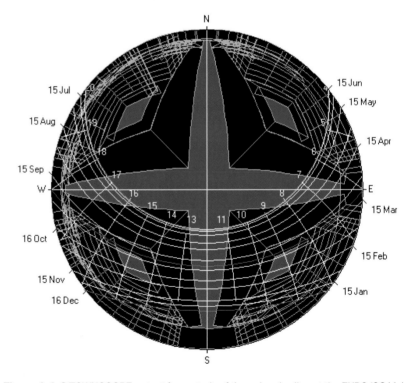

Figure 1.1.3 TOWNSCOPE output from study of the solar shading at the EXPO '98 Lisboa site. © University of Liege

Figure 1.1.4 The EXPO '92 case study site, Seville, Spain. © University of Seville

References to section 1.1

[1.1.1] Santamouris M & Wouters P. Energy and indoor climate in Europe: past and present. *Proceedings 1st European Conference on Energy Performance and Indoor Environment,* Lyon, 1996.

[1.1.2] Akbari H, Davis S, Dorsano S, Huang J & Winett S. *Cooling our communities: a guidebook on tree planting and light colored surfacing.* Washington, Office of Policy Analysis, Climate Change Division, US Environmental Protection Agency, January 1992.

[1.1.3] University College Dublin for CEC. *Project Monitor: case studies in passive solar architecture.* University College, 1989.

[1.1.4] Goulding J R, Lewis J O & Steemers T C. *Energy in architecture.* London, Batsford, 1992.

[1.1.5] NBA Tectonics. *A study of passive solar housing estate layout.* Report S 1126, Harwell, Energy Technology Support Unit, NBA Tectonics, 1988.

[1.1.6] Crisp V H C, Littlefair P J, Copper I & McKennan G. *Daylighting as a passive solar energy option: an assessment of its potential in non-domestic buildings.* BRE Report BR 129. Garston, CRC, 1988.

1.2 How to use this book

This book is divided into six main chapters. Chapter 1 sets the scene, outlining the importance of each of the main environmental factors affecting site layout. Chapters 2–6 then cover the urban design process, from the selection of a site for a new development to the design and landscaping of individual buildings and the spaces around them.

Chapter 2 begins by considering the environmental issues affecting site location. It will be particularly valuable for urban planners setting out environmental structure plans for their cities and towns. It will also be of value to developers who have a range of different sites from which to choose the location of a development. Chapter 3, on public open space, is also principally aimed at urban planners and designers of multi-building developments. It covers a range of issues concerned with the design of groups of buildings and the external spaces they generate around them.

Chapter 4 focuses on the design of individual groups of buildings. It will be of particular interest to building designers and development control officers. A key issue, dealt with fully here, is how the new building affects the environmental quality of existing buildings nearby. Chapter 5 links in with this, showing how built form can impact the quality of the building itself and its immediate surroundings.

Warm (cooling-dominated) climates

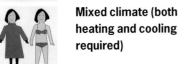

Cool (heating-dominated) climates

Mixed climate (both heating and cooling required)

Finally, Chapter 6 will be of particular interest to landscape designers. It deals with the selection and design of vegetation and hard landscaping to modify microclimate in the spaces immediately surrounding buildings.

Europe covers a wide range of climate types and not all the techniques described in this book will be applicable to all of them. Throughout the book, the symbols (left) show which climate types the advice is aimed at.

Section 1.13 (at the end of this chapter) will be especially useful here. It describes the range of climate types in Europe and the heating and cooling requirements in each, with a summary of layout strategies. Designers without detailed local knowledge of an area may find it helpful to start with this chapter.

The book refers to a range of prediction tools which can help evaluate the environmental impacts of buildings and groups of buildings. These are described briefly in Appendices A and B and full references are given. Finally, Appendix C contains a glossary of technical terms used.

1.3 Urban climate

The city creates its own climate. Air temperatures in densely built urban areas are higher than the temperatures of the surrounding rural country. This phenomenon known as 'heat island', is due to many factors:
- the geometry of city streets means long wave radiation is exchanged between buildings rather than lost to the sky, and short wave radiation is more likely to be absorbed,
- heat stored in the fabric of the city,
- anthropogenic heat released from combustion of fuels and from people and animals,
- long wave radiation is trapped in the polluted and warmer urban atmosphere (the urban greenhouse),
- less evaporative cooling by vegetation,
- less wind cooling within streets.

In colder climates the heat island effect can be beneficial, reducing heating demands. Towns like Trondheim have created artificial 'heat islands' by covering over streets. But in warmer climates the heat island effect can significantly worsen outdoor comfort and the energy consumption of buildings.

The intensity of the heat island can be up to 10 °C or more. The bigger the city, the more intense the effect (Figure 1.3.1)[1.3.1]. The expected heat island intensity for a city of one million inhabitants is close to 8 and 12 °C in Europe and the US, respectively. Higher values for the American cities arise from the taller buildings and higher densities in the city centres.

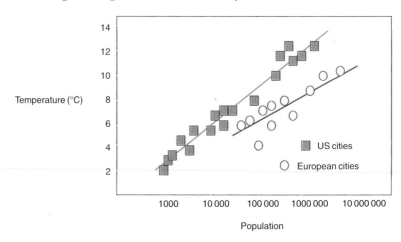

Figure 1.3.1 Maximum difference in urban and rural temperatures for US and European cities. Data from Oke[1.3.1]

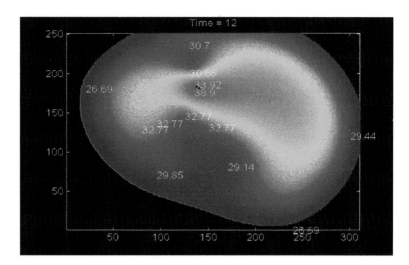

Figure 1.3.2 Temperature distribution around the central Athens area at 12:00, 1st August 1996. © University of Athens

The results from our monitoring in Athens agree with these temperature differences. Figure 1.3.2 shows the spatial temperature distribution in the central Athens area at noon on 1 August 1996. The central Athens area is about 7–8 °C warmer than the surrounding area, while at Ippokratous street, with its high traffic density, the temperature difference is close to 12–13 °C. An important finding was that the biggest temperature differences between the city and its surroundings occurred on the hottest days.

Worryingly, it appears that the heat island effect is getting worse. Analysis[1.3.2] of average and maximum annual temperatures in cities in the USA and Asia shows a steady increase over the years (Table 1.3.1).

The rise in temperature in cities results in much higher cooling loads. Table 1.3.2 compares cooling degree days for urban and rural stations[1.3.3]. Cooling degree days can be almost doubled in some city centres. This has a tremendous impact on the energy consumption of buildings for cooling. The higher temperatures also result in lower efficiency of cooling plant.

However, results from the POLIS project have shown that urban design can have a significant impact on urban climate. By appropriate urban design it is possible to limit or even reverse the heat island effect. In the Athens studies, the national park, located at the centre of the city, had much lower temperature differences compared with the suburbs, while low temperature differences were also recorded in a main pedestrian street.

Results from monitoring of the Santa Cruz district in Seville (Figure 1.3.3) were even more startling. During the day the average air temperature was

Table 1.3.1 Measured temperature trends in selected cities.
Data from Akbari et al[1.3.2]

City	Trend (°C /decade)	Type of temperature data
Los Angeles	0.7	Highs
Los Angeles	0.4	Means
San Francisco	0.1	Means
Oakland	0.2	Means
San Jose	0.2	Means
San Diego	0.4	Means
Sacramento	0.2	Means
Washington	0.3	Means
Baltimore	0.2	Means
Fort Lauderdale	0.1	Means
Shanghai	0.07	Means
Shanghai	0.1	Minima
Tokyo	0.3	Means

Table 1.3.2 Increase of the cooling degree (°C) days due to urbanization and heat island effects. Averages for selected locations for the period 1941–1970.
Data from Taha[1.3.3]

Location	Urban	Airport	Difference (%)
Los Angeles	368	191	92
Washington DC	440	361	21
St Louis	510	459	11
New York	333	268	24
Baltimore	464	344	35
Seattle	111	72	54
Detroit	416	366	14
Chicago	463	372	24
Denver	416	350	19

Figure 1.3.3 The Santa Cruz district of Seville. © University of Seville

some 4–8 °C lower than at the reference station at the airport. This is an area with traditional architecture and narrow pedestrian streets.

Further details on the impact of urban layout on temperature are contained in sections 2.2 and 2.7. The following sections describe techniques to reduce or reverse the effects of urban climate: 4.5 (mutual shading), 5.3 (courtyard design), 6.2 (shading by vegetation), 6.4 (ponds and fountains) and 6.5 (albedo).

References to section 1.3

[1.3.1] Oke T R. Overview of interactions between settlements and their environments. *WMO experts meeting on Urban and building climatology.* WCP-37. World Meteorological Organization (WMO), Geneva, 1982.

[1.3.2] Akbari H, Davis S, Dorsano S, Huang J & Winett S. *Cooling our communities: a guidebook on tree planting and light colored surfacing.* Washington, Office of Policy Analysis, Climate Change Division, US Environmental Protection Agency. January 1992.

[1.3.3] Taha H. Urban climates and heat islands: albedo, evapotranspiration, and anthropogenic heat. *Energy and Buildings* 1997: **25**: 99–103.

1.4 Light from the sky

In a wide range of building types, access to natural light is vital. People generally prefer to work by daylight[1.4.1] and to have their homes lit by daylight. Daylight enhances the appearance of a space, providing good diffuse modelling without harsh shadows. The changeability of daylight gives an interior variety and interest. Natural light has excellent colour rendering and does not buzz or flicker. A daylit building gives contact with the outside world either directly through a view out, or indirectly as the changing moods of daylight reflect the seasons, time of day and weather conditions.

Daylight also represents an energy source. It helps reduce the need for electric lighting, particularly in dwellings where natural light alone is often sufficient throughout the day. In commercial and industrial buildings too, there is often enough daylight provided suitable control of electric lighting is available to exploit it[1.4.2, 1.4.3]. It is estimated[1.4.4] that the active use of daylight in this way could save 4–8 million tonnes of coal equivalent each year throughout the EU.

Daylight provision depends on the building design: windows, internal reflectances and the type of glass. But the external environment is also important. Large obstructions outside reduce the amount of daylight entering

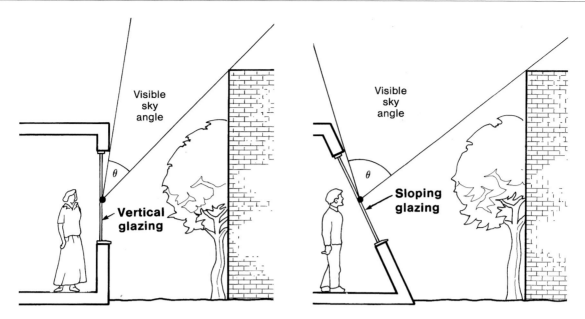

Figure 1.4.1 Daylight received is proportional to θ, the angle of visible sky

a window. Consider a room with a wide continuous obstruction outside, like a terrace of houses or apartments (Figure 1.4.1). Under cloudy conditions the amount of light entering the window is proportional to θ[1.4.5], the angle of visible sky measured in a vertical plane looking out through the centre of the window. So a 45° obstruction could halve the daylight available, compared with an unobstructed window.

Outside obstructions can also affect the distribution of light in a room. Areas very near the window may still get a view of the sky above the obstruction. But further in, no direct sky light can be received. Areas which have no direct view of the sky tend to look gloomy compared with areas near the window[1.4.6].

Loss of daylight due to obstructions is a particularly important issue in existing buildings. Large new developments close by can make adjoining properties gloomy and unattractive. With an existing building there is little or no opportunity to make design changes to counteract the effect of loss of light, so the extra obstruction can result in serious loss of amenity. Sensitive design of new buildings should try to minimize the impact on nearby existing properties.

In this Guide, section 4.1 explains how to manage the spacing and height of buildings to ensure enough daylight reaches windows, both in the new development itself and in existing buildings. Appendices A1, A2 and A8 describe calculation techniques for daylighting.

References to section 1.4

[1.4.1] Cakir A E. *An investigation on state-of-the-art and future prospects of lighting technology in German office environments.* Berlin, Ergonomics Institute for Social and Occupations Sciences Research, 1991.

[1.4.2] Building Research Establishment. Lighting controls and daylight use. *BRE Digest 272.* Garston, CRC, 1983.

[1.4.3] Slater A I, Bordass W T & Heasman T A. People and lighting controls. *BRE Information Paper IP6/96.* Garston, CRC, 1996.

[1.4.4] Crisp V H C, Littlefair P J, Cooper I & McKennan G. *Daylighting as a passive solar energy option: an assessment of its potential in non-domestic buildings.* BRE Report BR 129. Garston, CRC, 1988.

[1.4.5] Lynes J A. A sequence for daylighting design. *Lighting Research & Technology* 1979: **11**(2): 102–106.

[1.4.6] Littlefair P J. *Site layout planning for daylight and sunlight: a guide to good practice.* BRE Report BR 209. Garston, CRC, 1991.

1.5 Sunlight

Sunlight has an important amenity value. Surveys of householders in Switzerland[1.5.1], The Netherlands[1.5.2] and the UK[1.5.3] revealed that over 75% wanted plenty of sun in their homes, with less than 5% wanting little sun. Sunlight is also valued in the workplace. In a survey of UK office workers[1.5.4], 86% wanted some sunshine in the office all year round.

The sun is seen as providing light and warmth, and also having a health-giving effect. It gives a high intensity light which helps maintain the body's rhythms, promoting alertness. It aids the synthesis of vitamin D in the body and can kill germs.

Sunlight is also valued out-of-doors. In cooler climates it makes outdoor activities like sitting out and children's play more thermally comfortable[1.5.5]. In winter it can melt frost, ice and snow, and dry out the ground, reducing moss and slime. Even in southern Europe sunlight is valued throughout the year for activities like sunbathing, swimming and drying clothes. Sunlight encourages plant growth, and enhances the appearance of outdoor spaces.

Site layout is the most important factor affecting the duration of sunlight in buildings and open spaces. Because of the changing path of the sun (Figure 1.5.1) orientation of windows and open spaces is critical (sections 4.2, 5.1).

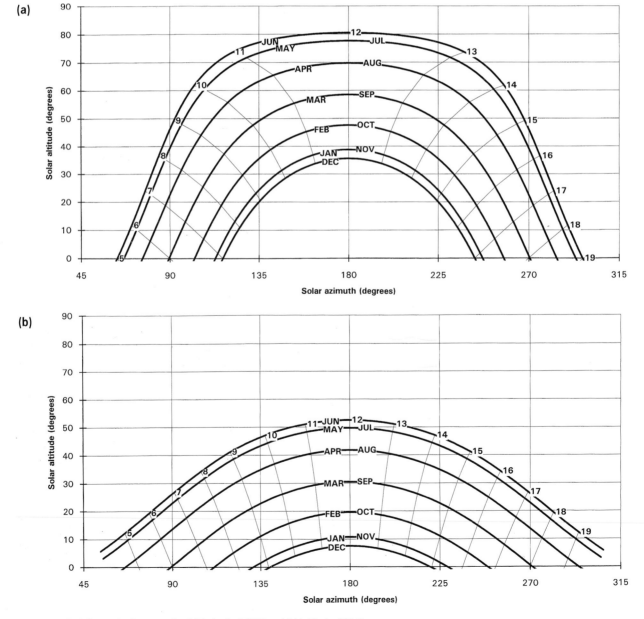

Figure 1.5.1 Sunpath diagrams for (a) latitude 36° N and (b) latitude 60° N

Figure 1.5.2 This play area in London is in continuous shadow for 10 months of the year. It is dark and underused

Overshadowing by other buildings is also very important. Inappropriately designed groups of buildings can give rise to unappealing outdoor spaces, in deep shade almost all the year (Figure 1.5.2). Section 4.4 explains the pitfalls, and how to ensure good access to sunlight in open spaces where it is required.

Overshadowing also affects buildings. It is a particular issue where new development shades existing homes nearby. Since householders value sunlight they will resent losing it. Section 4.2 gives guidance; section 4.5 supplements this with a real case study of the negative impact of a new building on adjoining properties.

Sunlight is not always an unmitigated blessing, particularly in warmer climates. With sunlight there should also be some form of solar control. This is discussed in the following section.

Sunlight calculations can be complex. Appendices A1 and A2 outline tools for computing solar access. B2 describes measurement in models.

References to section 1.5

[1.5.1] Grandjean E & Gilgen A. *Environmental factors in urban planning.* London, Taylor & Francis, 1976.

[1.5.2] Bitter C & van Lerland J F A A. Appreciation of sunlight in the home. *Proceedings CIE Conf Sunlight in Buildings,* Newcastle, 1965. Rotterdam, Bouwcentrum International. pp 27–38. 1967.

[1.5.3] Neeman E, Craddock J & Hopkinson R G. Sunlight requirements in buildings: 1 Social survey. *Building and Environment* 1976: **11**: 217–238.

[1.5.4] Markus T A. The significance of sunshine and view for office workers. *Proceedings CIE Conference on Sunlight in Buildings,* Newcastle, 1965. Rotterdam, Bouwcentrum International. pp 59-93. 1967.

1.6 Solar shading

Solar shading is valuable for reducing the heat entering buildings and therefore improving comfort and reducing cooling costs. On a clear day in summer an unshaded window can admit 3 kilowatt hours per square metre of glass; this is equivalent to leaving a single bar electric fire running for three hours. Overheating is likely to be more of a problem if:

● the windows face the southern half of the sky,
● the building has high internal heat gains,
● the building needs to be kept cooler than normal.

Solar shading is also important for protecting outdoor spaces. Ideally the shading of the building itself should be integrated architecturally with the shading of the spaces around it. Reflective glass will reduce the solar gain entering the building but at the cost of worse conditions outside.

Figure 1.6.1 At Demoulin's house, Liege, Belgium, an overhang provides shade to the south-facing windows. An extension to the side of the terrace provides shading from the summer sun. © University of Liege

(a)

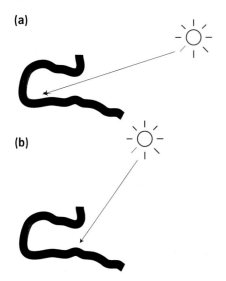

(b)

Figure 1.6.2 Early cave dwellings could be oriented to allow the sun in winter (a) but exclude it in summer (b)[1.6.1]. The colonnade (c) provides a similar function

Sometimes buildings themselves can provide shading of the spaces surrounding them (section 4.5). Special building forms involving overhangs (Figure 1.6.1) and covered walkways can increase shaded areas, and trap pools of cool air. Alternatively, vegetation can provide the shade (section 6.2). Vegetation also helps cool a space by transpiration and evaporation of moisture from the leaves.

In intermediate climates sunlight may be welcome at some times of the year but not others. Some form of variation of the degree of shading provided is desirable. This can either be a passive control, for example:

● overhangs, blocking summer sun, letting through low angle winter sun,
● colonnades (section 5.4) providing a shaded semi-outdoor space in summer, a sunny space in winter (Figure 1.6.2),
● deciduous trees, shedding their leaves in winter to let through more sunlight (section 6.2).

Alternatively, shade control could be modified by people's behaviour. Examples are:

● moveable screens and shutters (Figures 1.6.3, 1.6.4),
● patterns of sun and shade, so people can choose whether to sit in the sun,
● alternative circulation routes, one in sun, the other in shade.

References to section 1.6
[1.6.1] **Brown R D & Gillespie T J.** *Microclimatic landscape design.* New York, Wiley, 1995.

Figure 1.6.3 Moveable shading of a courtyard in Seville. © University of Seville

Figure 1.6.4 Shutters and balconies in Seville, Spain

Figure 1.7.1 Passive solar housing at Giffard Park, Milton Keynes

1.7 Solar energy

Solar energy in its various forms is potentially the most important renewable energy source in Europe. The following can all make important contributions.

- *Passive solar* (Figure 1.7.1), where the form, fabric and systems of a building are designed and arranged to capture and use solar energy. UK studies[1.7.1] have shown passive solar can reduce house heating energy consumption by 11%.
- *Active solar thermal* (Figure 1.7.2), using solar collectors with fans and pumps to provide space heating.
- *Photovoltaic systems* (Figure 1.7.3)[1.7.2] with solar cells to convert sunlight into electricity.
- *Daylight* (section 1.4).
- *Passive cooling* (section 1.9).

For passive solar buildings site layout is of particular importance (Figures 1.7.4 and 1.7.5). Because thermal solar collectors are often roof-mounted, they are in general less susceptible to overshadowing, although orientation is still an important issue. Low-level collectors, such as those used for swimming pools, can however be vulnerable to overshadowing.

Photovoltaic panels, too, are often mounted high on a building. However, there is a trend towards using these as wall cladding[1.7.2], with some low-level photovoltaic cells. Where overshadowing occurs it can have a serious impact on the output of photovoltaic arrays. Even if only one of the cells in an array is shaded, an electrical mismatch can occur and the whole array loses power output. Annual energy losses due to shading averaging 20% have been measured in building integrated photovoltaic arrays in Germany[1.7.3].

Section 4.3 deals with issues of site layout for solar access and also gives guidance on the important issue of overshadowing of existing buildings which have solar collectors, either passive or active. Section 5.1 includes additional material on orientation. Section 2.3 gives information on the effects of site slope. Appendices A1–A3 describe tools to calculate the impact of site layout on passive solar buildings.

Figure 1.7.2 Two types of solar collector at Demoulin's house, Liege, Belgium: passive collection using an attached greenhouse (conservatory) and active collection with liquid-filled solar panels (top of roof). © University of Liege

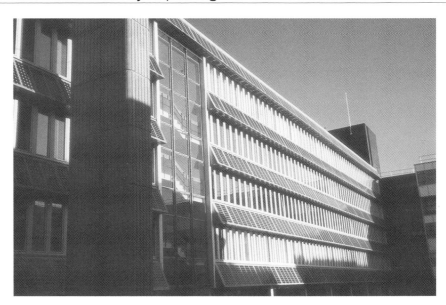

Figure 1.7.3 Photovoltaic cladding at the Northumbria Building, Newcastle-upon-Tyne

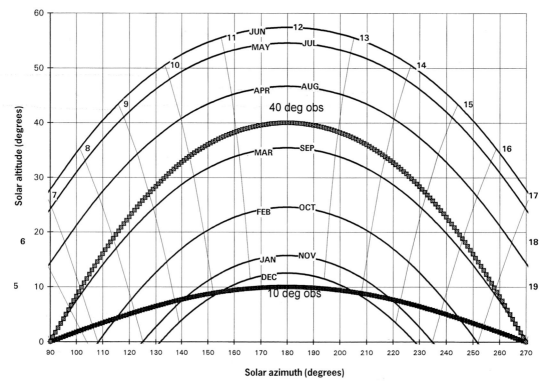

Figure 1.7.4 Sunpath diagram for latitude 55°, showing impact of obstructions

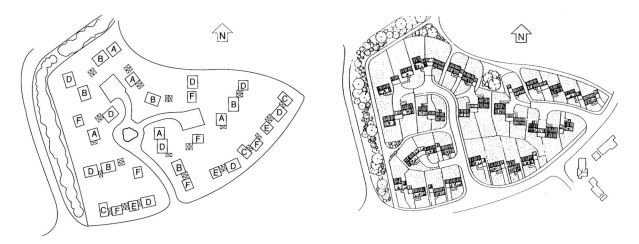

Figure 1.7.5 A site layout design study by NBA Tectonics for ETSU. The conventional layout of detached houses (left) would need 8900 kWh/year for space heating, 8500 kWh/year with passive solar features. The passive solar site layout (right), redesigned by Stillman Eastwick-Field, would require only 7900 kWh/year, a saving of over 10%

References to section 1.7
    [1.7.1] NBA Tectonics. *A study of passive solar housing estate layout.* Report S-1126. Harwell, ETSU, 1988.
    [1.7.2] Sick F & Erge T. *Photovoltaics in buildings.* London, James and James, 1996.
    [1.7.3] Kovach A & Schmid J. Determination of energy output losses due to shading of energy-integrated photovoltaic arrays using a ray tracing technique. *Solar Energy* 1996: **57**(2): 117–124.

1.8 Wind shelter

In northern Europe one of the main aims of building design is to mitigate the cold, wind and wet of the relatively long cool season. Site layout (section 4.6), built form (section 5.1), external materials and landscape design (section 6.1) can all help create a sheltered environment. For maximum effect the various elements need to be well integrated into the overall design.

Reduction of wind speed by wind control should improve the microclimate around buildings. This can be direct, in terms of reduced mechanical and thermal effects on buildings and on people, and indirect, by avoiding the dissipation of external heat gains by mixing with colder air. Wind control implies the choice of built forms least likely to disturb wind-flow patterns near the ground, and the use of wind-sheltering design elements such as courtyard forms, windbreak walls and fences and shelterbelts.

Key wind protection strategies[1.8.1] involve:
1 protecting space and buildings from important wind directions
    (eg dominant winds, cold winds),
2 preventing buildings and landscape features from generating unacceptable
    wind turbulence,
3 protecting space and buildings from driving rain and snow,
4 protecting space and buildings from cold air 'drainage' at night,
while retaining enough air movement to disperse pollutants.

Providing wind shelter offers a range of benefits, including reduced space-heating energy costs[1.8.2, 1.8.3] and better comfort and usefulness of the spaces around buildings[1.8.4, 1.8.5]. A variety of processes are involved as follows.
● *Increased air temperature*: if the external air surrounding buildings remains warmer the internal/external temperature difference will be smaller, reducing heat loss by both conduction and ventilation/infiltration. Some influence on air temperature may be possible by deliberately 'storing' solar heat in external thermal mass, and by wind control to limit the mixing of cold and warm air.

- *Increased surface temperatures*: if the external surfaces of buildings are warmed by direct or reflected solar radiation, or by long-wave radiation emitted by other warmed external surfaces, the internal/external surface temperature difference will be smaller, reducing the amount of heat lost by conduction.
- *Reduced air change rate*: wind shelter such as trees or windbreaks can reduce high rates of pressure-difference-driven infiltration of external air into the building (most significant for older buildings, less so for modern buildings with good draughtproofing).
- *Increased surface resistance*: wind shelter can increase surface resistance through reduced air movement and mixing (important for poorly insulated areas such as glazing).
- *Reduced moisture effects on thermal performance of envelope*: wind control can reduce the wetting of the building fabric (which would otherwise increase its thermal transmittance) by wind-driven rain[1.8.6]. Reduced air movement will also reduce the rate of evaporative heat loss from damp materials, so these two factors interact.

References to section 1.8

[1.8.1] **BRE.** Climate and site development. *BRE Digest 350*, Parts 1–3. Garston, CRC, 1990.

[1.8.2] **Huang Y T, Akbari H, Taha H.** The wind-shielding and shading effects of trees on residential heating and cooling requirements. *ASHRAE Transactions* AT-90-24-3. pp 1403-1411. 1992.

[1.8.3] **O'Farrell F, Lyons G, Lynskey G.** Energy conservation on exposed domestic sites. Final report of contract EEA-05-054-EIR(H). Brussels, CEC, 1987.

[1.8.4] **Arens E, Bosselmann P.** Wind, sun and temperature-predicting the thermal comfort of people in outdoor spaces. *Building and Environment* 1989: **24**(4): 315–320.

[1.8.5] **Yannas S.** *Solar energy and housing design.* London, Architectural Association/ETSU, 1994.

[1.8.6] **Penman J.** *Energy saving through landscape planning.* Volume 2: The thermal performance of rain-wetted walls. Croydon, PSA, 1988.

1.9 Ventilation — passive cooling

In Europe, the use of air-conditioning equipment is increasing significantly; in southern Europe the market is now close to 1.7 billion Euros per year. In Greece, for example, sales of packaged air-conditioning units jumped from around 2000 in 1986 to over 100 000 in 1988. Significant growth rates are also registered in northern Europe.

The extensive use of air conditioning together with relatively low energy prices have contributed to a high increase in energy consumption of buildings in southern Europe. The impact of air conditioning on peak electricity demand is a serious problem for almost all southern European countries, except France. Because of peak electricity loads, the utilities have had to build extra plants to satisfy demand, increasing the average cost of electricity.

Alternative passive-cooling techniques[1.9.1] are based on improved thermal protection of the building envelope and the dissipation of the building's thermal load to a lower temperature sink. These have proved to be very effective and have reached a level of architectural and industrial acceptance. Compared with air conditioning, passive cooling can give important energy, environmental, financial and operational benefits.

Site layout has an important impact on the effectiveness of passive-cooling systems in a number of ways as follows.

- Shading of buildings provides solar protection (sections 4.5, 6.2).
- Site layout affects the flow of wind through the city, in some cases increasing natural ventilation (section 4.6).
- Conversely, in very warm climates buildings can be arranged to trap poorly ventilated pools of cool outdoor air which act as heat sinks in the daytime (sections 4.6, 5.3).

● Some layouts can promote the dispersal of pollutants, improving the viability of natural ventilation (section 4.7).
● Earth sheltering provides additional thermal mass reducing temperature swings of the building (section 5.5).
● Important temperature and wind-flow differences can occur over the same building facade (sections 3.2, 5.3). Openings for passive cooling can be arranged to take advantage of this (section 5.6).
● Heat sinks like vegetation (section 6.2), lakes and fountains and sprays (section 6.4) can lower outdoor air temperature, making passive cooling more effective.

Reference to section 1.9
[1.9.1] Santamouris M & Asimakopoulos D (eds). *Passive cooling of buildings.* London, James & James, 1996.

1.10 Urban air pollution

Urban areas are often the major producers of man-made pollutants, with the highest levels of ambient pollution. This affects human health and mortality rates[1.10.1], damages and modifies flora, fauna and water courses, and causes excessive erosion and defacing (usually by blackening) of buildings[1.10.2]. Since most of the world's people live in cities, urban air is the dominant contributor to human exposure to pollution.

The problems of urban pollution are not new. Brimblecombe[1.10.3] notes the blackening of buildings by urban pollution in ancient Rome; and evidence of increased levels of sinusitis in Romano-British and subsequent skulls in the London area and complaints about odour, blackening and fumes from industrial processes and fires for domestic heating in London since early medieval times[1.10.4]. From the 17th century onwards, growing industrialization increased both the sizes of urban areas and the scale of their polluting emissions. This continued largely unabated until the end of the 19th century (Figure 1.10.1) when significant levels of pollution control began. The present century, especially its second half, has seen increasing regulation of polluting emissions on local, national and global scales. One of the important

Figure 1.10.1 A view of the Potteries (Stoke-on Trent) UK in about 1910. Many urban areas still look like this. Because the smoke in the multitude of discharges makes them clearly visible, their dispersion and merging to form the polluting background over larger scales is apparent. The same behaviour occurs in more highly regulated environments, the only difference is that the mix of pollutants has changed, the smoke has gone and the dispersion process is no longer visible.

triggers for air pollution control in the UK was the major smog episode in London in 1952, during which it was estimated that about 4000 premature deaths occurred in a single week.

Elsom[1.10.1] quotes estimates that, worldwide, about 1.6 billion city dwellers are exposed to small particles or SO_2 in excess of the World Health Organization (WHO) guidelines, and that premature deaths due to these two pollutants probably exceed 750 000 per year. Despite increasing levels of pollution control in the more developed countries, their urban pollution problems have tended to change in character rather than diminish entirely. Smoke and SO_2, the major pollutants from coal and heavy oil burning processes, have diminished, only to be replaced by nitrogen oxides, ozone, photochemical smog and fine particles as matters of major concern. Traffic is commonly identified as the major contributor to pollution in urban areas, but the more intensive use of energy and the greater consumption of goods and services also contribute.

Urban pollution levels also depend on meteorological and topographical factors. Since pollutants are usually removed by being carried away and diluted by the wind, these factors can be critical. The highest pollution levels are usually associated with light winds, stable atmospheric stratification and the blocking of large-scale air movements by topographic features. Mexico City, Los Angeles and Athens are well-known examples of urban areas with high pollution levels resulting from a combination of these factors. High levels of solar radiation also contribute to the formation of photochemical smog, so urban areas in sunny climates are more prone to these problems.

Urban pollution control is thus of great current concern and seems likely to remain so. Until now control has been by the regulation of polluting discharges in various ways. Regulation may include:

● operational limits on processes discharging pollutants or the fuels used (eg the sulphur content of oil and coal),
● the use of abatement to control polluting discharges (for example, the use of electrostatic precipitators to remove small particles from industrial discharges or of exhaust catalysts in motor vehicles),
● the requirement of minimum discharge stack heights to control local pollution problems,
● limits to discharges according to meteorological conditions.

In the more developed countries, including the European Community, there are now very high levels of regulation and control of polluting discharges. However, in many parts of the world there are negligible controls and this situation is unlikely to change quickly.

This approach to urban pollution control is essentially reactive, responding to pollution problems as they arise with direct controls. However, it can be a costly approach as abatement plant now represents a significant fraction of the capital and operating costs of many polluting processes. One contributory approach that has received only limited attention is that of urban design to minimize air pollution problems on both macro and micro scales. This might, for example, be by siting static pollution sources or major roads to minimize impacts within the urban area (section 2.6), by the layout of urban areas to take advantage of specific meteorological factors (section 2.6), or by the layout of buildings to encourage rapid ventilation of near-ground sources (section 4.7).

There have been examples of pollution control by zoning. In medieval times it was common for producers of black smoke to be sited outside the city walls. New towns designed in the UK have included zoning of industrial areas, but the effects on urban air pollution could not have been readily predicted. It is now common for modelling studies to predict the polluting effects of major changes in fuel usage or new road developments.

The advantages of using small-scale urban design to encourage the rapid ventilation of pollutants have received little attention. High building densities and particular styles of building layout can significantly reduce rates of pollutant dispersion near the ground. For example, courtyards and enclosed spaces, which are amongst the most common architectural forms, can store locally generated pollutants (section 4.7).

References
[1.10.1] Elsom D. *Smog alert — managing urban air quality.* London, Earthscan Publications, 1996.

[1.10.2] DOE. *The effect of acid deposition on buildings and building materials.* Building Effects Review Group, UK Department of the Environment. London, The Stationery Office, 1989.

[1.10.3] Brimblecombe P. *The big smoke.* London, Methuen, 1988.

[1.10.4] Evelyn J. *Fumifugium, or the inconvenience of the aer and smoke of London dissipated.* 1661. Reprinted by the National Society for Clean Air, Brighton, UK.

1.11 Comfort in outdoor spaces

The duration and intensity of the use of outdoor spaces is closely linked to how comfortable they are. It is possible to control the climate of outdoor spaces, but compared with the air-conditioning of buildings there are big differences as follows.

● *The number of variables to be manipulated.* Outside, wind and rain can be important.
● *The relative influence of each variable.* For example, direct sun on people is generally much more important out-of-doors since it may not penetrate far inside a building. Indoors, air temperature has more influence.
● *How far each variable can be manipulated.* For example, it is more difficult to achieve still conditions out-of-doors on a windy day. Indoors, the temperatures of surrounding surfaces are likely to be relatively stable, whereas outdoors they can vary a lot if the surfaces are sunlit.
● *The comfort level required.* Out-of-doors, people can be comfortable in a wider range of conditions because they can usually move about more easily and carry out a different range of activities.

Figure 1.11.1 shows the major heat flows over the human body. H is the direct (H_D) diffuse (H_d) and reflected (H_r) solar radiation absorbed by the subject; ΔR represents the long wave radiation exchange with surrounding surfaces; C is the convection with the air and E represents evaporation.

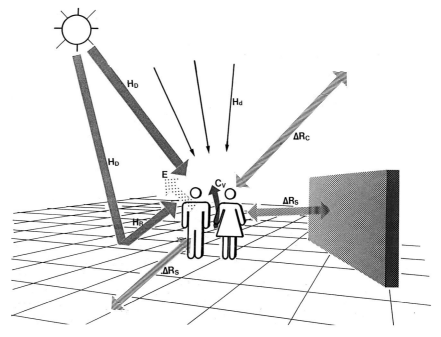

Figure 1.11.1 Heat flows over the human body in an outdoor space

	Component	Contribution to heat gains (%)	External controllability
Table 1.11.1 The thermal balance in figures			
Heat gains of a person	Net heat generation	24	Not controllable
	Total radiation (direct+ diffuse+ reflected)	55	Controllable
	Long-wave interchange	14	Controllable. Likely to be negative on cooler days
	Convection	7	Controllable. Likely to be negative on cooler days
	Total gains	**100%**	

If the net heat flow between a person and their exterior surroundings is positive, they have to compensate and balance it by the cooling effect of sweating. Table 1.11.1 shows the resulting values of the relative energy gains for a human subject in a typical unshaded situation on a hot summer hour.

Thus to improve the level of comfort on a hot day means reducing the unfavourable heat gains, eliminating them whenever possible, or even, for convection and long wave exchange, changing them into favourable heat losses. Conversely, on a cold day it is best to increase heat gains and reduce heat losses.

The criteria for designing a thermally comfortable urban site are therefore complex and sometimes contradictory. They include solar control in summer, but also solar gains in winter, wind protection in winter but generally wind access in summer (section 4.6).

Strategies to provide thermal comfort in an outdoor urban environment on a hot summer day can be divided into three groups:
● control of direct and diffuse solar radiation,
● reduction of the radiant temperature,
● reduction of the air temperature.

Narrow streets (section 4.5) and courtyards provide extra shade as they stop the access of direct solar radiation at ground level for most of the day, especially in orientations NE–SW or NW–SE (section 3.3). This blocking of solar radiation also produces low temperatures on the surfaces surrounding the pedestrian, reducing the infrared radiation. However, narrow streets can lead to high pollution levels due to the poor ventilation at the bottom of the street canyon (section 4.7), high noise levels where there is traffic and a very hot environment when air-conditioning systems release waste heat onto the street.

Wider streets can become efficient in terms of summertime thermal comfort if they include awnings or other shading devices which protect the occupied spaces from solar radiation. An advantage of wide streets from the thermal point of view is that they can include streetscape elements (such as street furniture, seating, vegetation, trees, shelters, canopies, structures and water features) to promote shading and good comfort conditions.

Avenues of trees (section 6.2) are appreciated by pedestrians and allow the use of wide and sunny streets in urban planning with good summer comfort for pedestrians. In cities where rain protection is important, trees can be replaced by colonnades (section 5.4).

In cold climates, thermal comfort is highly influenced by wind flows. The form (section 5.1) and layout (section 4.6) of buildings, particularly tall buildings, can have a big impact on air flow and therefore the comfort of pedestrians. Vegetation and windbreaks (section 6.1) can also help. Sunlight in the spaces between buildings (section 4.4) will aid thermal comfort here.

1.12 Vegetation, heat sinks

Trees, green spaces and areas of water can significantly cool the built environment and save energy. Their impact depends on their size and location.

1 *Large-scale* = surrounding land, or large areas within a city such as forests, urban parks, sea, lakes or rivers
2 *Medium-scale* (at the urban layout level) = planting strategies and the distribution of green, non-built and built up areas
3 *Small-scale* = local features such as trees, green areas or fountains at street level and in adjacent or enclosed open areas of a building

For groups 1 and 2, the major effects in vegetation are due to evapotranspiration of plants and trees that regulate their foliage temperature. Water also maintains a low level of temperature due to evaporation and to thermal inertia. In both cases, a reduction of the air temperature can be achieved. Lower air temperatures result in a decrease of the heat gains to the building and an increase of the efficiency (COP) of air-conditioning systems.

Numerical studies to simulate the effect of additional vegetation on urban temperatures have been performed by various researchers. Huang et al[1.12.1] report from computer predictions that increasing the tree cover by 25% in Sacramento and Phoenix, USA, would decrease air temperatures at 2:00 pm in July by 6–10 °F (3–6 °C). Taha[1.12.2] reports simulation results for Davis, California, using the URBMET PBL model. He found that the vegetation canopy produced daytime temperature reductions and night-time increases compared with non-vegetated areas nearby. The temperature reduction is caused by evaporative cooling and shading of the ground, whereas the temperature increase at night is the result of the reduced sky factor within the canopy. Results of the simulations show that a vegetative cover of 30% could produce a noon-time oasis effect (temperature reduction) of up to 6 °C in favourable conditions, and a night-time heat island of 2 °C.

Other numerical simulations reported by Gao[1.12.3] show that green areas decrease maximum and average temperature by 2 °C, while vegetation can decrease maximum air temperatures in streets by 2 °C. Givoni[1.12.4] recommends spacing trees and public parks throughout the urban area rather than concentrating them in a few spots. Honjo & Takakura[1.12.5], using numerical simulations of the cooling effects of green areas on their surrounding areas, have also suggested that smaller green areas spaced at intervals are preferable for effective cooling of surrounding areas.

For group 3, apart from the evapotranspiration, other major qualitative effects are:
● shading effects due to trees: mitigation of the solar heat gain,
● reduction of surface temperatures: decreasing convective and conductive heat loads,
● reduction of short-wave and long-wave radiation from soil to environment or to building by ground cover plants or water films,
● windbreak effect or insulation effect: wind speed and infiltration mitigation in winter.

Shading from trees can significantly decrease energy for cooling. Parker[1.12.6] reports that trees and shrubs planted next to a South Florida residential building can reduce summer air-conditioning costs by 40%. Reductions in summer power demand of 59% during morning and 58% in afternoon were also measured. According to Heisler[1.12.7], shading from trees of a small mobile home can reduce air conditioning by up to 75%. Akbari et al[1.12.8] monitored peak power and cooling energy savings from shade trees in two houses in Sacramento, USA. They found that shade trees at the two monitored houses yielded seasonal cooling energy savings of 30%, corresponding to average daily savings of 3.6 and 4.8 kWh/day. Peak demand savings for the same houses were 0.6 and 0.8 kW, (about 27% savings in one house and 42% in the other).

Akbari et al[1.12.9] also carried out computer simulations to study the combined effect of shading and evapotranspiration of vegetation on the energy use of typical one-story buildings in various US cities. By adding one tree per house, the cooling energy savings range from 12 to 24%, while adding three trees per house can reduce the cooling load by 17–57%. According to this study, the direct effects of shading account for only 10–35% of the total cooling energy savings. The remaining savings result from temperatures lowered by evapotranspiration.

Experimental results carried out during the POLIS project reveal a significant decrease of the air temperature (3–5 °C) in courtyards with tall and dense trees compared with those without vegetation.

In a complementary context, trees also help mitigate the greenhouse effect, filter pollutants, mask noise, prevent erosion and have a calming psychological effect.

References to section 1.12

[1.12.1] Huang Y J, Akbari H, Taha H G & Rosenfeld A H. *The potential of vegetation in reducing summer cooling loads in residential buildings.* LBL Report 21291. Berkeley, California, Lawrence Berkeley Laboratory, 1986.

[1.12.2] Taha H. *Site specific heat island simulations: model development and application to microclimate conditions.* LBL Report 26105. Berkeley, California, Lawrence Berkeley Laboratory, 1988.

[1.12.3] Gao W. Thermal effects of open space with a green area on urban environment. Part 1: a theoretical analysis and its application. Journal of Architecture, Planning and Environmental Engineering (AIJ) 1993: (488) .

[1.12.4] Givoni B. *Climate considerations in building and urban design.* New York, Van Nostrand Reinhold, 1998.

[1.12.5] Honjo T & Takakura T. Simulation of thermal effects of urban green areas on their surrounding areas. *Energy and Buildings* 1990/1991: **15–16**: 443–446.

[1.12.6] Parker J H. Landscaping to reduce the energy used in cooling buildings. *Journal of Forestry* 1983: **81**(2): 82–83.

[1.12.7] Heisler G M. Energy savings with trees. *Journal of Arboriculture* 1986: **12**(5): 113–124.

[1.12.8] Akbari H, Kurn D M, Bretz S E & Hanfold J W. Peak power and cooling energy savings of shade trees. *Energy and Buildings* 1997: **25**: 139–148.

[1.12.9] Akbari H, Davis S, Dorsano S, Huang J & Winett S. *Cooling our communities — a guidebook on tree planting and light colored surfacing.* Washington, Office of Policy Analysis, Climate Change Division, US Environmental Protection Agency, January 1992.

1.13 Layout strategies

Warm (cooling-dominated) climates

Cool (heating-dominated) climates

Mixed climate (both heating and cooling required)

This book aims to provide guidance on site layout for improved environmental conditions both within and around buildings. Clearly the requirements will vary according to local climate. In the rest of the book the guidance is grouped according to its suitability for different climate types. The icons (left) are used.

Where possible, detailed data on the local climate should be obtained at the outset. The key parameters are as follows.

(a) Temperature

Temperature is important for passive solar design and also for the design of outdoor spaces. In northern Europe winter temperatures affect the heating requirement. Although the lowest temperatures occur in the early morning, solar gain contributes most around mid-day. It follows, then, that the places where solar gain can make an important contribution will be those where the temperature just after mid-day is below the threshold for heating, eg 16 °C, for a significant part of the year.

In the south, the summer temperatures and high solar radiation cause the need for shade. Passive cooling techniques like shading can make their biggest impact around the middle of the day. So the temperature during the day could be the critical parameter here too. Where this exceeds 24 *C for a significant part of the year, buildings would need extra cooling which passive measures could avoid. External conditions can be uncomfortable too and shade and other passive cooling measures will be welcome.

Figure 1.13.1 shows areas of Europe where passive solar heating and shading are likely to be of value. The brown contour shows areas where the average temperature in the early afternoon is 16 °C or less for three months of the year. North of this line passive solar gain in winter is likely to be of benefit. The blue contour shows areas where the average summer temperature in the early afternoon exceeds 24 °C for three months of the year.

The contours divide Europe into three zones:

1 A heating-dominated zone with cool winters and mild summers, north of both contours. Here the following site layout strategies are likely to be particularly useful:
   ● use of passive solar gain (sections 2.3, 3.3, 4.3, 5.1),
   ● sunlight as an amenity both indoors (section 4.2) and outdoors (section 4.4),
   ● wind shelter (sections 2.4, 4.6, 6.1),
   ● daylighting (section 4.1).

2 A cooling-dominated zone with mild winters and warm or hot summers, south of both contours. This includes the Algarve, southern Spain, most of the Mediterranean islands and the very south of Italy and Greece. Here the dominant strategies are:
   ● lower heat island effects by siting (sections 2.2, 3.2),
   ● use ventilation for cooling and encourage winds in open sites (sections

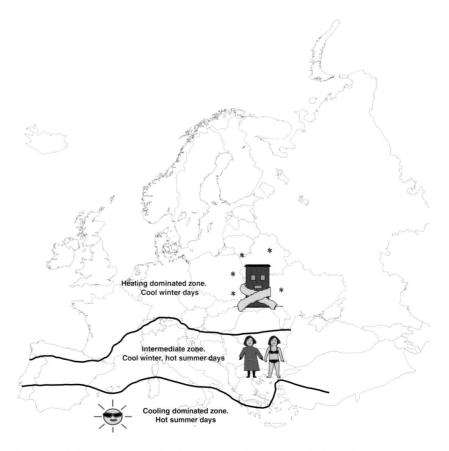

Figure 1.13.1 Map of Europe showing contours of temperature in the early afternoon

2.5, 3.2, 4.6, 5.6),
- use narrow streets and courtyards for deeply shaded areas (sections 4.5, 5.3),
- use vegetation as heat sink and to provide extra shading (sections 2.7, 6.2),
- water features: lakes, ponds and sprays for cooling (sections 2.7, 6.4),
- high surface albedo to prevent heat absorption (section 6.5).

3 An intermediate zone with cool winters and warm or hot summers, between the two contours. This covers most of Portugal and Italy, central Spain, southern France, northern Greece and the Balkan states. Here, passive solar heating is welcome in winter but shade and cooling is needed in summer. Specialized site layout techniques are needed to cope with both requirements simultaneously:
- use vegetation for winter wind shelter (section 6.1) and summer shade and cooling (section 6.2),
- deciduous trees for summer shade (section 6.2),
- colonnades for shade in summer and shelter in winter (section 5.4),
- overhangs and other forms to shade buildings in summer (section 5.6),
- daylighting through shaded side windows or north-facing apertures (section 4.1),
- high surface albedo for summer cooling and light reflection all year (section 6.5).

(b) Wind speeds

Although not as important as temperature, wind speed has a considerable effect on site layout strategy. In the north, windy locations need more shelter. In the south breezes can provide cooling, and the need for mutual shading is less important. The effect of wind speed is therefore to make the site appear more northerly as far as site layout strategy is concerned. In cold areas with little wind, the best strategy is to open up the site layout for maximum sun (sections 4.3, 4.4). Where winds are stronger, the provision of shelter (sections 4.6, 6.1) becomes much more important. Wind speeds therefore need to be treated as an independent variable. Figure 1.13.2 shows average wind speeds in Europe. However, wind exposure also depends considerably on the precise position of the site (in a valley, on the crest of a hill, etc.). Section 2.2 gives guidance.

(c) Building type and heating and cooling needs

The need for heating and cooling inside a building depends on its purpose. This in turn determines:
- the range of internal temperatures required,
- the internal heat gains,
- weight of construction and hence thermal heat storage,
- typical plan depths: deep plan buildings usually need less heating and more cooling.

Figures 1.13.3–1.13.6 illustrate this for two common building types: residential and offices. For housing, the heating load over the whole year always exceeds the cooling load, even in the far south of Europe. Much of this heating load will occur in the early morning and therefore cannot be provided by solar heat gain. For offices the reverse is true. Even in northern France, the cooling requirements over the year exceed the heating requirements. These results should also be typical of other medium–large non-domestic buildings like supermarkets and light industrial factories.

Site layout issues can still be important for these non-domestic building types. Key strategies are:
- use of natural ventilation, perhaps as part of a mixed mode cooling strategy (sections 2.5, 3.2, 4.6, 5.6),
- management of pollutant levels to aid ventilation (sections 2.6, 4.7),

Wind at 50 metres above ground level			
Sheltered terrain ms⁻¹	Open plain ms⁻¹	At a sea coast ms⁻¹	Hills and ridges ms⁻¹
> 6.0	> 7.5	> 8.5	> 11.5
5.0 – 6.0	6.5 – 7.5	7.0 – 8.5	10.0 – 11.5
4.5 – 5.0	5.5 – 6.5	6.0 – 7.0	8.5 – 10.0
3.5 – 4.5	4.5 – 5.5	5.0 – 6.0	7.0 – 8.5
< 3.5	< 4.5	< 5.0	< 7.0

Figure 1.13.2 Average wind speeds in Europe

● other passive cooling strategies (section 5.6) including overhangs and evaporative cooling strategies,
● daylighting (section 4.1) coupled with appropriate control of electric lighting inside the building to reduce heat gains,
● heat sinks like vegetation (sections 2.7, 6.2) and water features (sections 2.7, 6.4, 6.5),
● managing visual impact of a building (sections 3.5, 5.8).

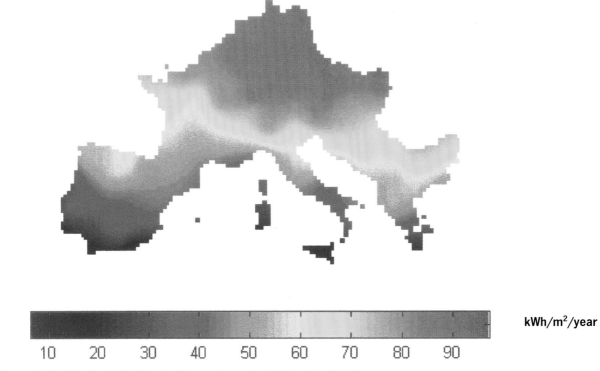

kWh/m²/year

Figure 1.13.3 Residential building heating requirements. © University of Seville

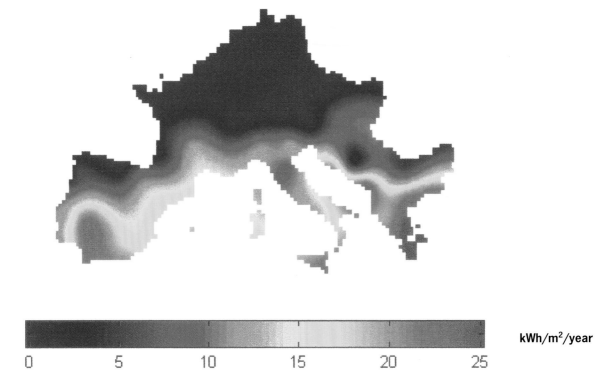

kWh/m²/year

Figure 1.13.4 Residential building cooling requirements. © University of Seville

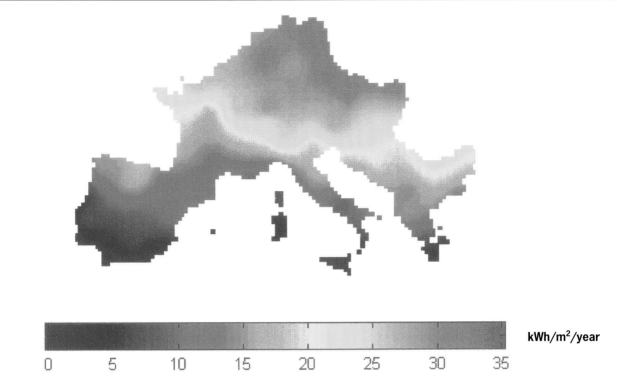

Figure 1.13.5 Office building heating requirements. © University of Seville

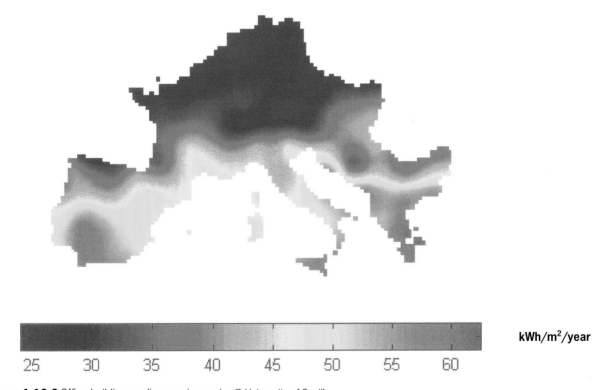

Figure 1.13.6 Office building cooling requirements. © University of Seville

2 Site location

The climate of a particular site will often differ in several respects from the 'area average' indicated by maps or tables. Ideally, microclimate and passive solar considerations should be a factor in selecting sites for many types of building. However, with the restricted availability of development land in many parts of Europe, this is not always possible. Nevertheless, there may be situations where a choice of sites is possible. In any case, a knowledge of the microclimatic character of the site is valuable because it can help designers and urban planners to develop a strategy to improve the site microclimate, and to decide to what extent solar gains can be exploited.

2.1 Urban development strategy

Strategy: Balance accessibility and energy demands

Urban development patterns are a primary factor in sustainable energy policies. In traditional compact cities, for instance, private building energy consumptions are usually smaller because of the thermal benefits of sharing party walls. However, changes in transport patterns mean that compact cities need no longer be the norm. Long home to work distances are no longer a major impediment for people with cars or easy access to public transport. Thus, several new types of urban pattern have emerged. They are illustrated in Figure 2.1.1[2.1.1]. These six models are based on data collected in eastern central England, and are examples of major tendencies that can be observed elsewhere.

Real cities are a mix between these theoretical models. Nevertheless, they provide a simple typology for urban developments. Some of these patterns result from stringent development control (patterns 0, 1 and 3). Others are almost spontaneous (patterns 2, 4 and 5). Each has its own advantages and constraints, in terms of domestic building energy consumptions, travel costs, accessibility and congestion, individual access to private home ownership and other issues.

The existing pattern (pattern 0) appears to be convenient under present oil conservation and domestic building policies. Yet this could be dramatically modified if energy costs rose substantially.

Reduction of transport fuel consumptions
Pattern 1, in which all new developments are directed into the existing city, appears to be the most appropriate for major fuel savings: reduced trip length, improved accessibility, an estimated 18% reduction in the total passenger-kilometres travelled. Pattern 5 gives similar, but slightly inferior fuel savings.

Reduction of domestic building energy consumptions
Pattern 1 is again the most appropriate, partly due to reduction of private space, closely followed by patterns 3 and 5.

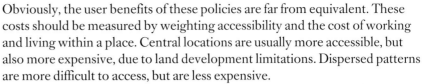

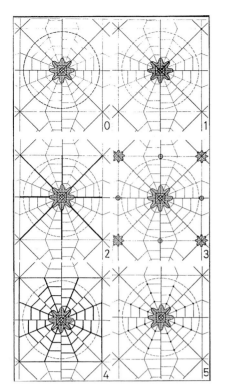

Figure 2.1.1 Six theoretical regional settlement patterns. One as existing (pattern 0) and five variants: concentration of new developments into the central city (pattern 1), along the main road system (pattern 2), into satellite towns (pattern 3), along secondary roads (pattern 4) and into existing villages (pattern 5).
© University of Liege

Obviously, the user benefits of these policies are far from equivalent. These costs should be measured by weighting accessibility and the cost of working and living within a place. Central locations are usually more accessible, but also more expensive, due to land development limitations. Dispersed patterns are more difficult to access, but are less expensive.

Considering these factors, pattern 3 would provide energy benefits at twice the cost of pattern 1, and pattern 5 at half the price of pattern 1. Consequently, from a sustainability point of view, pattern 5 (dispersed villages) would probably be the most promising solution.

New developments in transport and energy supply (electric cars, district heating systems, etc.) could however change the relative benefits of each city type. Development of major light railways along main axes would obviously benefit the third scenario. And active solar devices would lessen differences between concentrated and dispersed configurations since they are not easily achievable in very dense areas like pattern 1 (44.5 persons/hectare).

Urban development strategy also affects pollution levels. This is discussed in section 2.6 below.

Reference to section 2.1

[2.1.1] Rickaby P & Steadman P. *Towards a spatial energy model: a theoretical comparison of accessibility and energy-use in regional settlement patterns.* Final report. Centre for Configurational studies, The Open University, Milton Keynes, 1985.

2.2 Temperature

Strategy: choose or modify site to enhance heat island effect (in cool climates) or reduce it (in warm climates)

Urban and suburban sites will experience different climates. Towns and cities can show marked increases in temperature (the 'heat island' effect) both in winter and, especially, in summer. Studies on the intensity of the heat island have been performed for a number of European cities. Lyall[2.2.1] mentions that the heat island in London at night in June–July 1976 increased temperatures by around 2.5 °C on average. This is not far below a daily upper decile limit of 3.1 °C found by Chandler[2.2.2] for London in 1951–1960. Eliasson[2.2.3] reports data on the heat island intensity in Goteborg, Sweden. Urban–rural temperature comparisons show a well-developed urban heat island increasing temperatures by up to 3.5 °C in winter and even 6 °C in summer. During summer nights the heat island intensity was nearly always greater than 0.5 °C and on 40% of the night hours it was greater than 1 °C. In Malmo, Sweden, during winter and spring, a mean heat island temperature increase close to 7 °C has been found (Barring et al[2.2.4]). Limited data on the heat island intensity in Essen, Germany, are reported by Swaid & Hoffman[2.2.5] for September 1986. The observed temperature increase was between 3 and 4 °C for both day and night. A maximum horizontal temperature gradient between Paris and its suburbs close to 14 °C has been recorded[2.2.6].

In cool climates, the heat island effect is generally beneficial. It can reduce building heating costs and improve thermal comfort in outdoor spaces. The primary concern is to mitigate the cold, wind and wet of the relatively long cool season. It is better, then, to enhance at a local level, as far as practicable, the heat island effect. Site layout, built form, external materials and landscape design are all elements that can help to create a sheltered environment, exploiting favourable climatic influences and protecting against unfavourable ones. For maximum effect the various elements need to be well integrated into the overall design. In site selection, the following factors will help:
● site integrated into built-up area,
● site well sheltered from prevailing winter winds (section 2.4),
● site with good solar exposure: eg a south-facing slope (section 2.3) or with

low obstructions to the south,
● site neither on an exposed hill top or at the base of a valley where mist can form and cold air collect.

In warm climates, the reverse strategy is needed. Urban design should aim to reduce the heat island effect if possible. Once again, site layout and position, built form, external materials and landscape design are all important. In the POLIS research project, 20 temperature and humidity stations were installed in the Athens region from June 1996. The number of stations had been extended to 30 by June 1997. High temperature differences between the urban and reference stations were recorded during summer 1996, up to 18 °C during the day and, in particular, between a station suffering from high traffic density and the reference station. It was found that the higher the temperature in the urban station, the higher the temperature difference. This is mainly due to extra heat from traffic and other sources in the city centre.

During the day temperature differences can vary widely (0–18 °C) with the urban layout, traffic load, anthropogenic heat and the overall energy balance of each particular area. A mean temperature difference is close to 7–8 °C. The national park, located at the very centre of Athens has much lower temperature differences with the suburbs, while the lowest temperature differences are recorded in a main pedestrian street. In general the city centre has much higher temperatures during the day time than the surrounding area. This becomes clearer when the spatial distribution of the temperature is plotted. Figure 2.2.1 visualizes the spatial temperature distribution at the central Athens area at noon on the 1st August 1996. As shown, the central Athens area is about 7–8 °C warmer than the surrounding area, while at the high traffic station of Ippokratous the temperature difference is close to 12–13 °C.

The following site factors will therefore help mitigate the heat island effect:
● location close to major heat sinks like the sea and lakes, forests and parks (section 2.7), preferably downwind of these,
● areas of low traffic density like pedestrian streets,
● shading from summer sun by trees or buildings,
● access to prevailing winds (section 2.5),
● using materials with low heat capacity,
● use of highly reflective surfaces to increase the albedo (section 6.5).

The two most cost-effective methods to reduce the heat island effect are by increasing the amount of vegetation in the cities and using light-coloured facades instead of dark building materials. Vegetation can reduce the heat island by directly shading individual buildings and by evapotranspiration. The

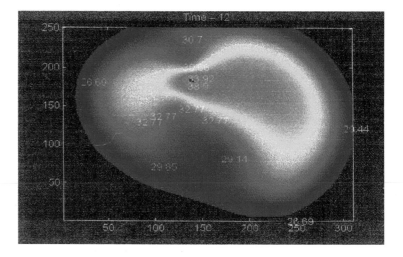

Figure 2.2.1 Temperature distribution around the central Athens area at 12:00 of the 1st August 1996. © University of Athens

albedo of the city surfaces determines the amount of solar radiation absorbed or reflected which is the main reason for the high surface temperatures observed in the urban environment. The implementation of these techniques can be applied in a whole urban area or in individual locations like pedestrian streets.

References to section 2.2

[2.2.1] Lyall I T. The London heat-island in June–July 1976. *Weather* 1977: **32**(8): 296–302.

[2.2.2] Chandler T J. City growth and urban climates. *Weather* 1964: **19**: 170–171.

[2.2.3] Eliasson I. Urban nocturnal temperatures, street geometry and land use. *Atmospheric Environment* 1996: **30**(3): 379–392.

[2.2.4] Barring L, Mattsson J O & Lindqvist S. Canyon geometry, street temperatures and urban heat island in Malmo, Sweden. *Journal of Climatology* 1985: **5**: 433–444.

[2.2.5] Swaid H & Hoffman M E. Prediction of urban air temperature variations using the analytical CTTC model. *Energy and Buildings* 1990b: **14**: 313–324.

[2.2.6] Escourrou G. Climate and pollution in Paris. *Energy and Buildings* 1990/1991: **15–16**: 673–676.

2.3 Site slope

Strategy: Consider effects of site slope on solar access, temperature and daylight

Solar access

Site slope[2.3.1] and surrounding mountains may reduce the daylight, sunlight and solar heat gain (Figure 2.3.1) buildings can receive. For slopes of all orientations, daylight will be lost to windows facing up the slope (Figure 2.3.2). Rows of buildings need to be spaced further apart to achieve the same amount of mutual obstruction. Figure 2.3.3 shows the extra spacing (see Figure 2.3.2) required for different site slopes and latitudes, to meet the daylight access recommendations in section 4.1. On steep slopes, consider having the main window walls facing down the slope. In warmer climates, earth sheltering (section 5.5) is a possible strategy, with buildings being recessed into the hillside.

For access to sunlight, particularly for passive solar gain, a south-facing slope is best. Buildings can be closer together and still achieve the same solar access, and the ground is warmer because it faces the sun for most of the year. Conversely, a north-facing slope may result in a loss of sunlight, particularly at high latitudes. To achieve the same solar access, buildings need to be spaced further apart. Figure 2.3.4 quantifies this. It is based on the recommendations for solar access in section 4.3. The spacings are based on achieving sun at mid-day on January 21 north of 50° N, and on December 21 south of 46.5° N. Figure 2.3.4 assumes south-facing buildings, and that the site slope is measured in a north–south vertical section. An east- or west-facing slope will result in loss of sun at particular times of day but will have little impact on the

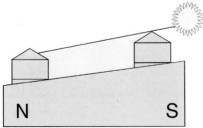

In northern latitudes, south-facing slopes can enable good solar access with reduced spacing

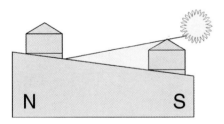

Steep north-facing slopes are unfavourable for passive solar designs

Figure 2.3.1 The slope of the site has a significant effect on overshading

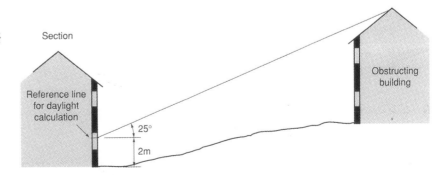

Figure 2.3.2 To achieve the same obstruction angles and hence daylight access, greater spacing is required on sloping sites

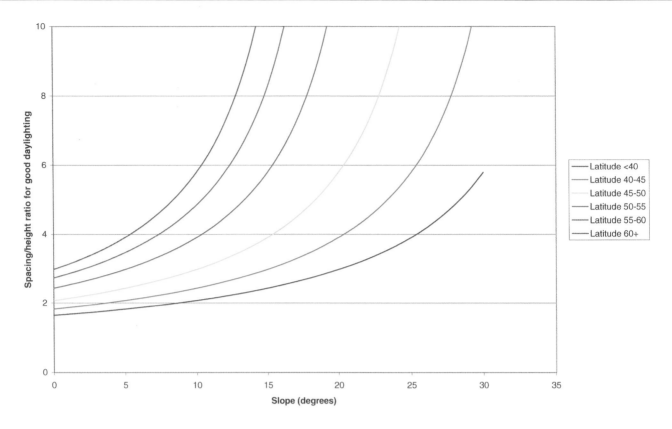

Figure 2.3.3 Spacing:height ratios for rows of houses (Figure 2.3.2) to achieve good access to daylight (section 4.1)

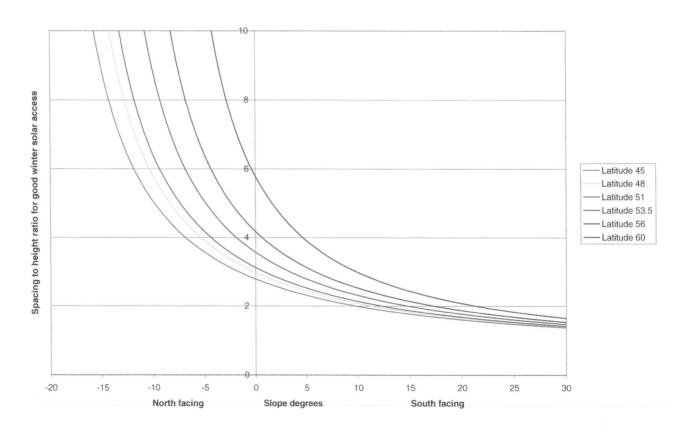

Figure 2.3.4 Spacing:height ratios for rows of houses, to achieve good access to winter solar heat gain (section 4.3)

Figure 2.3.5 Maison Herzet, Belgium, is sited on a north-facing slope. To improve solar access living areas are at first-floor level, and the conservatory has high level curved glazing

Figure 2.3.6 This passive solar school in Modane, France, is surrounded by mountains. It experiences some loss of winter sun for this reason.

sun around noon which in winter forms the major contributor to passive solar heating.

Where a north-facing sloping site must be chosen, it may be possible to improve solar access by using sloping glazing and having main living rooms on an upper floor (Figure 2.3.5)[2.3.2]. Alternatively, if the required building spacings are impractical it may be best to abandon a passive solar approach and instead concentrate on highly insulated buildings and to seek ways to improve site microclimate. This could involve opening out spaces to the available sun (section 4.4), and providing wind shelter (section 4.6), with enough daylight for amenity purposes (section 4.1).

Even if the site is level, solar access can be lost if it is surrounded by mountains (Figure 2.3.6). This can be quantified by treating the mountains like any other obstruction and comparing angles in sections 4.1 and 4.3. If the site itself is level, the nearby mountains do not affect the required spacing of buildings to achieve access to daylight and solar gain.

Air flows

The movement of air up or down a slope, even a modest one, can be important, especially for sites at or near the bottom. This effect is due to buoyancy: air warmed by the ground on a calm, sunny day will rise up a slope (anabatic flow), while air cooled by the ground on a calm, clear night will drift down it (katabatic flow). Typical speeds for such flows are from 1 to 2 m/s, depending on the extent and steepness of the slope. Much stronger flows can occur in mountainous regions. Katabatic flows are more important for site development: they render hollows and valley floors colder than locations part-way up the sides and, especially, increase the severity and persistence of frosts where cold air is trapped. It is important to recognize where such flows are likely, to avoid creating cold air traps at unsuitable points in the layout of buildings or landscape features.

The most favourable location in a valley is often referred to as the 'thermal belt', lying just above the level to which pools of cold air build up, but below the point at which the chilling effects of the wind become dominant[2.3.3].

References to section 2.3
[2.3.1] Simpson B J & Purdy M T. *Housing on sloping sites: a design guide.* London, Construction Press, 1984.
[2.3.2] Yannas S. *Solar energy and housing design* (Volumes 1 and 2). London, Architectural Association, 1994.
[2.3.3] Brown G Z. *Sun, wind and light architectural design strategies.* New York, Wiley, 1985.

2.4 Wind shelter

Strategy: Identify site exposure to cold winter winds

The wind regime in and around cities can be defined in two layers. The 'urban air canopy', is extended from the ground surface up to the building height, h_b, while the 'urban air dome' is extended above the roof tops, to about 2–3 times the building height. Above this level, the wind is not affected by the details of the surface, only its drag force.

Wind speeds in the two layers are quite different. The urban air canopy has its own wind-flow field which depends on the wind-flow field above but also on local effects such as topography, building geometry and dimensions, street patterns, traffic and other local features, like the presence of trees.

Generally, significantly larger average wind speeds exist in the urban air dome. The urban edge, or areas close to large open spaces or lakes or the sea will also experience more severe winds. Air flows in the urban air dome depend on the aerodynamic roughness length z_0. Typical values of z_0 are given by Oke[2.4.1], Table 2.4.1.

Table 2.4.1 Typical roughness length, z_0, of urbanized terrain. Data from Oke[2.4.1]	
Terrain	z_0 (m)
Scattered settlement (farms, villages, trees, hedges)	0.2–0.6
Suburban	
Low density residences and gardens	0.4–1.2
High density	0.8–1.8
Urban	
High density < 5-storey row and block buildings	1.5–2.5
High density plus multi-storey blocks	2.5–10

Figure 2.4.1 Tree shape revealing wind exposure

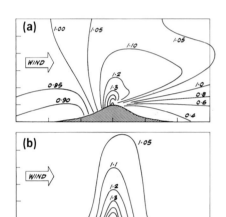

Figure 2.4.2 Typical velocity profiles at crest of steep hill: (a) steep slope, (b) shallow slope

The CEC Wind Atlas[2.4.2] gives a methodology for estimating site wind conditions quantitatively. It is particularly helpful for assessing the impacts of the stronger winds that are typical of winter. Basic data are given for a large number of regions in Europe. In the atlas calculation method, these are then corrected for terrain roughness. Both wind speed spectra and wind direction are given.

The greater wind exposure of upland sites, eg hill-tops and moorland, is usually evident on all but the calmest days. Even if the altitude is insufficient to result in markedly reduced air temperatures, the greater frequency of days when winds are stronger affects both external comfort and energy use in buildings. Severe wind exposure will often be revealed in the form of trees and hedges (Figure 2.4.1).

The crests of hills and ridges can present particular problems due to the way wind flows over them. The wind velocity:height profile is compressed, compared with that above level ground, and strong winds can occur very near ground level. For example, around the crest of a 1 in 3 hill, gust speeds only a few metres above the ground will be about one-third greater than those at a height of 10 m above a level situation upwind of the hill (Figure 2.4.2). Because of this, attempts to establish natural shelter, such as trees, may have limited success. The exposure of an upland site will depend on the adjoining terrain in different directions. For example, sites facing prevailing winds will generally be more exposed than those sloping away from them; a site on an isolated hill will tend to be more exposed than on a hill within a group. In summary, although exposed hilltop sites may receive unrivalled solar radiation, they will be very difficult to shelter from the wind.

In exposed urban edge sites, shelterbelts and windbreaks can provide considerable improvements in site microclimate. Section 6.1 gives full details. Building spacing (section 4.6) and form (section 5.1, 5.5) are also important.

References to section 2.4

[2.4.1] **Oke T R**. *Boundary layer climates*. Cambridge, Cambridge University Press, 1987.

[2.4.2] **Troen I & Peterson E L**. *CEC European wind atlas*. Roskilde, Denmark, Ris National Laboratory, 1989.

2.5 Wind cooling: ventilation

Strategy: Consider site access to natural ventilation, and factors affecting it like noise and pollution

Natural ventilation can provide fresh air for building occupants, to maintain acceptable air quality levels and also to provide cooling. Natural ventilation processes are caused by naturally produced pressure differences across openings due to the wind or temperature differences. The flow of air through large openings such as windows and doors in naturally ventilated buildings is mainly due to the effect of the wind. Thermal forces attributed to temperature differences also play a significant role, especially when ambient wind speeds are low.

Various methods, both simplified and detailed, have been proposed to calculate the effects of the building location on the effectiveness of natural ventilation. The methods, in general, propose techniques to find the reduction of either the wind speed or the air-flow rate due to the relative location of the building and the characteristics of nearby buildings.

A simplified but quite comprehensive method has been developed by the Florida Solar Energy Center[2.5.1, 2.5.2]. The method proposes a Terrain Correction Factor (TCF) to multiply the design air change rate, to take into account the reduction of wind speed because of the building location. The proposed values are given in Table 2.5.1 for 24-hour and night ventilation strategies.

The same method proposes a reduction coefficient to take into account the effect of nearby buildings. The coefficient is based on the wall height of the upwind building, h, as well as on the gap between the building and the adjacent upwind building, g. Values of the Neighbourhood Correction Factor (NCF) are given in Table 2.5.2. as a function of the ratio g/h.

The final air-flow rate can then be calculated as the product of the design air-flow rate multiplied by the NCF and the TCF.

A number of other methods have been developed based on measurements in urban environments. These either propose a correction factor to decrease the wind speed in urban canyons or give analytical expressions to calculate the wind speed as a function of the wind and canyon characteristics. A comprehensive review of these methods is given in section 4.6.

Natural ventilation is an appropriate technique for almost all types of environment. However, special attention should be given to urban and industrial environments where outdoor pollution may be a serious constraint. Section 2.6 below gives details. In very dirty or polluted locations sealed windows and mechanical ventilation with filtration or air-conditioning may be necessary. Alternatively, it may be possible to admit natural ventilation from a less polluted side of the building.

Similar problems can occur in very noisy environments, with a conflict between acoustic protection and ventilation. An open window gives very little sound insulation. Trickle vents tend to reduce the performance of a double-

Table 2.5.1 Terrain Correction Factor (TCF)		
Terrain type	TCF, 24-hour ventilation	TCF, Night-only ventilation
Oceanfront or > 3 miles water in front	1.30	0.98
Airports, or flatlands with isolated, well-separated buildings	1.00	0.75
Rural	0.85	0.64
Suburban or Industrial	0.67	0.50
Centre of large city	0.47	0.35

Table 2.5.2 Neighbourhood Correction Factor (NCF)	
Ratio g/h	NCF
0	0.00
1	0.41
2	0.63
3	0.77
4	0.85
5	0.93
6	1.00

glazed unit to that of a single-glazed window. It may be possible to admit ventilation air from a quieter side of the building, if there is one, or to site acoustically sensitive tasks on the quieter side. In extreme cases mechanical ventilation, through specially designed vents, may be necessary.

References to section 2.5
[2.5.1] Chandra S, Fairey P W & Houston M M. *Cooling with ventilation.* Report SERI SP-273-2966, DE 86010701. Solar Energy Research Institute, Golden, Colorado, 1986.

[2.5.2] Chandra S, Fairey P W & Houston M M. *A handbook for designing ventilated buildings.* Final Report FSEC-CR-93-83. Florida Solar Energy Centre, Cape Canaveral, Florida, 1983.

2.6 Pollution sources

Pollution sources in urban areas are not fundamentally different from those elsewhere, there are more of them in a small area. The most important effects of pollution are:
● adverse health effects,
● erosion or blackening of buildings,
● nuisance,
● damage to flora or fauna.

A single pollution source may contribute to one or more of these effects. Health effects are of greatest concern due to both the high levels of exposure in urban areas and to the relatively high numbers of people exposed (see section 1.10). Erosion and blackening of buildings is a long-running aesthetic problem and very important for historic structures of architectural or archaeological importance. The most common causes of nuisance are dust and odour. Damage to flora and fauna is common in urban areas.

Subdivided by type of discharge, the most important source groupings are:
● road traffic,
● combustion plant (eg heating systems, power generation and waste incineration),
● discharges from industrial processes,
● accidental discharges from industrial processes and other sources,
● building ventilation exhaust discharges.

Vehicle emissions are probably the major local pollution source in urban areas[2.6.1, 2.6.2]. However, other sources are often the principal component of the overall pollution level. Of the pollutant discharges from different sources, most are usually only known approximately. This applies especially to odours, which are difficult to quantify. Pollution sources in cities are released at different heights. Discharges from road traffic are mostly (but not always) at the ground, while those from combustion and process discharges are usually above the local building heights. In the latter cases there is often a regulatory requirement for minimum discharge stack heights to ensure that pollution levels at the ground from these sources are within acceptable levels. Accidental and ventilation exhaust discharges are at heights and positions that are largely arbitrary.

Subdividing pollution sources by types of pollutant is more complex as an enormous range of pollutants are discharged to the atmosphere. The most important are usually the subject of monitoring and their emissions are often controlled. The most important groups of pollutants are given in the box, left[2.6.3].

Pollutants discharged into the air are carried away as a slender plume by whatever wind may be blowing. The plume spreads and dilutes with increasing distance. This process is known as dispersion. The contaminant concentration in plumes is roughly inversely proportional to both the windspeed and to the square of the distance.

Important groups of pollutants

● **Acid gases.** Mainly sulfur and nitrogen oxides from combustion processes, but there are contributions from other sources, eg hydrogen chloride and hydrogen fluoride from incineration.
● **Small, inhalable, particles** (including soot).
● **Metals,** especially heavy metals, mercury, cadmium, and lead. Mainly produced by incineration and industrial processes. A major source of lead is vehicle emissions, though this is diminishing rapidly within Europe with lead-free fuel.
● **Volatile organic compounds (VOCs).** There is an enormous variety of these, discharged directly (eg from paint spraying or vehicle fuel evaporation) and also as products of combustion, from industrial processes and other sources.
● **Dioxins and other toxic and carcinogenic organic compounds** from combustion and industrial processes.

In urban areas, the dispersing plumes from the multitude of sources merge together at longer distances to form the 'background' pollution. Sources close by will contribute high contaminant concentrations, but there will probably be few of them. Exposure levels critically depend on the local meteorology, not only the windspeed and direction, but also the degree of stratification (stability) of the atmosphere, and the effects of topography. Dispersion from sources near the ground is also affected strongly by surface obstacles, usually buildings. They can both increase or slow down dispersion and modify windspeeds near the ground (which in turn affects plume concentrations). A variety of surface features affect this, the proportion of the surface occupied by buildings, their heights and widths, layout patterns and variability in shape (see section 4.7).

Sources at different distances will give different exposure patterns as follows.

● The *far-field regime*, beyond about 1 km distance, where the plume cross-section is large compared with individual buildings and structures.
● The *intermediate-field regime*, in which the plume cross-section is large enough to encompass a few buildings or structures. This typically covers distances from a few hundred metres up to about a kilometre.
● The *near-field regime*, in which the plume cross-section is small compared with buildings and other obstacles. This extends typically from very short ranges up to distances of a few hundred metres.

The far-field regime

When a dispersing plume has reached a size where its cross-section is large compared with the surface obstacles, only the overall atmospheric turbulence controls the rate of dispersion. Figure 2.6.1 shows a sketch of this dispersion regime. At these large scales, the details of the surface obstacles are unimportant, it is only their overall effect that matters.

Manins et al's recent review of Australian work in this area[2.6.4] remarks that 'urban form does matter' in its effects on air pollution. They describe studies of real and hypothetical large-scale urban layouts and the effects of these on the levels and distributions of air pollutants from various sources. Figure 2.6.2 shows a diagram of the inputs required for this type of study. Figure 2.6.3 shows diagrams of six styles of urban area investigated in this way, with different population densities and patterns of land use. The types are described broadly as given in the box, left.

The study showed that urban form had significant effects on pollution levels and patterns of distribution, though none was superior for all pollutants. *Business-as-usual* gave, overall, a continuing deterioration. The *compact city* was good for fuel usage and energy saving (reducing CO_2 emissions) but exposure to pollutants increased. Thus, this option would require higher levels of emission control. The other city designs all offered reduced exposure to pollutants in various ways, but little change in fuel usage and CO_2 emissions. Thus, the balance between urban form and pollution is complex but can be subject to change by deliberate design.

The intermediate-field regime

Here, a dispersing plume cross-section is large enough to spread across a number of buildings. It corresponds typically to source distances between a few hundred metres and one kilometre. Figure 2.6.4 shows a sketch of this regime. Dispersion depends on the area density (the proportion of the surface area occupied by obstacles), the mean building heights and widths and their variability in a given area. The layout of surface structures and the wind direction over them is also important as some patterns can greatly alter the rates of lateral and vertical dispersion. For example, for releases near the ground, plumes within urban areas mix rapidly vertically to the height of the buildings and beyond and laterally to the widths of the buildings.

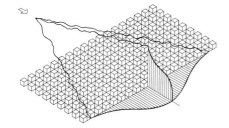

Figure 2.6.1 The far-field regime

Categories of urban layout[2.6.4]	
Business-as-usual	Extrapolation of current patterns into the future
Compact city	Increased population density of inner suburbs
Edge city	Increased population and density of an inner group of suburbs
Corridor city	A focus of growth along linear radial corridors supported by improved public transport and infrastructure
Fringe city	Additional growth, predominantly at the outer boundaries
Ultra city	Additional growth in secondary cities within 100 km, linked by high-speed transport

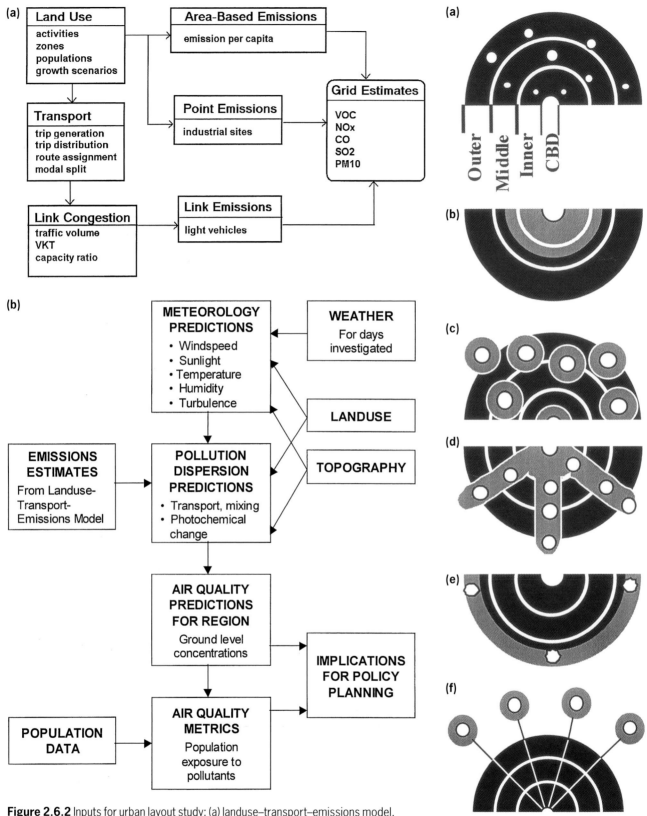

Figure 2.6.2 Inputs for urban layout study: (a) landuse–transport–emissions model, (b) prognostic meteorological and airshed models

Figure 2.6.3 Types of urban area: (a) business-as-usual, (b) compact city, (c) edge city, (d) corridor city, (e) fringe city, (f) ultra city

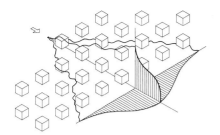

Wind
direction

Figure 2.6.5 The near-field regime

Figure 2.6.4 The intermediate-field
regime

The near-field regime

This regime covers plume dispersion over short distances, up to perhaps a few hundred metres. Here the width of a plume will be of the order of tens of metres or less (at distances of 10–20 m the plume width may only be a few metres). Thus, a locally discharged contaminant plume can only affect a limited region at one time, there will be either no exposure or a relatively high concentration when the plume impacts on a particular site. It is quite common for there to be very high levels of fluctuation in concentration at a single position, over time-scales of seconds. However, there is also a capacity for increased mixing to occur downwind of buildings, over areas of the order of the cross-section of the buildings. Concentrations are reduced but exposure is more likely to occur. Figure 2.6.5 shows sketches of these types of dispersion behaviour.

From a local point of view there may be no way to avoid large polluting sources at long distances, which pervade the whole urban area. However, there are greater possibilities for avoiding and controlling local sources so that their effects can be diminished by planning and regulation. There is a potential for further minimizing the effects of local pollution sources by the choice of urban layout and design (section 4.7), especially if this is done with regard to the local weather patterns.

References to section 2.6

[2.6.1] QUARG (Quality of Urban Air Review Group). *Urban air quality in the United Kingdom. UK Department of the Environment.* London, The Stationery Office, 1993.

[2.6.2] QUARG (Quality of Urban Air Review Group). *Diesel vehicle emissions and urban air quality. UK Department of the Environment.* London, The Stationery Office, 1993.

[2.6.3] Salway A G, Eggleston H S, Goodwind J W L & Murrels T P. *UK emissions of air pollutants, 1970–1995.* National Emissions Inventory: National Environmental Technology Centre Report AEAT-1746/Issue 1. Culham, UK, AEA Technology, 1997.

[2.6.4] Manins P C, Cope M E, Hurley P J, Newton P W, Smith N C & Marquez L O. The impact of urban development on air quality and energy use. *Paper presented at 14th International Clean Air and Environment Conference,* 18–22 October 1998, Melbourne, Australia.

2.7 Heat sinks: sea, lakes and forests

Thermal performance of water bodies

Compared with most land surfaces a water body exhibits very little change in surface temperature during the day. Water is different because (i) solar radiation can be transmitted deep within it and then absorbed, (ii) heat can also pass deep within the water by convection and mixing, (iii) water loses heat by evaporation. So although water absorbs a lot of heat because of its low albedo (section 6.5), it is such a good heat sink that the heat transfer to its surroundings is small. By day, sensible heat flux is small because most of the energy is stored or evaporated off; at night it is small because the long-wave radiative cooling is largely offset by heat stored deep in the water. Little heat flows to and from the air by convection so atmospheric warming and cooling rates are relatively small over water bodies. In contrast, the convective heat flows and rates of temperature change over land are large and vary a lot during the day.

Land and sea (lake) breezes

Land and water surfaces therefore have different thermal responses, and this is the driving force behind the land and sea (lake) breeze circulation system encountered near ocean or lake shorelines. By day, the land is warmer and air above it rises. This is replaced by air from the relatively cool sea (the sea breeze). At night the air flow is reversed; air rises over the warm water and is replaced by air from the relatively cool land (land breeze) (Figure 2.7.1). Thermal breeze systems of this type develop most quickly in anticyclonic summer weather with light winds and high solar radiation. These conditions produce the greatest differences between sea and land. Increased cloud or stronger winds modify or swamp these local winds.

Daytime sea breezes (Figure 2.7.2) are more powerful than the land breeze at night. During the day the sun warms the land up quickly giving large temperature differences. Commonly, the sea breeze blows at 2–5 m s^{-1}, extends inland as far as 100 km, and affects the air flow up to a height of 1–2 km. The horizontal extent of the breeze may allow it to be deflected by the rotation of the earth so that by late afternoon the inflow can end up being almost parallel with the coast. On the other hand, the land breeze is usually about 1–2 m s^{-1} in strength and smaller in both horizontal and vertical extent.

During the sea breeze cool moist air from the sea reaches the land where it rises. This can often cause cumulus clouds to form on the landward side, further cooling the coastline compared with areas further inland.

Ponds and rivers

The influence of a pond or a river on the air of the surrounding built-up area is a surface cooling process that depends on three things:
● length of the mass of water in the direction of the prevailing winds,
● air velocity,
● situation of the area downwind where the cooling effect is examined.

Several authors have investigated this subject. Ishii et al[2.7.1] performed experimental research on the thermal effect of a pond on the surrounding

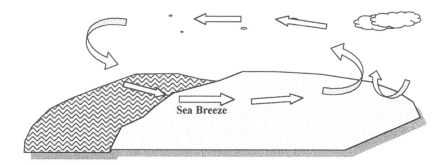

Figure 2.7.1 Night-time land breezes

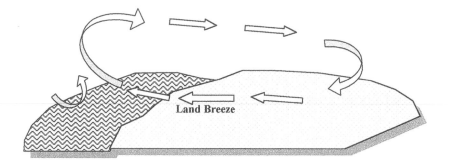

Figure 2.7.2 Daytime sea breezes

built-up area. Two surveys were conducted and compared, when water filled the pond and after the pond was drained. The area surrounding the pond was kept cooler when the pond was filled with water. The greatest difference found on the day when the pond was full, was about 3 °C in the early afternoon. The air temperature distribution demonstrated the cool island effect of the pond.

Murakawa et al[2.7.2] measured the temperature distribution near a river and studied the influence on the air temperature of the surrounding areas. It appeared that the influence of the river on the microclimate varied with the width of river and road and the building density in the surrounding area. They also analysed the effects of wind velocity on the drop in air temperature. The air temperature difference between the river and the city area was about 3–5 °C on a fine day. The analysed wind velocity was about 1–5 m/s.

Katayama et al[2.7.3] examined the cooling effects of a river and a sea breeze on the thermal environment in a built-up area in summer. The measurements were made along the river and an avenue which went in the direction of the sea–land breeze. The air temperature was lower above the river than above the avenue. The air temperature difference increased almost in proportion to the surface temperature difference. The river was found to be a useful open space to introduce the sea breeze into an urban area.

In the POLIS project, computational fluid dynamics (CFD) numerical analysis was performed with results very close to those of the literature mentioned. The results were presented as the relative temperature drops (actual temperature drop/maximum temperature drop) at and after the mass of water as a function of the air velocity and the length of mass of water (in the wind direction). The results were applied to different situations such as the influence of the Tagus river (14 km of cooling length) on the EXPO '98 ground in Lisbon (600 m in the wind direction). Figure 2.7.3 shows the results for a

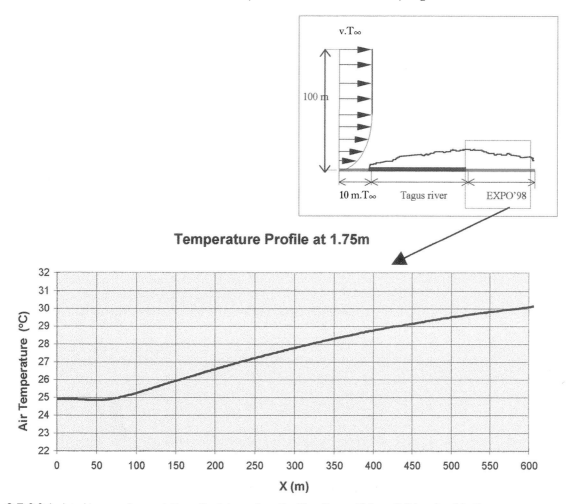

Figure 2.7.3 Calculated temperature variation with distance from the River Tagus, Lisbon. © University of Seville

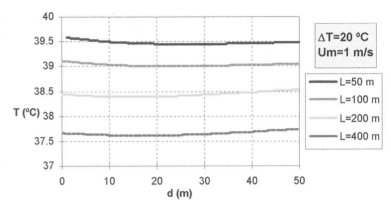

Figure 2.7.4 Variation of temperature with distance d from lakes of various widths.
© University of Seville

wind velocity of 1 m/s. There is a temperature drop of about 6 °C in the first 100 m due to the presence of the river. From this point, there is a progressive heating of the air so that, at the edge of the site, its temperature is roughly the same as without the cooling effect of the mass of water.

For smaller areas of water, however, there is less impact on the surrounding air temperature. Figure 2.7.4 shows the influence of a lake on the temperature of air flowing over it at 1 m/s. The lake is assumed to be 20 °C cooler than its surroundings. However, even a 100 m lake only has a 1 °C temperature impact on the air leaving it. This result is for a lake in a large open area. In an enclosed street or courtyard, a pond will have a larger impact, particularly if it replaces low albedo hard surfaces which would heat up in the sun.

Forests and urban parks

Forests or other green areas tend to be cooler and produce a cooling effect downwind. Plants absorb radiation and cool the air through evapotranspiration. They also slow down-air-flow, trapping the cooler air[2.7.4]. By day, there is a temperature maximum at the top of the leaf canopy with heavier cool air forming a stable layer beneath. Experimental results[2.7.4] indicate that inside the canopy and downwind, the daytime drop in temperature can reach 6 °C, especially in clear weather. Further, wind speed was reduced by around 2 m/s in mild conditions and by as much as 6.7 m/s during cyclonic weather when open-field wind speed was in the region of 8 m/s.

There is poor agreement on the effect of the green area on its built surroundings. Some authors[2.7.5] state that the effect of urban parks extends only a short distance into the surrounding urban area. They view parks primarily as providing a pleasant climate for people actually visiting them or living very near by. However, some experiments[2.7.6] prove that the temperatures of the air leaving an orchard remained low for a distance five times the height of the trees. POLIS experiments by Santamouris et al in Athens reveal that the cooling influence of the National Garden extends well beyond the immediate area. Consistent results have been obtained in similar field measurements such as that conducted in West Berlin[2.7.7].

POLIS CFD simulations treated a forest as a porous medium with a heat sink. The results downwind are characterized by a dimensionless variable that is the efficiency of the cooling effect:

$$\varepsilon = \frac{T_1 - T}{T_1 - T_F}$$

where:

$T_1 =$ incoming air temperature,
$T_F =$ forest temperature,
$T \ =$ temperature at a point.

Table 2.7.1 Influence of forest length on cooling efficiency					
Forest length (m)	Distance from the downwind edge, x (m)				
	10	30	50	100	150
50	0.83	0.64	0.55	0.42	0.36
100	0.86	0.70	0.60	0.46	0.39

Table 2.7.2 Influence of forest length on downwind temperature (°C)					
Forest length (m)	Distance from the downwind edge, x (m)				
	10	30	50	100	150
50	21.7	23.6	24.5	25.8	26.4
100	21.4	23.0	24.0	25.4	26.1

$T_1 = 30\,°C$, $T_F = 20\,°C$

Graphs showing the influence of the forest length and the forest porosity have been obtained. It has been demonstrated that the efficiency decreases exponentially with the distance from the downwind edge of the forest. The tables below show the cooling efficiency and an example of the corresponding downwind temperatures (assuming an inlet temperature of 30 °C and a forest temperature 10 °C below it).

For both tables two forest lengths of 50 m and 100 m, respectively, have been considered. There is a small increase in efficiency with increasing forest length. As the temperature dropped sharply within the first few metres inside the canopy, we can conclude that a large forest or vegetation stand is not necessary.

The characteristic distance where the cooling effect could still be detected, can be estimated by extrapolating the obtained results, and assuming that the effect is not worthwhile when efficiency is equal to either 0.5 (or 0.3). Thus, for an orange orchard, 50 m in length, an external wind velocity of 10 m/s, 5 m height, we obtain a characteristic distance of 70 m (160 m). This characteristic distance is 14 times (32 times) the height of the trees, which means that it is not necessary to place the trees very close to buildings in order to benefit from their microclimates.

However, an increasing density of forest produces a larger pressure drop at the downwind edge. Then the behaviour is very different because of a recirculating vortex (see Figure 2.7.5). Cooling efficiency drops sharply downwind of the forest, and the vertical temperature profile is different.

Finally, external wind velocity has some influence: the simulations showed that efficiency increases with the velocity, but this influence is only important at low-flow velocities.

References to section 2.7
[2.7.1] **Ishii A, Iwamoto S, Katayama T, Hayashi T, Shiotsuki Y, Kitayama H, Thutsumi J & Nishida M.** A comparison of field surveys on the thermal environment in urban areas surrounding a large pond: when filled and when drained. *Energy and Buildings* 1990/1991: **15–16**: 965–971.

[2.7.2] **Murakawa S, Sekine T, Narita K, Nishina D.** Study of the effects of a river on the thermal environment in an urban area. *Energy and Buildings* 1990/1991: **15–16**: 993–1001.

[2.7.3] **Katayama T, Hayashi T, Shiotsuki Y, Kitayana H, Ishii A, Nishida M, Tsutsumi J, Oguro M.** Cooling effects of a river and sea breeze on the thermal environment in a built-up area. *Energy and Buildings* 1990/1991: **15–16**: 973–978.

[2.7.4] **Oke T R.** *Boundary layer climates.* Cambridge, Cambridge University Press, 1987.

[2.7.5] **Givoni B.** *Climate considerations in building and urban design.* New York, Van Nostrand Reinhold, 1998.

[2.7.5] **Taha H, Akbari H & Rosenfeld A.** Heat island and oasis effect of vegetative canopies. Micro-meteorological field measurements. *Theoretical and Applied Climatology* 1991: **44**: 123–129.

[2.7.6] **Horbert M & Kircheorg A.** Climatic and hygienic aspects in the planning of inner city open spaces: Berliner Grosser Tiergarten. *Energy and Buildings* 1982: **5**(1): 11–22.

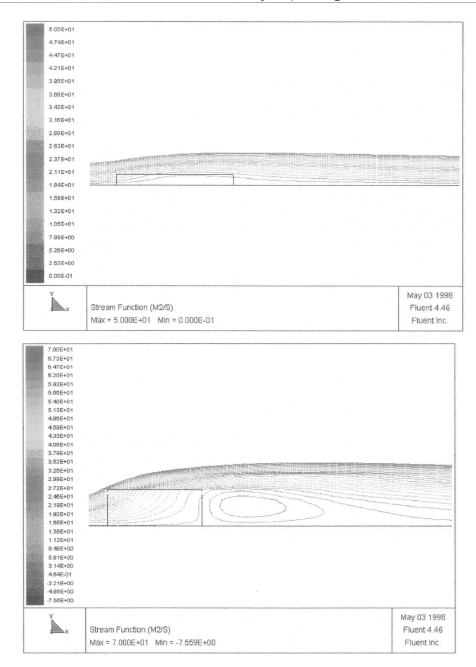

Figure 2.7.5 Stream function: low and high density forest. © University of Seville

2.8 Conclusions

Even within the space of a few kilometres, the climate of different sites can vary considerably. Where there is a choice of site or where different activities take place in different areas the following should be borne in mind.

Cool and intermediate climates

● City centre sites are warmer than rural or suburban sites (section 2.2).

● Sites should be well-sheltered from prevailing winter winds (section 2.4). Hilltop and coastal sites tend to be most exposed.

● A south-facing slope will be warmer and give better solar access (section 2.3).

● For best solar access, the site should not be heavily obstructed to the south (sections 4.2, 4.3, 4.4).

Warm climates
● Sites near heat sinks like the sea, lakes and forests will be cooler
  (section 2.7).
● Natural ventilation will be easier if the site can catch prevailing
  summertime winds (section 2.5).
● Sites with low traffic density will be cooler.

As well as the thermal aspects of site position there are a range of other factors
which need to be borne in mind as follows.
● Choose a site away from major pollution sources (section 2.6).
● Activities likely to cause air pollution should be sited away from areas
  where dispersion could be poor.
● Natural ventilation will be more difficult to achieve in noisy or polluted sites
  (section 2.5).
● On a city-wide level, energy savings from better microclimate and solar
  access on greenfield sites can be outweighed by increased transport use.
  Environmental planning needs to take into account the layout of urban
  development (section 2.1) as well as the provision of public transport.

3 Public open space

In cities, open spaces are often heavily used and so the design of open spaces has a big impact on the comfort of city dwellers. The layout of the space can affect thermal comfort and exposure to pollution through its effects on temperature and air flows. There are also important psychological issues like feelings of security, enclosure and views. Since an open space is largely defined by the buildings surrounding it, this chapter may be of interest to designers of individual buildings as well as to those planning major developments with their own open spaces.

3.1 People and open spaces

Strategy: Facilitate natural surveillance, personal control and visibility through open space design and equipment

It is widely acknowledged that urban design can have significant effects on people's perceptions (for example, thermal comfort) and behaviour. Energy-related concerns form only one aspect of the general quality of open spaces. There are a number of other factors, sometimes conflicting, that should be considered alongside them. Personal safety is a very important issue in open space design for people, and therefore deserves special care.

Though personal insecurity concerns may seem subjective, they are neither entirely irrational nor totally unpredictable. In environments where fear and victimization are high, features of the exterior environment can either aggravate or lessen the problem, from both the objective and subjective point of views.

In such situations, people naturally tend to scan their environment in search of danger signals. Consequently physical deterioration, or lack of any public investment in the open space, act as physical cues for fear of crime. Some morphological characteristics of urban open spaces can also play this role.

Design: prospect, refuge and escape
Prospect, refuge and escape are three exterior site features that can influence our perception of a place's safety.

Prospect
This can be measured by the view length distribution in all directions from a specific viewing point. A low prospect will reduce the possible control of a given area by potential victims. As such it is often considered as a cue for insecurity. When designing an open space, one should consider the 'social distances' in Table 3.1.1. For instance, medieval squares had average dimensions of 57×140 metres.

Table 3.1.1 Common social distances	
Distance (m)	
0–0.5	Smell and thermal radiation perception
0.5–1.25	Maximum distance for touching
2.1–3.6	Conversation distance
9	Maximum individual contact distance
12	Maximum distance to perceive facial expressions
24	Maximum distance for recognizing a face
135	Maximum distance for seeing any human movement
1200	Maximum distance for seeing a human silhouette
4000	Horizon distance for a person whose eye is 1.65 m above ground

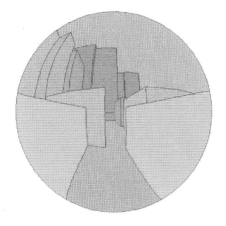

Figure 3.1.1 TOWNSCOPE's orthogonal projections and sky opening calculations of area A. It has highly enclosed spaces (its sky opening is 37%) with cross paths hidden by high planters and vegetation on either side. To pass through, pedestrians would have to turn into one of these blind alleyways. They would lack prospect into potential areas of refuge for an offender

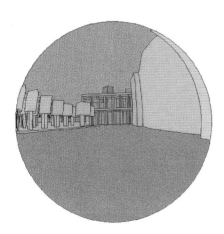

Figure 3.1.2 TOWNSCOPE's orthogonal projection in site B shows a high-prospect area which offers a wide panoramic view (the sky opening is 81%). The area on the left of the orthogonal projection is moderate in refuge. Offenders can hide in the vegetation, but passers-by can move away from the vegetation to reduce refuge. The central open area is low in refuge

Refuge

This parameter defines how easy it is for a potential attacker to hide in or next to the open space. It is also an insecurity cue. Refuge can include hiding places, dark spots, trees and shrubs, parked cars and building enclosures[3.1.1].

Escape

Finally, the individual's feeling of safety is influenced by the degree to which a space affords an opportunity for escape: either an exit route from a potential threat, or by reaching someone else who could respond in case of an attack. Escape places (shops, bars) are safe areas where a potential victim could find possible refuge in case of fear of aggression. If a space offers no escape (in terms of escape routes or escape places) the person can feel unsafe.

The combination of prospect, refuge and escape can help show how different exterior design features affect perceptions of safety. They have been correlated to both objective and subjective security through on-site social surveys by Nasar & Fisher[3.1.1]. These authors checked and validated their method on the site around the Wexner Center, a museum complex for visual arts at Ohio State University. Areas labeled A and B correspond to two zones surveyed by Nasar & Fisher. Area A (Figure 3.1.1) is considered as low prospect and high refuge; area B (Figure 3.1.2) is considered as high prospect and low refuge.

Prospect considerations may clash with energy-related concerns, especially in southern latitudes. Trade-offs between security and energy concerns are sometimes difficult to resolve.

Equipment: public lighting design

The lack of public lighting at night can be another physical cue for personal insecurity. Users of the space should encounter consistent, well-lit, clean spaces, enhancing their feeling of safety. The purpose of the lighting must be properly identified. If the lighting is to enhance the security of an area[3.1.3, 3.1.4] it should be sufficient to support the *principles of natural surveillance.*

In pedestrian areas, the main objective should be to allow people to identify the intentions of a passer-by and react appropriately. A semi-cylindrical illuminance of 0.8 lux computed at 1.5 metres above ground allows identification of another person's intentions at 4 metres distance. The semi-cylindrical computation method is given in Figure 3.1.3.

Nevertheless, the *application of lighting should not necessarily tend to uniformity.* Optimizing ground illumination is often not the best way to consider security concerns. Overlighting some strategic areas, like building entrances, parking lots and underground passages can be very efficient when it clearly responds to peoples' subjective concerns. A detailed survey of an area should be carried out before any major changes to the public lighting. This should include the likely night-time occupancy, natural pedestrian routes, dark areas, local landmarks, strategic areas, and high crime areas.

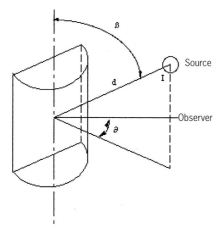

Figure 3.1.3 Semi-cylindrical illuminance calculation method

E (semi-cylindrical)

$$= [I/(\pi d^2)] * (1 + \cos\alpha) * \sin\beta$$

where:

I = source intensity in candela,

d = distance (m) between a source and the target,

α = the angle projected on a horizontal plane between the direction of the observer and that of the incident light ray.

The design should then specify these public lighting parameters:

● colour,
● orientation,
● intensity,
● design,
● type and position of light sources, and
● the definition of the lighted area.

Lighting provides night-time landmarks that may or may not coincide with day-time ones.

References to section 3.1

[3.1.1] Nasar J L, Fisher B, Grannis M. Proximate physical cues to fear of crime. *Landscape and urban planning* 1993: **26**: 161–178.

[3.1.2] Appleton J. *The experience of place.* London, Wiley, 1975.

[3.1.3] Painter K. Value for money: street lighting and crime reduction. *Lighting Journal* 1998: **63**(6): 24–27.

[3.1.4] Hargroves R, Hugill J R & Thomas S R. Security, surveillance and lighting. *Proceedings CIBSE National Lighting Conference*, Bath, 1996. pp 209–216. London, CIBSE, 1996.

3.2 Canyon effects

Strategy: use street design to limit heat build-up and promote ventilation

Tall buildings lining a street turn it into an 'urban canyon' with its own microclimate. According to Oke[3.2.1], the air space above a city can be divided into the 'urban air canopy', and the boundary layer over the city space called 'the urban air dome'. The urban air canopy is the space bounded by the city buildings up to their roofs. This layer includes local microclimates generated by the various building configurations. The specific climatic conditions at any point within the canopy depend on the immediate surroundings and in particular the geometry, materials and their properties. The upper boundary of the urban canopy varies from one spot to another because of the variable heights of the buildings and the wind speed.

The air dome layer is defined by Oke[3.2.2], as 'that portion of the planetary boundary layer whose characteristics are affected by the presence of an urban area at its lower boundary', and is more homogeneous in its properties over the urban area.

The temperature distribution in the urban canopy layer is highly affected by the city's radiation balance. Solar radiation incident on the urban surfaces is absorbed and then transformed to sensible heat. Most of the solar radiation strikes roofs, and the vertical walls of the buildings, and only a relatively small fraction may reach the ground level.

Walls, roofs and the ground emit long-wave radiation to the sky. The intensity of the emitted radiation depends on the view factor of the surface to the sky. Under urban conditions most of the sky dome viewed by walls and surfaces may be blocked by other buildings, and in these cases the long-wave radiation exchange does not result in significant losses.

The net balance between solar gain and heat loss by emitted long-wave radiation determines the thermal balance of urban areas. Because the radiant heat loss is slower in urban areas, the net balance is more positive than in the surrounding rural areas and thus higher temperatures are obtained. A comprehensive description of the urban canyon thermal regime is given by Mills[3.2.3]. Canyons can be modelled by dividing them into zones and calculating the heat flows between each one.

Air flow is an important issue in city streets as ventilation may be much lower than in open space. Further information on this issue is given in section 4.6.

Canyon layout and temperature increase

As one cause of the heat island effect is the restricted view of the sky from ground and buildings, its magnitude will depend on street geometry. Park[3.2.4] discusses the relationship between population and sky view factor for the different regions, characterized by different heights of buildings and different canyon widths.

Oke[3.2.5] has proposed an analytical expression to correlate the maximum heat island intensity during clean and calm nights with the geometry of the 'urban canyon', as expressed by the relationship between the height of the buildings, H, and the distance between them, W:

$$DT_{max} = 7.45 + 3.97 \ln (H/W)$$

It is valid for $H > W$.

Various studies have investigated the relationship between the canyon layout and especially the sky-view factor with the heat island intensity as well as with surface temperatures. Yamashita et al[3.2.6] report a clear correlation of urban air temperature and sky view factor for some Japanese cities. Barring et al[3.2.7] studied the relationship between the street surface temperature and the sky-view factor in Malmo, Sweden. They report a strong correlation between the surface temperature pattern and the street geometry; the highest sky-view factors gave the lowest surface temperatures. Higher surface temperatures are recorded in low sky-view factor canyons outside the city as well. However, a clear correlation between the urban temperature and the sky-view factor has not been found. This clearly indicates that the standard level air temperature of the streets is governed by more complex and regional factors than their surface temperature, even if the local canyon geometry is of importance.

Similar results were found in Athens in measurements for the POLIS research project. There was a clear variation in surface temperature between urban sites of different layout. Similar results have been reported by Eliasson[3.2.8, 3.2.9] for the city of Goteborg in Sweden. It is found that during the winter period, the surface temperature was highly influenced by the city structure. In a similar study, Arnfield[3.2.10], reported a surface temperature difference of 4 °C between urban sites of different density (H/W ratio of 0.5 and 2.0, respectively). Both studies show clearly that important variations in surface temperature exist between urban sites of different geometry. On the other hand, there is a relatively weak connection between geometry and air temperature. This is because the air temperature also depends on wind flows within the canyon.

Air flows in a street canyon

Urban canyons are characterized by three main parameters (see Figure 3.2.2):
H = the mean height of the buildings in the canyon,
W = the canyon width, and
L = the canyon length.

Three geometrical measures can help describe the air flows. These are:
● the aspect ratio H/W,
● the ratio L/H, and
● the building density $j = A_r/A_L$ where A_r is the roof area on plan of the average building and A_L is the 'lot' area or unit ground area occupied by each building.

The flow-over arrays of buildings has been the subject of many studies. When the predominant direction of the airflow is approximately normal (say ± 30°) to the long axis of the street canyon, three types of air-flow regimes are observed as a function of the building (L/H), and canyon (H/W), geometry[3.2.11] (see Figure 3.2.2).

When the buildings are well apart (H/W > 0.05), their flow-fields do not

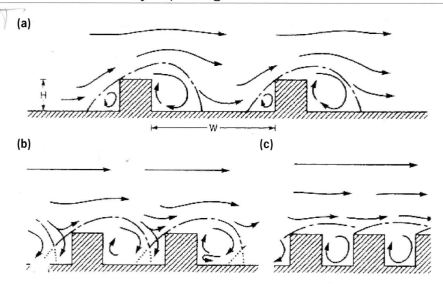

Figure 3.2.1 The flow regime associated with air flow over building arrays of increasing H/W: (a) isolated roughness flow, (b) wake interference flow, (c) skimming flow. Reproduced from Oke[3.2.12]

interact. At closer spacings (Figure 3.2.1a), the wakes are disturbed and the flow regime is known as 'isolated roughness flow'. When the height and spacing of the array combine to disturb the eddies at the back of the first building and the front of the second, the regime changes to wake interference flow (Figure 3.2.1b). This has secondary flows in the canyon space where the downward flow of the wind, after it has passed over the first building, is reinforced by deflection down the windward face of the next building downstream. At even greater H/W and building density, a stable circulatory vortex is established in the canyon and transition to a 'skimming' flow regime occurs where the bulk of the flow does not enter the canyon (Figure 3.2.1c). However, this skimming flow is easily broken up by variations in the heights of buildings.

The transitions between these three regimes occur at critical combinations of H/W and L/W. Oke[3.2.12], has proposed threshold lines dividing flow into three regimes as functions of the building (L/H) and canyon (H/W) geometry. The proposed threshold lines are given in Figure 3.2.2.

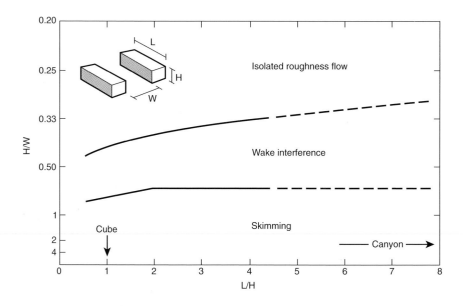

Figure 3.2.2 Threshold lines dividing flow into three regimes as functions of the building (L/H) and canyon (H/W), geometry. Reproduced from Oke[3.2.12]

The flow regime inside a canyon has been measured in many experiments. Comparison of the wind components measured in the canyon with the winds above the roof has shown that[3.2.13]:

● a vortex in the canyon appears to exist at all finite windspeeds across the canyon,
● the transverse vortex speed $(u^2+w^2)^{0.5}$ across the canyon is proportional to the transverse wind component above the roof and is independent of the component of the wind along the canyon, v. Here, u is the cross-canyon wind velocity, v is the velocity along the canyon and w is the vertical velocity in the canyon.

Air-flow measurements reported in ref.[3.2.13] have also shown that a vortex is created in the street canyon for flows perpendicular to the canyon down to 10–20° to the axis parallel to the canyon. Under these conditions, there is enough cross-canyon flow to drive the vortex. Also, the along-canyon flow component, v, roughly followed the equation $v = V\cos\theta$, where V is the overall wind speed over the buildings and θ is the angle between the wind flow and the canyon axis.

It was also found that the vortex was rarely static with time. It would repeatedly form, accelerate and suddenly collapse due to variations in local wind speed and direction and to interactions with other local canyon flows.

Design parameters

It is very difficult to offer specific guidance on planning canyons in the urban environment. However, in order to promote air flow inside the canyon, the height-to-width ratio should be lower than unity[3.2.1]. To enhance air flow and natural ventilation of urban buildings the following procedure is appropriate.

● Calculate the mean air speed inside the canyon based on the wind-speed data collected by the nearest meteorological station. The calculation methods given in other sections of this book may be applied. However, as a rule of thumb the wind speed inside the canyon can be expected to be an order of magnitude lower than the undisturbed external wind speed.
● Using a network air-flow calculation model like AIOLOS or BREEZE[3.2.14], evaluate the natural ventilation potential of the initial design.
● Optimize the size of the openings in order to achieve the design air changes per hour.

References to section 3.2

[3.2.1] Oke T R. *Boundary layer climates.* Cambridge, Cambridge University Press, 1987.

[3.2.2] Oke T R. The distance between canopy and boundary layer urban heat island. *Atmosphere* 1976: **14**(4): 268–277.

[3.2.3] Mills G M. Simulation of the energy budget of an urban canyon. 1 Model structure and sensitivity test. *Atmospheric Environment* 1993: **27B**(2): 157–170.

[3.2.4] Park H S. City size and urban heat island intensity for Japanese and Korean cities. *Geographical Review of Japan (Sep. A)* 1987: **60**: 238-250.

[3.2.5] Oke T R. Canyon geometry and the nocturnal urban heat island: comparison of scale model and field observations. *Journal of Climatology* 1981: **1**: 237–254.

[3.2.6] Yamashita S, Sekine K, Shoda M, Yamashita K & Hara Y. On the relationships between heat island and sky view factor in the cities of Tama River Basin, Japan. *Atmospheric Environment* 1986: **20**(4): 681–686.

[3.2.7] Barring L, Mattsson J O & Lindqvist S. Canyon geometry, street temperatures and urban heat island in Malmo, Sweden. *Journal of Climatology* 1985: **5**: 433–444.

[3.2.8] Eliasson I. Urban geometry, surface temperature and air temperature. *Energy and Buildings* 1990/1991: **15–16**: 141–145.

[3.2.9] Eliasson I. Urban nocturnal temperatures, street geometry and land use. *Atmospheric Environment* 1996: **30**(3): 379–392.

[3.2.10] Arnfield A J. Canyon geometry, the urban fabric and nocturnal cooling: a simulation approach. *Physical Geography* 1990: **11**: 209–239.

[3.2.11] Oke T R. Overview of interactions between settlements and their environments. World Meteorological Organization (WMO) experts meeting on Urban and building climatology.

Report WCP-37. Geneva, WMO, 1982.

   [3.2.12] Oke T R. Street design and urban canopy layer climate. *Energy and Buildings* 1988: **11**: 103-113.

   [3.2.13] Geomet. *Kfz: Schadstoffbelastungen in Strassen-schluchten.* Final Report. Berlin, Geomet, 1985.

   [3.2.14] BRE. BREEZE software package for estimating ventilation rates. BRE package AP55. CRC, Garston.

3.3 Road layout and orientation

Strategy: consider solar access, pollution dispersion and shade for pedestrians when planning road layout.

Road layout can have a significant impact on the environmental and energy performance of a site.

● Passive solar housing needs to face as near to due south as possible (Figure 3.3.1).
● In dense urban layouts some road layouts can help disperse localized pollutants, like traffic fumes.
● In hot summers in cities some road layouts can provide more shade for pedestrians.

Road layout for passive solar design
In passive solar layouts the main facades of the buildings should face within 30° of due south (section 4.3). In housing estates the easiest way to achieve this is to have east–west roads. Then the main solar facade can either face the

North

Figure 3.3.1 At Willow Park, Chorley, UK, careful road layout design means all the passive solar homes can have a south orientation

road (south-entry houses), or away from it (north-entry houses) (Figure 3.3.2)[3.3.1].

If roads have to run north-south there are various techniques to give the houses a southerly orientation (Figure 3.3.3)[3.3.2]:

● spacing out larger detached houses one plot deep along the road,
● placing higher density housing around short culs-de-sac leading off the north-south roads,
● innovative house designs, including the use of roof-space solar collectors.

On diagonal roads (NW–SE or NE–SW) solar access can be improved by placing houses at an angle to the road (Figure 3.3.4)[3.3.3]. North and south entry types will be required on different sides of the road.

Road layout to disperse pollutants

Pollutants are most easily dispersed if the road is aligned at around 30° to the dominant wind. Polluting discharges released in streets aligned with the wind tend to be kept within the width of the street at first, limiting their dispersion. Streets at right angles to the wind flow also have poor dispersion unless they are wide compared with the height of buildings. Section 4.6 gives further details.

Sun penetration into urban streets

In hot climates in summer, thermal comfort in outdoor areas is improved if shade is provided. To avoid sunlight penetrating to the ground, one approach is to have very tall, narrow streets. Street orientation is also important. Sunlight penetration was calculated for four possible street orientations in Rome (42° N) and Athens (38° N), for a long street, of height to width (H/W) ratio 2. Table 3.3.1 gives the percentage of annual sunlight hours for which the sun could penetrate to ground level at some point on the street. For times when the sun is shining this is the probability that it will reach the base of the street canyon. The sunshine hours are divided into the summer (22 March–21 September) and winter months (22 September–21 March). They were calculated using the BRE sunlight availability indicators produced for the POLIS project (see Appendix A2).

The results show that east-west streets are to be avoided in hot climates. They have significantly higher annual sunshine penetration than the other street orientations, and all of this occurs in the six summer months. In mid-summer the sun can reach the north side of the street for nearly all the hottest part of the day. The only exception to this is if the street is very narrow indeed compared with its height. For Athens H/W would need to be at least 4, for Rome an H/W of 3.5 would be best to avoid sun penetration.

North-south streets have the least sun penetration, and around a third of it occurs in the six winter months when it will be more welcome. The sunlight is concentrated around the middle of the day, and at other times of day the whole of the street will be in shade. Over the six summer months, sunlight penetration is less than half that for an east-west street.

This lower sun penetration arises at the cost of sunlight on the building faces. The same amount of sun enters the top of each canyon. With the E–W street more reaches the ground, with the N–S street more reaches the building

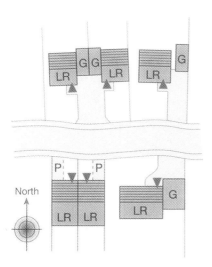

Figure 3.3.2 Housing along an east-west road. South-entry houses have the entry on the south, and the living room on the south (facing to road). North-entry houses have the entrance on the north but the living room on the south (facing away from the road)

Table 3.3.1 Probable annual sunlight hours (%) for which sun can reach the ground in long linear streets		
Canyon orientation	Rome	Athens
E–W	41 (41 summer 0 winter)	46 (46 summer 0 winter)
NE–SW	29 (22 summer 7 winter)	31 (24 summer 7 winter)
SE–NW	31 (24 summer 7 winter)	31 (23 summer 8 winter)
N–S	27 (18 summer 9 winter)	30 (20 summer 10 winter)

East-west roads give good solar orientation. Varying the orientation by up to 30° from due south can add visual interest to a scheme. Passive solar layouts do not need all the houses to be slavishly facing due south

North

On **diagonal roads**, houses and plots are angled 30° of south for better solar access

Culs-de-sac at right angles to **north-south roads** provide houses with good solar orientation

Bungalows used immediately south of two-storey houses minimise obstruction

Detached houses, one plot deep used on **north-south roads**

Figure 3.3.3 A passive solar layout showing good solar orientation of houses

faces. However, the sun for the N–S street is more likely to strike the east- and west-facing buildings at an oblique angle, resulting in less solar gain. Different solar-shading strategies will need to be adopted; overhangs will work less well and vertical fins and deep reveals will be better. Shading the upper storeys of the buildings could be a problem.

People have to move about the city somehow, and if all the streets run north-south then they have little opportunity to get from east to west or vice versa. If we consider the typical grid pattern of streets running at right angles to each other, a NE–SW/SE–NW grid (Figure 3.3.5) has significantly less sun penetration than an E–W/N–S grid. Adding the summer sun penetrations together gives a sunlight score of 46 for Rome and 47 for Athens, compared with 59 for Rome and 66 for Athens with the E–W/N–S grid.

References to section 3.3

[3.3.1] NBA Tectonics. *A study of passive solar housing estate layout.* Report S1126. Harwell, UK, Energy Technology Support Unit. 1988.

[3.3.2] Department of the Environment. *Passive solar estate layout.* General Information Report 27. Garston, UK, BRECSU, 1997.

[3.3.3] University College Dublin. *Smakkebo.* Project Monitor, Issue 25. Dublin, University College for CEC. 1988.

Figure 3.3.4 At Smakkebo, Snekkersten, Denmark, the solar houses are placed at an angle to the road for optimum orientation

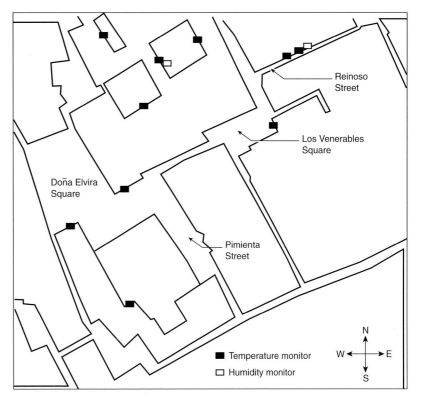

Figure 3.3.5 In the Santa Cruz area of Seville a NE–SW/SE–NW grid is the predominant street orientation. This, coupled with the reduced street width, results in low sun penetration. © University of Seville

3.4 Enclosure, views and landmarks

Strategy: Provide a clear definition of public open spaces through combinations of enclosure, views and landmarks.

Public open spaces are the core of urban cultural, social and economic life. They therefore deserve careful attention in urban design. Yet the shapes of open spaces would not be clear without an indication of their limits, whether real or virtual. The two main entities of urban environments are thus:

● *urban open spaces* (streets, squares, etc), and
● *built volumes* (dwellings, monuments, urban furniture, etc).

In traditional urban environments, these entities were totally interdependent. Any change in the external shape of buildings directly modifies the geometry of urban open spaces. On the other hand, precise limits to urban open spaces could not be defined without some constraints applied to the built elements. There are therefore two kinds of space: *dominant* and *residual* urban open space (Figure 3.4.1 and 3.4.2).

Spatial enclosure: floor, walls and roof

Traditional open spaces were often considered as 'urban rooms' whose walls are formed by buildings surrounding them. In these spaces the ceiling is left open, but it is very clearly defined by a 'ceiling line', which consists of the upper visual limit of the surrounding buildings (maybe rooftops or cornices) (Figure 3.4.3).

The enclosure of a city square focuses our attention on the space as an entity in itself, though it is connected to its urban surrounding. On an avenue, the enclosure may exist only on two sides, but it must be enough to hold our attention as a channel of space (Figure 3.4.4). When enclosure concentrates on the internal landscaping of open spaces, the design should also consider visual connections between spaces which are also important.

The enclosure of an open space can be characterized by a confinement level. Confinement describes the feeling of a visitor to a public space, between the extremes of claustrophobia and agoraphobia. This sensation depends on many factors of which some are purely subjective. To a first approximation,

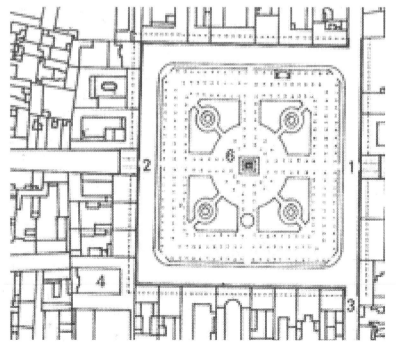

Figure 3.4.1 The square-shaped Place des Vosges (France) is dominant. The Figure illustrates how much the surrounding buildings and the cluster itself have been heavily constrained by the central open space, square-shaped geometry. © University of Liege

Figure 3.4.2 The irregular shape of Piazza della cisterna e del duomo in San Gimignano (Italy) is a residual open space delineated by surrounding buildings including the church. © University of Liege

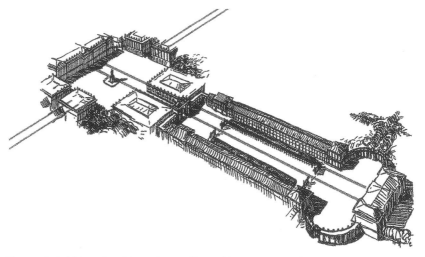

Figure 3.4.4 Place Stanislas in Nancy (France) is an example of an avenue where an enclosure is clearly delineated on the two long sides by trees and buildings, and punctuated with triumphal arches and the Stanislas statue. © University of Liege

however, the sensation of confinement at any point depends on the open-space sky opening calculated for this point.

For instance the sky opening (SO) of three typical open spaces is given in Table 3.4.1.

The sky opening can also be computed in a systematic way, on a grid, to visualize sky-opening variations. TOWNSCOPE's sky-opening maps (Appendix A1) can show the general organization of an open space and how connected it is with adjacent spaces (Figure 3.4.5).

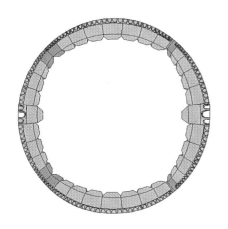

Figure 3.4.3 TOWNSCOPE's projection of the ceiling line of the Place des Vosges in Paris is entirely enclosed by surrounding buildings. The space is therefore very coherent. © University of Liege

Table 3.4.1 TOWNSCOPE's computations of the sky opening of three typical spaces			
Name	Average dimensions (m)	Mean height (m)	Sky opening (%)
Lucca	75 × 50	14	66
Arras Grand Place	190 × 100	10	88
Vosges	140 × 140	20	76

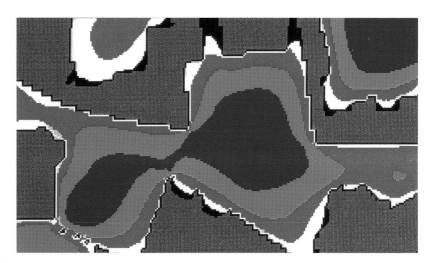

Figure 3.4.5 Illustration of a situation where the iso-sky-opening lines tend to merge two disconnected spaces (a square and an important parking area) because each space is not sufficiently enclosed by itself. © University of Liege

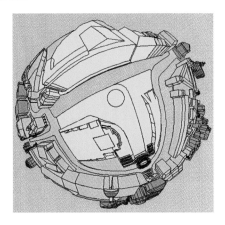

Figure 3.4.6 TOWNSCOPE's upside-down stereographic projection of a city square in Liège (Belgium) shows combinations of a view channel and a view termination in the upper-right corner of the Figure.
© University of Liege

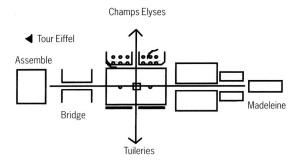

Figure 3.4.7 The French Baroque Place de la Concorde in Paris is a combination of long- and short-distance views. View channels and terminations include: the Champs-Elysées and Arc-de-Triomphe, the bridge and Parliament, the Tuilerie wall and the Louvre, the great buildings and the church of La Madeleine. © University of Liege

Views

By contrast with enclosure, views tend to create connections between adjacent and/or remote spaces. They are usually composed of a view channel and a view termination (Figure 3.4.6).
- View channel. Its purpose is to guide the observer's attention in a very specific direction. The channel could be a straight street, an alignment of trees, or even a bridge.
- View termination. Its purpose is to close the view on a specific focus which can be a monument or urban furniture (fountain, urban art, etc.).

By contrast with some suburban areas, mainly designed for car drivers, urban open-space networks should offer pedestrians attractive visual stimulation and useful cues for orientation and location.

Sixte-Quint's urban design for Rome is one of the pre-eminent examples of such spatial organization, where each square has been connected to others through the use of obelisks. Currently, views are used to improve the organization of urban spaces and perception of the city as a whole. La Defense in Paris was designed to comply with the historical major axis of Paris. It contains both short- and long-distance views (Figure 3.4.7).

Landmarks

Two main types of construction can be considered here:
- the traditional pattern, with regular units sharing a common typology and individualized by added decorations, and
- exceptional buildings (monumental architecture), either public or private, emerging from this urban pattern through their dimensions, their geometry or their position.

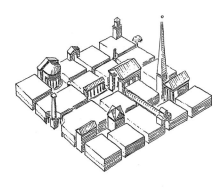

Figure 3.4.8 Landmarks become more easily identifiable if they have a clear form, if they contrast with their background, or if there is some prominence of spatial location

The first type gives the general reference ceiling line of the urban room described above, the second gives variability. Both contribute to the visual impression of the urban open space.

Landmarks are points of reference which most people experience from outside. By definition they are different from their surroundings, with some aspect that is unique or memorable in the context (Figure 3.4.8).

3.5 Sequences of spaces

Strategy: Urban design should consider how people move through the city

The way people perceive spaces is a dynamic activity. Even a static observer receives a myriad of instantaneous physiological perceptions which combine to give an overall impression of space. When combined with the observer's movement, this phenomenon becomes very complex.

Despite the growing importance of space occupied by cars in cities, pedestrian movement still deserves careful attention. Not only for its social and cultural value, but also because environmental conditions like temperature, air movement and ground surfaces become much more important.

The major characteristics of pedestrian movement
Speed and distance
Pedestrian speeds of movement are very low, around 1.3 m/s for adults. The design of road crossings usually assumes that 17% of pedestrians have a speed below 1 m/s. Nevertheless, pedestrian travel is preferable to other options for distances between 0 and 2 km. Bicycles are considered as competitive for distances up to 5 km. These two 'soft' modes of travel are therefore crucial since the average distance of all outdoor travel in a day is roughly 6 km.

Visual environment
Pedestrian travel allows optimal visual attention. The binocular visual field of a pedestrian is roughly 230° laterally and 150° vertically. This field is further increased by movement of the eyes and head. Consequently, pedestrians can easily observe their whole visible environment. By contrast, peripheral vision significantly disturbs the central vision when travelling at higher speeds. Car drivers have to concentrate on a smaller part of their visual field to foresee any possible difficulties.

Vulnerability
Pedestrians are highly vulnerable to physical accidents. As well as injuries caused by road accidents, the ground surface can be a major impediment for the disabled, elderly people and children. It therefore deserves careful attention.

Erratic pedestrian movement
Pedestrian movement is characterized by very frequent changes in direction, stops and reversing direction. Pedestrians usually tend to take the shortest route to their immediate goal, in spite of any impediment (legal or physical) that tends to force them to take a longer one. This is the reason why road crossings should not be located at more than 100 metre spacing. The road design should respect as much as possible 'natural movements' within its space. The same applies to time delays imposed by the layout of paths which should be reduced to a minimum.

Sequences of spaces
The attraction of pedestrian travel will largely depend on how varied and interesting the urban open space is. Sequential analysis is a way of defining variations in an observer's landscape as they move around. This type of technique is used in film making. For the urban designer, it gives a valuable framework to improve the visual richness of dynamic perception of an open space.

The basic idea behind this technique is to split up the continuous change of landscape caused by movement into several sequences. The reason for this is to avoid monotony, to give a sense of scale to the environment, to help people work out where they are, and to give a sense of movement when walking along a path.

Sequences: visual plan definition
Each sequence is characterized by a visual plan. This should be easy to identify, even though the components of the plan will vary with time and position within the sequence.

A plan should include stable relations between the following five factors despite small-scale variations within them:

- symmetry/asymmetry,
- lateral definition (objects of interest to one or both sides)/central definition (objects of interest straight ahead),
- frontal closure/open perspective,
- curved/narrowing/straight,
- aligned/zigzagging facades (folding screen)[3.5.1].

Sequence articulation
There are several ways of linking each sequence to the next one, to give the desired effect (Figures 3.5.1–3.5.3).

Visual connections
Direct links between totally separate sequences can be established through the use of landmarks (section 3.4). These landmarks help people work out where they are and which places they will reach next. Of course, landmarks may not be visible throughout the different sequences of movement.

Car driving and visual information
Motor car speeds are much higher than those of pedestrians, so traffic information usually tends to be much larger and concentrated on single focus points.

Concentrations of advertising hoardings and road signs can have significant effects on a driver's dynamic perception. The sequential design of streets should therefore consider how information is provided to drivers to make it as clear as possible.

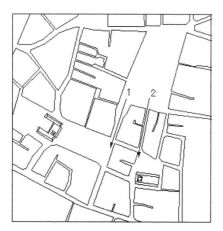

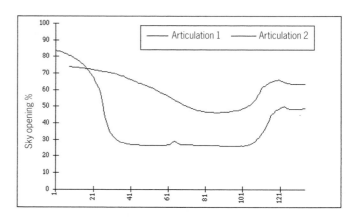

Figure 3.5.1 Connection of a funnel-shaped street with a space provides a gradual articulation between these two spaces. © University of Liege

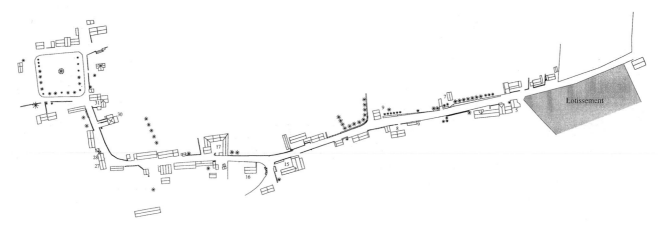

Figure 3.5.2 Articulation through a quick modification of one of the five plan areas and articulation through turning within a short distance maximize the surprise effect. © University of Liege

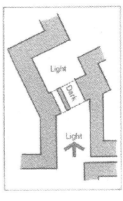

Figure 3.5.3 Key-hole, narrow openings and changes of direction maximize the attraction of the next sequence without revealing it. © University of Liege

Point saturation (Figure 3.5.4)

This happens when there are a great number of visual signs in the same place competing with each other. This often happens at decision points, where the drivers have to stop at road junctions or decrease their speed to choose which direction to go. Such information saturation mixes commercial and road information blindly. The two types of information compete for the driver's attention in a way that is very harmful to the overall clarity of the visual environment.

Longitudinal saturation (Figure 3.5.5)

Consists of the sustained presence of information all along a route. Even though the hoardings are quite distant from each other, their size, their great distance at which they can be seen, and the speed of the driver can lead to the accumulation in a very short space of time of a great number of visual stimuli.

Figure 3.5.4 Point visual information saturation at a crossroads in Liege, Belgium. © University of Liege

On the top of Figure 3.5.5 is the map of the urban space. The representation shows the following elements of the landscape: the road network, the building areas, the vegetation, the locations of the advertising hoardings, the commercial frontages and traffic signs.

At the centre of the Figure, three curves show the number of visual messages perceived at a given point on the route. The first applies to the road signs, the second to the hoardings and commercial frontages and the third is the combination of the two.

The lower part of the Figure shows, for each sign, the point from which it is seen, up to its own site. The bold lines represent the large hoardings (green lines) and the traffic lights and directional signs (blue lines).

This graphical representation shows, at each point on the route, the quantity and 'quality' of visual messages seen by the driver. It enables possible areas of visual information concentration to be located and identified on the map. It also shows longitudinal phenomena such as the origin and clustering of visual stimuli.

Reference to section 3.5

[3.5.1] **Greater London Council.** *An introduction to housing layout.* London, Architectural Press, 1978.

3.6 Conclusions

Open spaces form the major component of the urban environment and also affect the performance of the buildings which border them. They can be comfortable or uncomfortable places depending on their detailed design.

In cool and intermediate climates, open spaces should generally be:
● wide enough to allow adequate solar access (see sections 4.1–4.4),
● oriented to allow any solar buildings to receive solar gain; E–W roads give the most straightforward solar designs, but there are alternative techniques (section 3.3).

In warmer climates the emphasis will be more on providing cool, shady, well-ventilated spaces.
● Ventilation, and the heat trapped in a street, depend on the height to width ratio, H/W. For low H/W (< 0.3) there is good ventilation but little shading. As H/W increases, air flows become more turbulent. At H/W = 1 there is good ventilation with a vortex of air in the street. At street level this flows opposite to the wind direction. Finally, for large H/W there is very poor ventilation. A pool of stagnant air is created which can be cool in summer but can also trap pollutants.
● N–S streets will be less exposed to the sun than E–W streets. Where there is a grid of streets, NW–SE and NE–SW have lower solar exposure than other orientations (section 3.3).

In all climates, open spaces with pollution sources (like traffic) need to be wide enough to allow pollutants to disperse (section 3.3, see section 4.7). In general, spaces of this type need to be at least as wide as they are high.

The design of open spaces also needs to address the visual and psychological needs of the people using them. People need to feel secure; so spaces should not have hiding places for potential attackers or blind alleys where people feel trapped. Good night-time lighting should be provided (section 3.1).

People also need to be able to find their way about. Landmarks aid orientation, and specific views show direction and add interest. The sequences of spaces people experience need to be considered (section 3.5), with appropriate visual cues to act as signposts. Care is also needed to avoid a mass of conflicting information competing for the visual attention of people travelling by car (section 3.5).

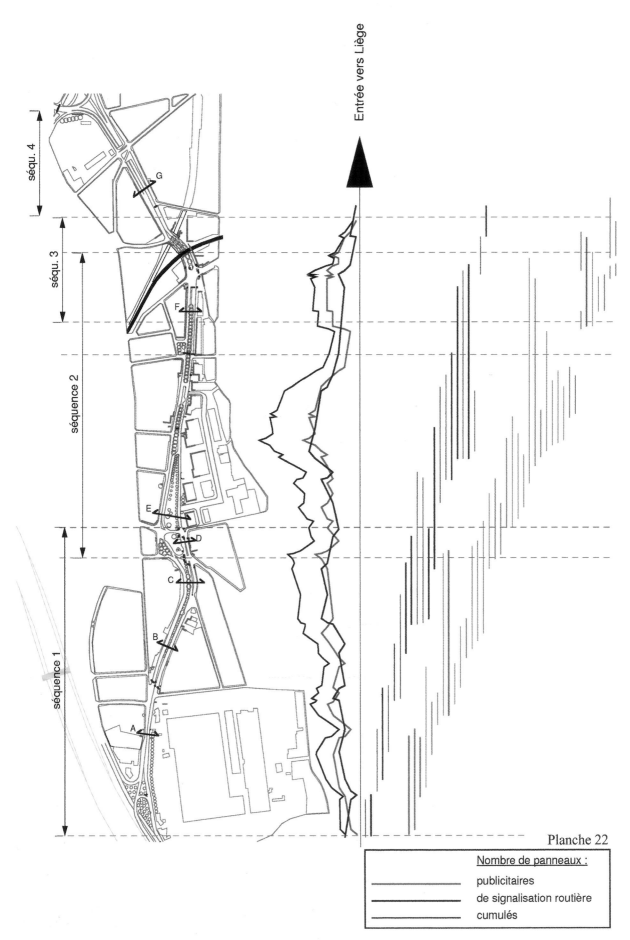

Entrée vers Liège

séqu. 4

séqu. 3

séquence 2

séquence 1

G

F

E

D

C

B

A

Planche 22

Nombre de panneaux :

publicitaires

de signalisation routière

cumulés

Figure 3.5.5 Visual information saturation in a city entrance. © University of Liege

4 Building layout

In urban areas building layout is the most important factor affecting the daylight, sunlight and solar heat gain reaching a building. It also affects sunlight in open spaces, ventilation, wind shelter and the dispersal of pollutants. When planning a new development, its impact on existing buildings nearby should be considered.

4.1 Spacing for daylighting

Strategy: Control the spacing and height of obstructions to allow good access to daylight for new and existing buildings

New development

Good daylight design starts at the site layout stage. If obstructing buildings are large or close by, adequate daylighting will be difficult to achieve. The distribution of light in the room will be affected as well as the total amount received.

At the site layout stage in design, window positions will often be undecided. A reference line 2 metres above ground level on each main face of the building (the likely level of the top half of windows) may be used. As a first check, draw a section in a plane perpendicular to each main face (Figure 4.1.1). If none of the obstructing buildings subtends an angle h to the horizontal (measured from the 2 metre reference line) greater than the critical values in Table 4.1.1, then there will still be the potential for good daylighting in the building.

If an obstructing building is taller than this, good daylighting may still be possible if it is narrow enough to allow adequate daylight around its sides. The vertical sky component[4.1.1] shows how much skylight falls on a vertical wall or window. It is the ratio of the direct sky illuminance on the vertical wall at a reference point, to the simultaneous horizontal illuminance under an unobstructed sky. The standard CIE Overcast Sky is used and the ratio is

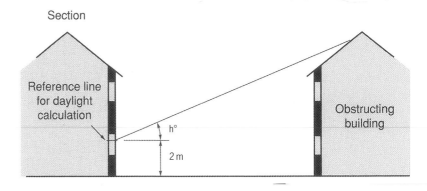

Figure 4.1.1 The angular height of obstructions should not exceed the critical value h

Table 4.1.1 Spacing angles for light from the sky		
Latitude (degrees)	Critical obstruction angle (degrees)	Critical vertical sky component (%)
up to 40	40	18
40–45	35	21
45–50	30	24
50–55	25	27
55–60	22	29
60+	20	30

Figure 4.1.2 Rooms looking out from the internal corners of courtyards can often be gloomy and lack privacy

usually expressed as a percentage. The maximum value is almost 40% for a completely unobstructed vertical wall. The vertical sky component on a window can be related to the average daylight factor in a room[4.1.2, 4.1.3]. Vertical sky components may be calculated using the skylight indicator (Appendix A2) or TOWNSCOPE (Appendix A1).

Table 4.1.1 gives critical vertical sky components which should be equalled or exceeded on the outside reference line if a building is to have good daylighting. Where the vertical sky component changes rapidly along a facade it is worthwhile, if possible, to site windows where most daylight is available. This situation often occurs at the internal corners of courtyards or L-shaped blocks. If windows are close to these corners they will result in poor levels of daylight as well as potential lack of privacy (Figure 4.1.2).

Obstructions can also affect the daylighting distribution in a building. Areas which cannot see the sky, since they receive no direct daylight, usually look dark and gloomy compared with the rest of the room, however bright it is outside. The no sky line[4.1.1] (Figure 4.1.3) divides points on the working plane which can and cannot see the sky. (In houses the working plane is assumed to be horizontal and 0.85 metres high; in offices 0.7 m high; in special interiors like hospital wards and infant school classrooms a different height may be appropriate). Supplementary electric lighting will be needed if a significant part of the working plane lies beyond the no sky line[4.1.2].

The guidance throughout this section needs to be interpreted flexibly since daylight is only one aspect of urban layout design. In a historic city centre, for example, it may be impossible to achieve the required building spacings. Where there is restricted space available in a layout, interior daylighting may be improved in a number of ways as follows.

● Increase window sizes, especially raising the window head height (Figure 4.1.4).
● Improve external surface reflectances with light-coloured building

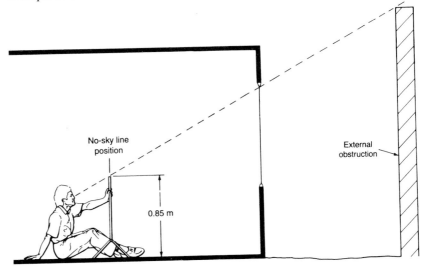

No-sky line position

0.85 m

External obstruction

Figure 4.1.3 The no sky line in a side-lit room

Figure 4.1.4 In Georgian streets (Cambridge, UK) the small spacing to height ratio is compensated for by tall windows. Note how window head height increases for rooms on the lower floors which are more heavily obstructed

materials and paving slabs on the ground. However, maintenance of such surfaces should be planned in order to stop them discolouring. And often the benefits may not be as great as envisaged, partly because of ageing of materials and partly because the obstruction itself may not receive much light.

● Reduce building depth (window wall to window wall).

Existing buildings

Safeguarding of the daylight to buildings adjoining a new development is very important. A badly planned development may make adjoining properties gloomy and unattractive. Some countries may have laws or planning regulations governing obstruction to existing buildings. These are not dealt with here but they need to be taken into account when designing new developments.

To find out whether an existing building still receives enough skylight, first draw a section in a plane perpendicular to each affected main window wall of the existing building (Figure 4.1.5). Measure the angle to the horizontal subtended by the new development at the level of the centre of the lowest window. If this angle is less than the critical value in Table 4.1.1 for the whole of the development, then it is unlikely to have a big impact on the daylight enjoyed by the existing building. If, for any part of the new development, this angle is more than the critical value, a more detailed check is needed.

Any reduction in the total amount of skylight can be calculated by finding the vertical sky component at the centre of the outside of each main window. (For a floor-to-ceiling French window or patio door, a point 2 m above ground on the centre line of the window may be used). If this vertical sky component is greater than the value in Table 4.1.1 then enough skylight should still reach the existing window. If the vertical sky component, with the new development in place, is both less than this value and less than 0.8 times its former value, then people in the existing building will notice the loss of skylight. The area lit by the window is likely to appear more gloomy, and electric lighting will be needed more of the time.

The impact on the daylighting distribution in the existing building can be found by plotting the no sky line (see above) in each of the main rooms. If, following construction of a new development, the area of the room which can receive direct skylight is reduced to less than 0.8 times its former value then the occupants will notice; more of the room will appear poorly lit. This is also true if the no sky line encroaches on key areas like kitchen sinks and worktops.

For domestic extensions to the front or rear of a house, a quick method can be used to check the diffuse skylight impact on the house next door. It applies where the nearest side of the extension is perpendicular to the window (Figure 4.1.6); but not for windows which directly face the extension, or for buildings opposite. On the elevation of the window wall, draw diagonally down at an angle of 45° away from the near top corner of the extension. On

Section

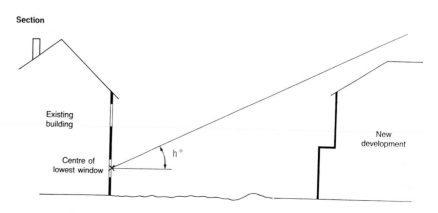

Figure 4.1.5 A new obstruction to an existing building

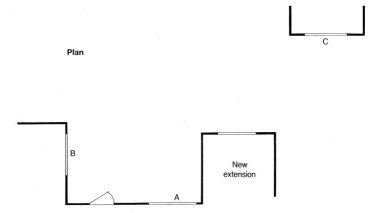

Plan

Figure 4.1.6 To assess the impact of the new extension, the 45° approach can be used for window A but not for windows B and C which directly face it

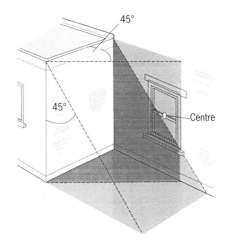

Figure 4.1.7 Application of the 45° approach to a domestic extension. If the centre of the window lies within the dark shaded area, a significant loss of light is possible

the plan draw diagonally back at an angle of 45° from the end of the extension towards the window wall. If the centre of the window next door lies on the extension side of both these 45° lines (Figure 4.1.7), the extension may significantly reduce the skylight received by the window. (For a floor-to-ceiling window, use a point 2 metres above the ground on the centre-line of the window).

Like most rules of thumb, this one needs to be interpreted flexibly. For example, if the extension has a much larger building behind it then the daylight from that direction may be blocked anyway. If the extension has a pitched roof then the top of the extension can be taken as the height of its roof halfway along the slope. Special care needs to be taken in cases where an extension already exists on the other side of the window, to avoid a 'tunnel effect' (Figure 4.1.8); it is then best to plot the no sky line in the obstructed room (see above).

As with the other guidelines in this section, the 45° approach deals with diffuse skylight only. Extra checks will need to be made for sunlight which may be blocked (section 4.2). Obstruction of light from the sky is just one of the ways in which a new development can affect existing buildings nearby.

Adjoining development land
It is possible to reduce the environmental quality of adjoining development land by building too close to the boundary. A well-designed building will stand a reasonable distance back from the boundaries so as to enable future nearby developments to enjoy a similar access to daylight. It will also then keep its own natural light when the adjoining land is developed.

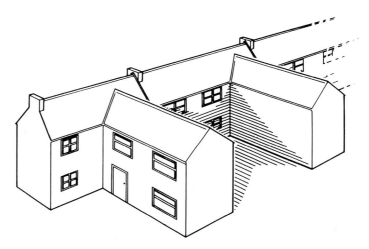

Figure 4.1.8 A 'tunnel effect' can occur if a window is obstructed by extensions on both sides

This is important when a main window wall, either of the current new development or of any probable future development on the adjoining site, will face over the boundary. The simplest way to ensure good access to skylight for a future development is to decide on the likely location of its window wall. This will often be the same distance from the boundary as the development on the other side. Then use the guidance for new developments above to check these future windows would receive enough light. Reference [4.1.1] gives more detailed guidance. A proposed building or group of buildings can also reduce the sunlighting of an adjoining site. If this is likely to be a problem, a good way to assess it is to draw the shadows cast by the new buildings at different times of year. Section 4.3 gives details.

References to section 4.1

[4.1.1] **Littlefair P J.** *Site layout planning for daylight and sunlight: a guide to good practice.* Building Research Establishment Report. Garston, CRC, 1991.

[4.1.2] **British Standards Institution.** *BS 8206:– Lighting for buildings. Part 2: Code of practice for daylighting.* London, BSI, 1992.

[4.1.3] **McNicholl A & Lewis J O (eds).** *Daylighting in buildings.* Dublin, University College for CEC, 1994.

4.2 Spacing and orientation for sunlight as an amenity

Strategy: Ensure access to sunlight for buildings where it is required, by orienting key spaces to the southern half of the sky and restricting obstructions

As section 1.5 shows, sunlight is highly valued as an amenity. In housing, the main requirement for sunlight is in living rooms, where it is valued at any time of day but especially in the afternoon. Sunlight is also required in conservatories. It is less important in bedrooms and in kitchens, where people prefer it in the morning rather than the afternoon[4.2.1]. Sunlight is also valued in non-domestic buildings. Generally the further north in Europe the more positive people are towards sunlight. However in southern Europe sunlight indoors is still welcome in the cooler months.

In the winter heating season solar heat gain can be valuable, reducing the need for space heating. Good design can make the most of this. This aspect of sunlight provision is dealt with in section 4.3; here, we concentrate on the amenity aspects of sunlight.

Site layout is the most important factor affecting the duration of sunlight in buildings. It can be divided into two main issues: orientation and overshadowing.

Orientation

A south-facing window will usually receive most sunlight while a north-facing one will only receive it on a handful of occasions (early morning and late evening in summer). East- and west-facing windows will receive sunlight only at certain times of the day. A dwelling with no main window wall within 90° of due south is likely to be perceived as insufficiently sunlit. This can be important in flats; ideally each individual dwelling should have at least one main living room with a reasonable amount of sunlight. In both flats and houses it is sensible to match internal room layout with window wall orientation. Where possible, living rooms should face south or west, and kitchens towards the north or east.

Overshadowing

Sunlight in a new development can be considerably improved if the buildings are designed to overshadow each other as little as possible. Access to sunlight can be improved[4.2.2] by:

● if possible, choosing a site on a south-facing slope rather than a north-facing one (section 2.3),

- having taller buildings to the north of the site with low-rise buildings to the south, but care must be taken not to overshadow a neighbouring property,
- similarly, having low density housing (semi-detached and detached) at the southern end of a site, with terraced housing to the north,
- placing terraces by east–west roads so that one window wall faces nearly south; semi-detached and detached houses can be located on north–south roads (section 3.3),
- opening out courtyards to the southern half of the sky,
- having garages to the north of houses,
- where window walls face predominantly east or west, avoiding obstructions to the south such as protruding extensions or other buildings,
- having low pitched roofs on housing.

Figure 4.2.1 illustrates some of these techniques.

It is recommended that, for rooms where the occupants require sunlight (at least one main living room per house):

- North of 50° N, the centre of a window should receive at least 25% of annual probable sunlight hours spread over at least 6 months of the year. Here 'probable sunlight hours' means the total number of hours in the year that the sun is expected to shine on unobstructed ground, allowing for average levels of cloudiness for the location in question. The sunlight availability indicator (see Appendix A2) can be used to calculate hours of sunlight received.
- Between 42° and 50° N, the centre of the window should receive at least 2 hours of possible sunlight on 19 February, and preferably earlier in the year. The sunpath indicator (see Appendix A2), TOWNSCOPE program or other sunpath diagrams can be used to check this. The 19 February date is not vital: this is only a rough guideline. When comparing borderline cases consider sunlight received at other times of year as well.

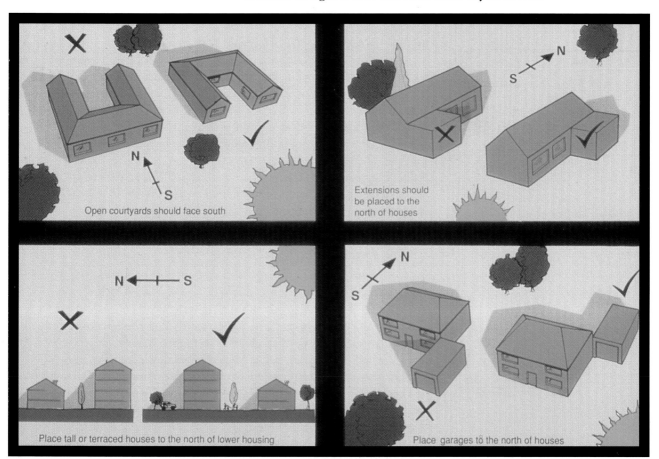

Figure 4.2.1 Good and bad examples of layout design for sunlight

In designing a new development care should be taken to safeguard the access to sunlight to existing buildings nearby. Particularly in northern Europe, people are likely to notice a loss of sunlight to their homes and if it is extensive it will usually be resented. Reference 4.2.3 gives more detail here.

References to section 4.2

[4.2.1] Bitter C & van Ierland J F A A. Appreciation of sunlight in the home. *Proceedings CIE Conference on Sunlight in Buildings,* Newcastle, 1965. pp 27–38. Rotterdam, Bouwcentrum International, 1967.

[4.2.2] NBA Tectonics. *A study of passive solar housing estate layout.* Report S 1126. Harwell, Energy Technology Support Unit, 1988.

[4.2.3] Littlefair P J. *Site layout planning for daylight and sunlight: a guide to good practice.* Building Research Establishment Report. Garston, CRC, 1991.

4.3 Passive solar access

Strategy: Where buildings rely on solar heat gain, orient near to due south and ensure the southern part of the sky has only small obstructions

In northern Europe, passive solar homes can have a heating energy consumption 1000 kWh per year lower than conventional housing – a 10% saving on the heating bill[4.3.1]. However these benefits depend on site layout. They may be halved if the site layout fails to optimize orientation and reduce overshadowing. Passive solar design is valuable for non-domestic buildings as well as for housing.

The advice in this section is also relevant to active systems like solar panels. However any overshadowing checks (see below) will need to be done at solar panel level.

When is passive solar design worthwhile?

● A climate with cold or cool winters where heating is required.
● A level or south-facing sloping site. On a sloping site which faces north it will be harder to reap the full benefits of passive solar design.
● Reasonable density of development. At high densities (above 40 dwellings per hectare) some houses may be seriously obstructed or have a poor orientation. Similarly, on a small site it may be impossible to achieve the best orientation for window walls or to avoid overshadowing by nearby buildings.
● Good natural ventilation in summer to avoid overheating in passive solar buildings; on a noisy or polluted site this may be hard to obtain.

None of these factors need necessarily rule out passive solar design. But they may make it harder to achieve substantial energy savings. It may be best to concentrate on providing daylight and sunlight as an amenity (sections 4.1 and 4.2), and introduce other energy measures such as improved insulation.

Passive solar site layout design can be divided into the two key issues: *orientation* and *overshadowing.*

Orientation

To make the most of solar gain the main solar-collecting facade should face within 30° of due south[4.3.2]. Orientations further east or west than this will receive less solar gain, particularly in winter when it is of most use. In non-domestic buildings a more easterly orientation may help provide solar heat in the morning, and avoid afternoon overheating in summer.

These orientation requirements influence site layout. Where possible, main roads should run east–west, with north–south link roads (see section 3.3) (Figure 4.3.1). A mixture of house types can help overcome the repetitive appearance of houses on an estate all facing the same way, as can careful design of the spaces between buildings (Figure 4.3.2).

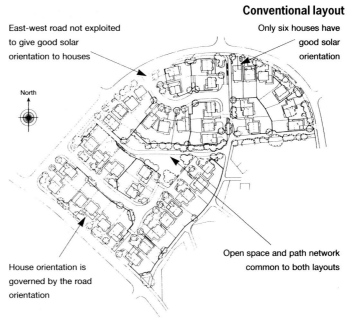

Conventional layout

East-west road not exploited
to give good solar
orientation to houses

Only six houses have
good solar
orientation

North

House orientation is
governed by the road
orientation

Open space and path network
common to both layouts

Passive solar layout

Houses on east-west road have
good orientation

North

Majority of houses
have south-facing
living rooms looking
out on to sunny
gardens

Small changes in orientation
produce an informal layout

Houses and plots
angled to road to
improve orientation

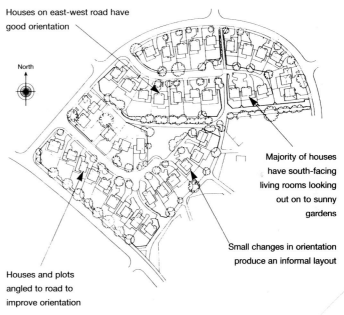

Figure 4.3.1 A case study by BTP Architects for Lovell Homes[4.3.4]. In the conventional layout (top) only six of the houses have good solar orientation. Realigning the roads enables two-thirds of the homes to face within 30° of due south and only four face due east or west

Figure 4.3.2 In Pennyland, Milton Keynes, UK, planting between buildings gives the estate an informal appearance

Overshadowing

Overshadowing by other buildings can spoil a passive solar design. This is because a solar-collecting facade needs access to low-angle sun in winter. In the worst case, with large obstructions to the south, a glazed area may be in shadow all winter but receive much unwanted solar heat gain in summer.

Building techniques can reduce overshading (Figure 4.3.3). Tree locations are also important; deciduous species are best because they are leafless when solar gains are most valuable, while providing some shade in summer.

To reap the full benefits of passive solar design, maximize winter solar gain as far as other site layout constraints allow. The most important area to keep lightly obstructed is within 45° of due south of a solar-collecting facade. This is the part of the sky from which most solar radiation comes in the winter months. To check solar access from this zone, draw a north–south section (not necessarily perpendicular to the facade). The altitude of any obstructions

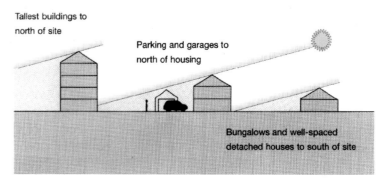

Figure 4.3.3 Avoiding overshading problems

Table 4.3.1 Limiting obstruction angles h to ensure reasonable winter solar access	
Latitude (° N)	Value of h (°)
50+	70 — latitude
46.5–50	20
< 46.5	66.5 — latitude

in it should not exceed the critical angle h (Figure 4.3.4) when measured from the centre of the solar-collecting glazing. Values of h are given in Table 4.3.1, in terms of site latitude. So at a site in London (51.5° N) then the maximum obstruction angle h would be 70 – 51.5 = 18.5°. These values will give sunlight at noon on January 21–November 21 north of 50° N, and sun at noon all year round south of 46.5° N. To achieve three hours of possible sun all year round requires an obstruction angle of 65° minus latitude (in London, this would be 13.5°) [4.3.3, 4.3.4].

This amount of open space in front of glazed areas may not always be feasible, particularly in the far north of Europe. And if an obstruction takes up only part of the 45° angular zone either side of due south, enough solar gain may still be available from other directions. To check this, use the solar gain indicator (Appendix A2) or TOWNSCOPE (Appendix A1).

A passive solar building also needs enough diffuse daylight (section 4.1). Special care should be taken to ensure good daylighting to the north side of the building as often minimal window areas are chosen on thermal grounds.

Where a proposed development of any type is near to an existing passive solar building, it is good practice to try to minimize loss of solar gain to the passive solar building. And when designing a passive solar building the

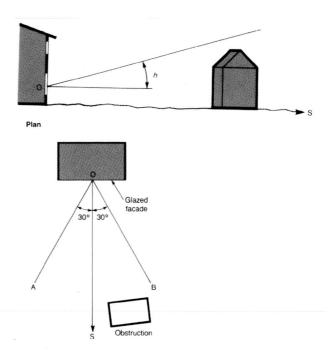

Figure 4.3.4 For solar access, the area of sky between south east and south west becomes important. Obstructions in this zone should not exceed the critical angle h. For latitudes above 50°, h is 70° — latitude; for latitudes below 46.5°, h is 66.5° — latitude; for intermediate latitudes h is 20°

possibility of future developments blocking solar access should be anticipated. The building(s) should stand well back from the southern boundary of the site unless no future development is to take place there. It is unreasonable to build very close to a southern boundary and expect future development to stand well back from it.

In a new solar estate, guard against the possibility of neighbours blocking each other's solar radiation by erecting large extensions and outbuildings. Legal agreements can protect solar access for each property. They need an unambiguous numerical criterion to assess the loss of solar gain. One possible procedure[4.3.5] might be:

● use the angular zone criterion outlined above (obstruction angle at centre of solar façade should be less than critical angle h within zone between SE and SW, Figure 4.3.4),
● if the above criterion is not met with the new building in place then calculate the heating season solar gain with and without the new building using a solar gain indicator (Appendix A2) or TOWNSCOPE (Appendix A1). If the solar gain is more than 0.9 times its former value then the reduction is small.

This technique is flexible but there are dangers, particularly in accepting what could be the first of a series of small losses to the available solar gain. This could happen where successive extensions are planned to the same building. Here the total impact on solar gain due to all the extensions needs to be calculated and compared with the guidance above.

References to section 4.3

[**4.3.1**] **NBA Tectonics.** *A study of passive solar housing estate layout.* Report S 1126. Harwell, Energy Technology Support Unit, 1988.

[**4.3.2**] **Goulding J R, Lewis J O & Steemers T C.** *Energy in architecture.* London, Batsford, 1992.

[**4.3.3**] **Littlefair P J.** *Site layout planning for daylight and sunlight: a guide to good practice.* Building Research Establishment Report. Garston, CRC, 1991.

[**4.3.4**] **Department of the Environment.** *Passive solar estate layout.* General Information Report 27. Garston, BRECSU, 1997.

4.4 Sunlight in spaces between buildings

Strategy: Ensure outdoor spaces like parks and gardens receive enough sunlight in cool climates

As section 1.5 showed, sunlight in the spaces between buildings has an important impact on the overall appearance and ambience of a development. Sunlight is particularly valuable in:
● gardens,
● parks and playing fields,
● children's playgrounds,
● outdoor swimming pools and paddling pools,
● sitting out areas such as those between non-domestic buildings and in public squares,
● focal points for views such as a group of monuments or fountains.

Requirements for sunlight will vary according to climate (see section 1.13). In the far north of Europe sunlight out of doors is almost always welcome. Further south, shade becomes more and more welcome, particularly in summer. For maximum amenity, both sunlit and shaded areas should be provided, for example:
● seating both shaded by trees and open to the sun,
● alternative circulation routes, one in sun, one in shade,
● use of deciduous trees to provide shade in summer, sun in winter,

Figure 4.4.1 Shaded areas are ideal for car parking

● overhangs and colonnades open to low-angle winter sun but not high-angle summer sun,
● the use of specific parts of a site can be planned with sunlight in mind. This could include reserving the sunniest parts of the site for gardens and sitting out, while using the shadier areas for car parking (in summer, shade is often valued in car parks) (Figure 4.4.1).

Where extra sunlight is needed, use some of the techniques described in the previous two sections. This could include siting low rise, low density housing to the south, with taller, higher density housing to the north of a site; and by opening out courtyards to the southern half of the sky. Special care needs to be taken in the design of courtyards in northern latitudes as often they can turn out to be sunless and unappealing (section 5.2).

With certain forms of layout it is difficult to achieve good sunlight provision outside[4.4.1]. Surprisingly, passive solar layouts can cause problems, as the buildings themselves receive most of the available sun. If a long face of a building faces within 10° of due north then there will be an area adjoining the building face which is permanently in shade at the equinox (and hence all winter). Areas of this sort can also occur if buildings form an enclosed or partly enclosed space which is blocked off from the southern half of the sky. Figure 4.4.2 illustrates some typical examples. It is usually possible to redesign the layout so as to minimize these areas, either by reorienting buildings or by opening up gaps to the south in courtyards.

Reference to section 4.4
[4.4.1] **Littlefair P J.** *Site layout planning for daylight and sunlight: a guide to good practice.* Building Research Establishment Report. Garston, CRC, 1991.

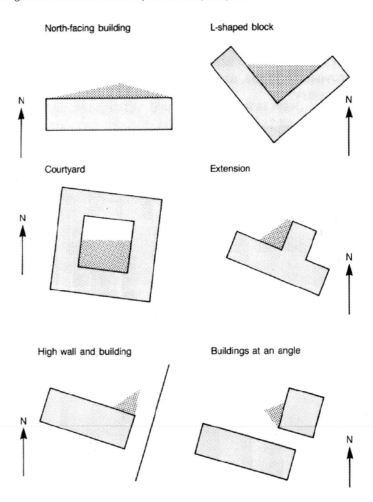

Figure 4.4.2 Examples of problem layouts where poor sunlighting on the ground can occur. The shaded areas will receive no sun at all for six months of the year

4.5 Mutual shading

Strategy: In cities in cool climates, check the overshadowing caused by large new developments by comparing with current levels of obstruction. In hot climates, mutual shading can be used deliberately, to keep building faces and the spaces between them cool.

As the previous sections have shown, proper geometrical design of open spaces in between buildings is very important. Mutual shading between buildings may determine if an outdoor space will be pleasant or undesirable during the different times of the day or throughout the year. It is also important to be able to locate windows and solar elements in an optimal way with regard to insolation. Moreover, shading of windows in summer in hot climates, is one of the most important ways to achieve good indoor climatic conditions with minimal energy consumption[4.5.1].

Overshadowing in city centres: a case study

The previous sections have emphasized the need for good sunlighting and daylighting in buildings and the spaces between them. Yet mutual shading is an unavoidable characteristic of dense urban areas. Although numerical guidelines are given above, these should be interpreted flexibly since natural lighting is only one of many factors in site layout design. In special circumstances the developer or planning authority may wish to use different target values. For example, in a historic city centre a higher degree of obstruction may be unavoidable if new developments are to match the height and proportions of existing buildings. Here, requirements for daylight and sunlight have to be evaluated carefully for each particular case. One possible strategy is to use comparisons with relevant local references, to define what level of overshading is common within the particular urban area under consideration. Simulation software, like TOWNSCOPE, can be used for such an analysis.

This approach has been followed for the Pierreuse redevelopment project in Liege (Figure 4.5.1). This project consisted of a major administrative building, located in front of an existing row of houses, remains of the city's mediaeval pattern. This street presently benefits from an exceptional situation, due to substantial demolitions that occurred during the 1970s: it is open on its south-west side, which provides a lot of sun to the neighbourhood.

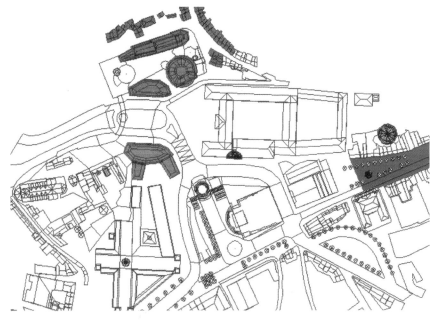

Figure 4.5.1 Axonometric of Pierreuse project in Liege. © University of Liege

From the solar point of view, the losses caused by the redevelopment are obvious[4.5.2]. Figures 4.5.2 and 4.5.3 show the decrease of the direct solar radiation reaching the facades. The value of this decrease is from 5% to 10% yearly mean value. At most, the loss of solar radiation can reach 25%.

Nevertheless, the levels reached with the new building in place are all favourable compared with common situations in the city of Liege (Figure 4.5.4). This was assessed using equivalent simulations for similar urban patterns in Liege. By agreement with the Liege municipal urban planning department, two spaces were used as references: a mediaeval square and an existing street. Mutual shading on these reference spaces is very similar to that obtained in the existing buildings, after re-development.

Mutual shading in hot climates

Mutual shading between surfaces is crucial for the thermal behaviour of an open space and for the internal spaces next to it. The two main factors for mutual shading are confinement and orientation. Figure 4.5.5 shows the shadow evolution for different solar times (15th of July) in a narrow NW–SE oriented street. Most of the time the shadowed areas are bigger than the sunny ones.

Figure 4.5.6 shows the daily evolution (15th of July) of the direct solar radiation impinging over one south-west surface. There are three curves in the graph. The first gives the value without shading (open land), the second one is for a surface shadowed by the opposite wall of a big avenue, and the third one is shadowed by the opposite wall of a narrow street placed in the Santa Cruz neighbourhood of Seville. For the Santa Cruz configuration the reception of solar radiation is much lower.

To visualize the influence of street orientation over the solar heat received, an appropriate measure is daily solar direct radiation ($kW \cdot h/m^2 \cdot day$). Figure 4.5.7 shows the angular values used for the different orientations of the ground and the wall of a typical street. For a vertical wall without shading the daily solar direct radiation varies considerably with orientation. Figure 4.5.8 shows these values for a vertical wall without shading, the big avenue and the narrow street in Santa Cruz. The minimum values are reached when the wall is facing north, but the maximum reductions of direct solar radiation due to the shading are when the wall is facing west or east.

References to section 4.5

[4.5.1] Shaviv E & Capeluto Y G. *The relative importance of various geometrical design parameters in hot-humid climate.* Atlanta, ASHRAE Transactions, V AN-92-1, 1992.

[4.5.2] LEMA — Laboratoire d'Etudes Methodologiques Architecturales. *Etude d'ensoleillement direct du quartier Pierreuse, Liege.* Liege, University of Liege, 1992.

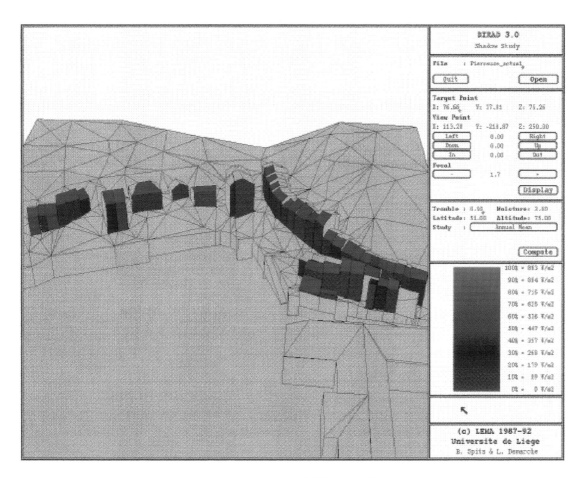

Figure 4.5.2 Direct solar radiation for the existing situation. © University of Liege

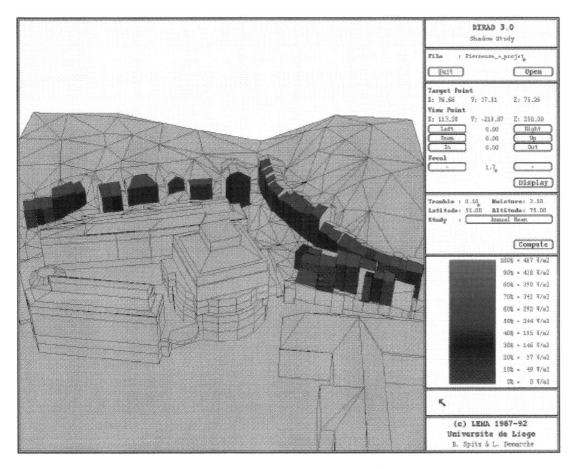

Figure 4.5.3 Direct solar radiation for the proposed situation. © University of Liege

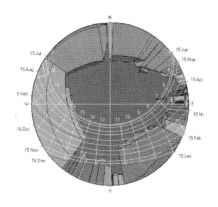

Figure 4.5.4 Stereographical projection of place du Marche (Liege, Belgium). © University of Liege

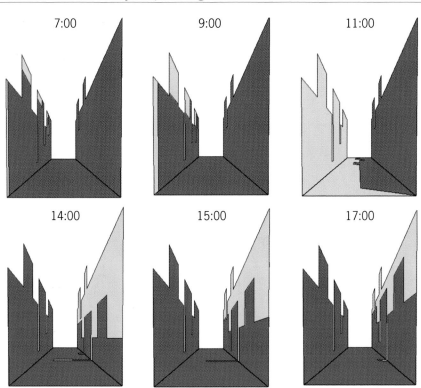

7:00   9:00   11:00

14:00   15:00   17:00

Figure 4.5.5 Shadow evolution of Pimienta Street, Santa Cruz, Seville, for the 15th of July (solar time). © University of Seville

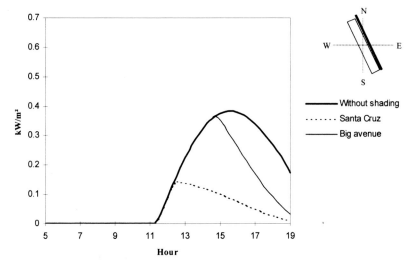

Without shading

Santa Cruz

Big avenue

Figure 4.5.6 Daily variation of direct solar radiation over the right wall of one street oriented in the Santa Cruz main orientation for the 15th of July (solar time). © University of Seville

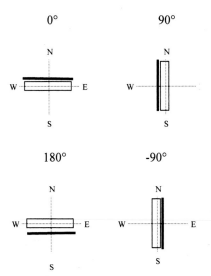

0°   90°

180°   -90°

Figure 4.5.7 Angular values for the different street orientations © University of Seville

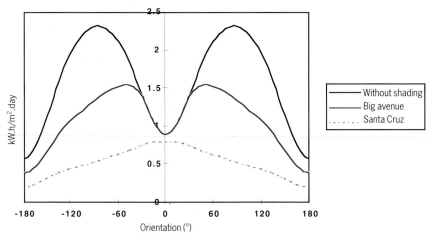

Without shading

Big avenue

Santa Cruz

Figure 4.5.8 Daily solar direct radiation over the vertical wall of one street as a function of the street orientation for the 15th of July (solar time). © University of Seville

4.6 Wind shelter, ventilation and passive cooling

Strategy: Lay out buildings to provide good access to ventilation while maintaining comfortable conditions for pedestrians

Air flows in the urban environment affect:
- ventilation and passive cooling of buildings,
- outdoor comfort, particularly in cold climates,
- pollution dispersal (see next section).

The layout of buildings can have an important impact on these air flows.

Ventilation and passive cooling

Previous chapters (sections 2.5, 3.2) have discussed the decreased potential for natural ventilation because of the reduced wind speeds in urban areas. Section 2.5 included a method to calculate the reduction in air flow because of the building's location and the characteristics of the neighbouring area.

As was mentioned in section 3.2, the air-flow velocity in a street canyon is strongly related to its aspect ratio and the wind velocity above the canyon. For good ventilation the wind velocity above the canyon should be high and nearly parallel to the canyon axis and the aspect ratio should be low. The worst case is when the wind above the canyon is weak and perpendicular to the canyon axis and the aspect ratio is high. In that case a vortex is formed and the air exchange at the bottom of the canyon is very poor.

Experiments in 10 deep canyons during the summer of 1997 in Athens and simulations using the AIOLOS natural ventilation simulation code gave the following conclusions.

- When the ambient wind speed is considerably higher than the wind speed inside the canyon and dominates buoyancy effects, the natural ventilation potential in single and cross-ventilation configurations is seriously decreased inside the canyon. In practice, this happens when the ambient wind speed is higher than 4 m/sec. For single-side ventilation configurations the air flow is reduced up to five times, while in cross-ventilation configurations the flow is sometimes reduced up to 10 times.
- When the ambient wind speed is lower than 3–4 m/sec, gravitational forces dominate the air-flow processes. In this case, the difference in wind speed inside and outside the canyon, does not play an important role, especially in single-sided configurations.
- The calculated reduction of the air flow inside the canyon is mainly a function of the corresponding wind direction. When the ambient flow is almost perpendicular to the canyon axis, the flow inside the canyon is nearly vertical and parallel to the window, the pressure coefficients and hence ventilation rate inside a building are much lower than would be calculated from ambient wind conditions. When the ambient flow is parallel to the canyon axis, a similar flow is observed inside the canyon, and the pressure coefficients are almost similar.

To show the reduction in the wind speed in streets and the corresponding reduction of the potential for natural ventilation, measurements of air flow have been made in urban canyons in Athens. The first set of experiments was performed at the urban canyon of Ippokratous Street, between 5th and 18th December 1996. The canyon is of S–N orientation, its width is close to 10 m while the mean height of the buildings is close to 20 m. During the experiments, the temperature distribution inside the canyon was measured at various heights. At the same time the wind speed was measured at two specific points and in particular 10 metres above the canyon and inside the canyon at about 10 metres from the ground surface. A cup anemometer was used to measure the undisturbed wind speed and direction. Inside the canyon a three axis anemometer was used. Measurements were taken every second.

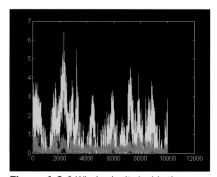

Figure 4.6.1 Wind velocity inside the canyon (red), and above the canyon (yellow). © University of Athens

The decrease in the wind speed inside the canyon compared with the undisturbed wind speed above it is especially important for ventilation purposes. Figure 4.6.1 shows a plot of the wind speed over and inside the canyon. For the period of comparison, the mean wind speed over the canyon was close to 0.9 m/sec, and the corresponding mean wind speed inside the canyon was close to 0.2 m/sec.

Analysis of the ratio of the wind speed inside and outside the canyon showed that the wind velocity ratio tends to be higher for lower wind speeds. This is mainly due to the fact that the wind speed inside the canyon was almost never higher than 1 m/sec. Thus, the higher the undisturbed wind speed, the higher the wind speed difference.

Comfort and wind shelter

Air flows in cities also affect outdoor comfort, particularly in cool climates in winter. Reduction of wind speed by wind control should improve the microclimate around the buildings.

The spacing of buildings has a considerable impact on site microclimate. Closely spaced buildings will shield each other, and the intervening spaces, from the wind. However, the spaces between the buildings, as well as the buildings themselves, will be less well sunlit.

Different sources give different guidance on spacing for wind protection. The BRE *Housing design handbook*[4.6.1] recommends a spacing 1.5–2.5 times the overall building height, Robinette[4.6.2] only 1.5–2 times height. This is too low for the spacing between passive south facades and buildings opposite if good winter solar gain is to be obtained, although reasonable daylighting could be achieved with a ratio of 2. However, spacings of this order could be used between the end-flank walls of passive buildings. The BRE handbook[4.6.1] warns against small gaps (up to 3 metres) between buildings, which can act as wind funnels. If buildings are close together there may be problems achieving good cross-ventilation in summer[4.6.3].

The *European Passive Solar Handbook*[4.6.4] quotes UK studies which indicate that for a spacing to height ratio of about 3 the pressure difference across a building is roughly halved compared with an isolated building. It suggests spacing to height ratios in the region 2.5 to 3.5. For most of Europe this would give reasonable daylighting and adequate winter sunlight. For low-rise housing a spacing to height ratio of 3.5 corresponds to an obstruction angle of just over 13° at ground floor window height. Brown[4.6.5] suggests that the area of reduced wind velocity on the leeward side of a building group extends to at least 3 to 4 times the building height. Evans[4.6.3] gives a table of the extent of 'wind shadow' from buildings. Depending on the width and shape of the building, this wind shadow can extend for 2–20 times the height of the building.

These studies assume that the wind is perpendicular to a main face of the building. Where the wind flow is parallel to rows of buildings the spaces in between the buildings will be much less well protected. For this reason long parallel rows of buildings should be avoided[4.6.1, 4.6.6]. For good wind protection in cool climates where straight streets are unavoidable, limit the length of flat facades to about 25 metres, or introduce steps and staggers.

Site tall buildings with care[4.6.7], as they can cause vortex flows[4.6.8] between the tall building and its small neighbours (Figure 4.6.2). For reduced site wind sensitivity building heights should be as uniform as possible[4.6.1, 4.6.6]. The effects of tall buildings can be evaluated using wind tunnel studies.

Avoid funnel-like gaps between buildings. Larger gaps (3–5 metres or greater) will aid solar access and avoid vulnerable passages where the wind rushes through. Alternatively such vulnerable areas can be avoided by overlapping the ends of blocks that meet at an angle: this may cause solar access problems near the internal corner (section 4.4).

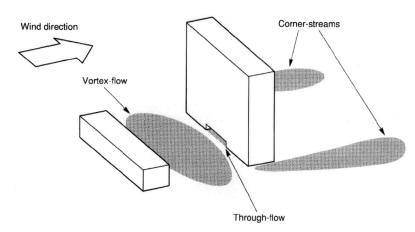

Figure 4.6.2 Vortex flows around a tall building

References to section 4.6

[4.6.1] BRE. *Housing design handbook*. Building Research Establishment Report (BR 253). Garston, CRC, 1993.

[4.6.2] Robinette G O (ed). *Energy efficient site design*. New York, Van Nostrand, 1983.

[4.6.3] Evans M. *Housing, climate and comfort*. London, Architectural Press, 1980.

[4.6.4] Goulding J R, Lewis J O & Steemers T C (eds). Energy in architecture. T*he European passive solar handbook*. London, Batsford for CEC, 1992.

[4.6.5] Brown G Z. *Sun, wind and light architectural design strategies*. New York, Wiley, 1985.

[4.6.6] BRE. Climate and site development. *Digest 350* (Parts 1–3). Garston, CRC, 1990.

[4.6.7] BRE. Wind environment around tall buildings. *Digest 392*. Garston, CRC, 1994.

[4.6.8] Penwarden A D & Wise A F E. *Wind environment around buildings*. Garston, BRE, 1975.

4.7 Pollution dispersal

Strategy: use the detailed layout of buildings to ensure that pollutants can be dispersed from local sources

The advantages of using small-scale urban design to encourage the rapid ventilation of pollutants have received little attention, even though urban form can significantly affect rates of pollutant dispersion near the ground. The area that can be influenced in this way is the urban canopy, ie the region up to 2–3 times the heights of the buildings where most urban pollutants are discharged (the main exception to this is large industrial discharges from tall stacks).

This effect is most important for pollution sources at short distances up to about 1 km, the 'near field' and 'intermediate field' described in section 2.6. Urban form at small scales does not greatly affect the dispersion of pollution sources from greater distances, the 'far field' concentrations described in section 2.6. Pollution sources from far away are generally well dispersed through the urban canopy and thus have quite small gradients of concentration which are not greatly altered by the details of the urban layout. Local sources of pollution provide an additional contribution to this slowly changing 'far field' concentration. Because of their proximity, pollutant concentrations from local sources within the urban canopy can be high and vary markedly in both time and space due to the unsteady local airflows, which are strongly affected by the buildings and surface topography. This behaviour is described in more detail by Hall et al[4.6.1].

These local pollution sources should be ventilated through the urban canopy as quickly as possible to minimize their locally high concentrations. Some features of the urban layout affect both rates of dispersion near the ground and the local windspeeds within the urban canopy (to which pollutant concentrations are inversely proportional). These are described below.

Area density

Area density is the proportion of the surface occupied by buildings and other obstructions. For area densities below 5–10%, the urban array is so sparse as to have no collective qualities and it is the effect of individual buildings which governs local windspeeds and dispersion patterns. Beyond 5–10% (a small proportion of covered surface), the collective characteristics of the buildings and other surface obstacles, rather than those of individual structures within it, affect windspeeds and rates of dispersion within the urban canopy.

Area density itself, beyond values of 5–10%, has only limited effects on the rates of dispersion of pollutants until quite high values of 80–90% are reached. However, windspeed within the urban canopy is markedly reduced as area density increases, up to about 80–90%, so that pollutant concentrations increase within the canopy for this reason. At the higher area densities, the buildings are so closely packed that they effectively produce a new, elevated, ground surface at roof height and most of the windflow is displaced upwards over the buildings. Windspeeds in this region then increase again and pollutant concentrations are reduced in the upper part of the urban canopy.

However, close to the ground between closely packed buildings windspeeds remain low. Pollutant concentrations can remain persistently high due to these low windspeeds and the slow rate at which pollutants are carried above roof level where higher windspeeds and more rapid dispersion occur. This is an alternative description of the behaviour of what are commonly described as 'street canyons', which are considered in section 3.2. 'Street canyons' are the deep spaces between buildings when the area density is high. They are not isolated, but a network of linked narrow spaces between the buildings, through which contaminants pass while dispersing relatively slowly and then ventilate through the tops of the 'canyons'.

Building heights and widths

Building heights and widths across the wind in the urban array directly affect both the spread of pollutants and local windspeeds. In general there is rapid dispersion of pollutants across the widths and heights of isolated buildings, so that the greater these are the greater the dispersion and the lower the concentration. This applies to building widths up to about eight times their height, beyond which there is only a limited further increase in the lateral dispersion. The way buildings are formed into groups, as rows and squares for example, affects this directly as it is the shape of their collective envelopes that governs aerodynamic effects.

Windspeeds within the urban canopy are markedly affected by building heights but less by their widths. Windspeeds near the ground generally reduce rapidly with increasing heights of building, so that pollutant concentrations are increased for this reason, while decreasing due to increased dispersion. Building width has its greatest effect on windspeeds at area densities around 20%. At higher area densities higher levels of sheltering occur and windspeeds near the ground are reduced as noted above. Also, the depth of the urban canopy is most affected by building heights as it is typically 2–3 building heights in extent. Overall, accounting for both rates of dispersion and windspeed, the greatest reduction in pollutant concentrations near the ground occurs when buildings are relatively wide and low, with low to moderate area densities.

Variation in building heights and widths

Some urban areas have buildings of relatively uniform height, while others show large variations. This difference has been regarded as important when area densities are high (greater than 20%) as large variations in building height encourage the penetration of higher windspeeds down to the ground. Despite this, a large variation in building height seems to have little effect on the overall dispersion of pollutants. However, it does have a significant effect on mean windspeed. Averaged over an area, windspeeds near the ground are reduced as height variability increases. However, this is accompanied by a greater local variation in windspeeds at the ground, so that there will be more regions with locally higher and lower windspeeds that the average. This is because the penetration of higher speed winds down to the ground (from above) in one place has to be accompanied by the displacement of lower speed winds upwards from another.

Alignment of buildings and the effects of wind direction

Buildings in urban areas may be laid out in orderly arrays with clearly defined long streets or in more random patterns with few clear passages of any length. The aerodynamic appearance of an urban area depends on the wind direction: an urban layout with clear streets running through it will appear blocked to the wind in some directions while open in others. Polluting discharges released in streets aligned or at acute angles to the wind tend to be restrained within the width of the street at first, limiting their dispersion. Discharges may also be carried along the lengths of the streets rather than in the wind direction, so that where the wind is skewed across the street pattern there can be lateral displacement of dispersing plumes across the wind direction.

If buildings are relatively wide, dispersion is increased when the wind is skewed at an acute angle to the long sides, reaching a maximum for angles of 30–45°. Vortices are generated which trail downwind and increase windspeeds and ventilation rates near the ground. There has been occasional comment on the advantages of aligning the streets of urban areas with the most frequently occurring wind directions in order to improve ventilation of pollutants at the ground. In fact, skew angles of about 30° to the wind should be more effective.

Courtyards and enclosed spaces are dealt with in section 5.3.

Urban ventilation and the retention of microclimates

The rest of this guide has presented ways to use urban layout to improve local climate. To maintain local cooling or heating, local ventilation rates need to be minimized. This is, of course, the opposite of increasing local ventilation rates to reduce pollutant concentrations. The principles discussed here for encouraging local ventilation can be used in reverse to aid the retention of microclimates. However, pollution levels from local sources can be increased as a result. A balance is required between the two opposing needs.

Reference to section 4.7

[4.7.1] **Hall D J, Spanton A M, Kukadia V, Walker S.** Exposure of buildings to pollutants in urban areas — a review of the contributions from different sources. *Atmospheric Environment* 1999 (in press).

4.8 Conclusions

Building layout has a big impact on daylight (section 4.1), sunlight (sections 4.2–4.5) and ventilation (sections 4.6–4.7) of buildings and the spaces around them.

In cool and intermediate climates, the best environmental strategy is usually to have buildings spaced far enough apart for good daylighting (section 4.1). This involves spacing-to-height ratios of 1.5–3 depending on latitude. Where sunlight is required, window walls should be oriented to the south (section 4.2). Where buildings are designed to make the most of solar heat gain, extra spacing will be required (typical spacing-to-height ratios of at least 3 and more at higher latitudes), with solar facades facing within 30° of due south.

This approach should give adequate ventilation for the dispersion of pollutants. The main conflict is with provision of wind shelter on cold days. Effective wind shelter can be obtained with spacing to height ratios of 2.5–3.5

which allows good daylighting, and solar gain in most of northern Europe (section 4.6). Detailed layout design (sections 5.1 and 6.1) can reduce the remaining wind exposure. In windy areas in the far north it may be best to concentrate on providing wind shelter and have daylit, superinsulated buildings rather than relying on passive solar design.

Another conflict can arise in city centres where the required spacings are not practicable (section 4.5). Here, passive solar techniques may be limited to the upper storeys and to roof space collectors. The loss of daylight can be partly compensated by raising window head heights, higher external reflectances and reduced building depths (section 4.1).

In northern Europe particular care is needed to safeguard daylight and sunlight to existing buildings near a new development. Sections 4.1 and 4.2 explain how to do this.

In the hotter parts of southern Europe a mixed approach to building layout is suggested. Outdoor spaces with pollution sources such as roads need to be adequately ventilated. This requires spacing to height ratios of at least 1, which should enable enough daylight to reach the upper storeys of buildings. Where there is likely to be a lot of pollution, wider streets are recommended (section 4.7). Shade for pedestrians can be provided by trees or colonnades (section 5.4).

Where there are no local pollution sources within an outdoor space, an alternative approach is to deliberately engineer a cooler local climate in it, involving the following techniques.

● *Restricting ventilation of the space:* this will happen if the width of the space is less than its height.

● *Shading the interior of the space:* unless the space is very narrow (less than a third its height) this is not always possible using building layout alone. Other forms of shading like fabric awnings, trees (section 6.3), or overhangs are needed. These will also reduce ventilation further.

● *Introducing heat sinks* like fountains and ponds (section 6.4) and vegetation (section 6.3).

5 Building form

This chapter develops two concepts in built form design. First, buildings need to harmonize with their surroundings climatically as well as visually. For example, tall slabs clad in reflective glass can cause turbulent gusts of wind at ground level, as well as unwanted solar glare and reflected heat. Secondly, some building forms can themselves generate a beneficial site microclimate: courtyards, colonnades and earth sheltering can all give outdoor areas protection from the extremes of the weather.

5.1 Building shape and orientation

Strategy: For best access to passive solar gain, buildings should face south. Choose building forms which do not cause adverse wind effects

As section 4.3 makes clear, there is considerable benefit from a southerly orientation for solar-collecting building facades[5.1.1]. A south-facing surface receives most solar radiation during the heating season, and is easier to shade in summer when excessive heat gain is unwanted. This requirement has a number of microclimate implications. In much of Europe, the prevailing winds tend to come from a south westerly direction[5.1.1]. To reduce air infiltration and heat loss to a building it is recommended[5.1.2, 5.1.3] that the long faces of the building be oriented parallel to the prevailing wind. Where the prevailing wind is westerly this is ideal because a south-facing main facade will be optimal for both solar access and wind resistance. Where the prevailing winter wind is south west there is more of a conflict because US studies[5.1.3] indicate that maximum air infiltration tends to occur when the wind is at 45° to the building faces. This conflict could be resolved by making the building construction more airtight and by planting shelter belts to the west of south-facing buildings; this may also help improve the environment in the spaces between the buildings.

Any building will itself tend to alter the microclimate in its immediate vicinity. For a passive solar building with a long south facade, there will be a sunny, pleasant area immediately to the south. However, outside its north face the building will shade the ground for nearly all of the day, producing a cooler and potentially less pleasant outdoor space (section 4.4). Its size can be reduced by sloping the building back to reduce the height of the north facade, and by avoiding sizeable projections from the north side of the building which can create chilly spaces in between them and the main face of the building (Figure 5.1.1). The main garden area should be situated to the south of the building if possible.

The overall proportions and detailed shape of a building can have an impact on the surrounding site microclimate as well as on the solar access to the surrounding buildings. In particular, large, inappropriately designed buildings may significantly worsen local wind conditions[5.1.4].

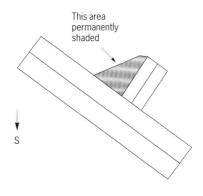

Figure 5.1.1 A projection from the north side of a building can give rise to an area of deep shade

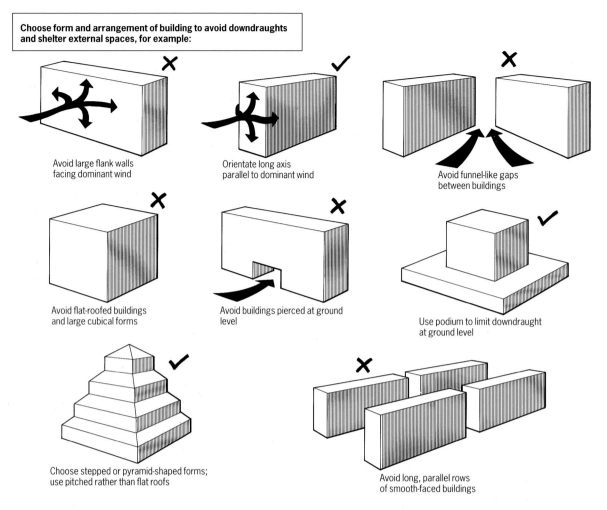

Choose form and arrangement of building to avoid downdraughts and shelter external spaces, for example:

Avoid large flank walls facing dominant wind ✗

Orientate long axis parallel to dominant wind ✓

Avoid funnel-like gaps between buildings ✗

Avoid flat-roofed buildings and large cubical forms ✗

Avoid buildings pierced at ground level ✗

Use podium to limit downdraught at ground level ✓

Choose stepped or pyramid-shaped forms; use pitched rather than flat roofs ✓

Avoid long, parallel rows of smooth-faced buildings ✗

Figure 5.1.2 Reducing the wind sensitivity of buildings

There are various ways[5.1.2] to reduce the wind sensitivity of buildings and their surroundings (Figure 5.1.2). These are briefly considered below.

● Avoid large flank walls facing the dominant wind; orientate long axis parallel to the dominant wind.

● Avoid flat-roofed buildings and large cubical forms; choose stepped or pyramid-shaped forms; use pitched rather than flat roofs. Although pitched roofs are better for wind deflection they may reduce solar access to adjoining buildings. The 'spacing angle' approach in section 4.3 can be used as a check here. Pyramid-shaped buildings tend to result in very good solar access and daylighting to the upper floors; however, this may become excessive and overheating could result. Meanwhile the lower floors will be less well daylit. If the glazing is sloping there may be problems with solar dazzle reflected from the glass (section 5.7). However, solar access to nearby buildings can be maintained if the pyramid is correctly placed and proportioned.

● Avoid buildings pierced at ground level. This has no significant passive solar implications.

● Use a podium to limit downdraughts at ground level. Where tall buildings are inevitable this is a sensible strategy; the tower part of the building will have good solar access, and the podium area can be lit by rooflights if required.

● Roughen building faces[5.1.2, 5.1.5] to provide resistance to the wind. This could include introducing steps and staggers into facades or features like external light shelves[5.1.6] which add 'roughness' to a building facade, decreasing its wind sensitivity as well as having a potential passive solar benefit.

The overall proportions of the building are important for both passive solar energy and microclimate. Generally speaking tall buildings have the best solar access. For example, if a large amount of commercial accommodation has to be provided on a site, its overall access to daylight and sunlight is greater if it is arranged in a number of tall shallow-plan buildings rather than as low-rise deep-plan buildings. However, tall buildings cause the greatest wind problems. These can be reduced, though not totally overcome, using the measures described above. In practice, other design considerations tend to influence decisions about building height more than passive solar energy or microclimate considerations do.

One particular building form which provides good wind shelter is the courtyard. This is dealt with in the next two sections.

References to section 5.1
[5.1.1] **Goulding J R, Lewis J O & Steemers T C.** *Energy in architecture.* London, Batsford, 1992.

[5.1.2] **BRE.** Climate and site development. *Digest 350:* Parts 1–3. Garston, CRC, 1990.

[5.1.3] **Robinette G O (ed).** *Energy efficient site design.* New York, Van Nostrand, 1983.

[5.1.4] **Westerberg U & Glaumann M.** Design criteria for solar access and wind shelter in the outdoor environment. *Energy and Buildings* 1990/1991: **15**(3/4): 425–431.

[5.1.5] **Yannas S.** *Solar energy and housing design* (Volumes 1 and 2). London, Architectural Association, 1994.

[5.1.6] **Littlefair P J.** *Designing with innovative daylighting.* Garston, CRC, 1996.

5.2 High density courtyards in heating-dominated climates

Strategy: Renewal of buildings around a courtyard requires changes to the design and layout of buildings. The aim is to find compromises between access, natural lighting, sunlight and privacy

In many cities in Europe, an urban block can contain up to four distinct concentric rings (Figure 5.2.1).

Zone 1: Setback
A zone between the buildings and the street imposed by the rules of town planning in force.

Zone 2: Built ring
The main buildings, facing streets and other public open spaces, form a built ring, which is mostly continuous in the urban environment.

Zone 3: Private gardens and courtyards
The size of this zone depends on the size of the cluster and the building density (this zone is thus smaller in urban areas). It contains extensions to the main buildings.

Zone 4: Interior of a cluster of buildings
Larger blocks can contain an additional zone which can contain parks, garages, small warehouses, etc. It can be private, semi-private or public.

Together, zones 3 and 4 form the cluster's core or courtyard area. In densely packed urban centres these cores can contain extensions to the built ring, or even additional built rows (sometimes up to three or four). The remaining open spaces were often devoted to internal circulation within the cluster. Over the years, therefore courtyards and private gardens have changed from being vast and mostly private, to confined and semi-public (Figure 5.2.2). Such an evolution is not without its problems given contemporary requirements for privacy, solar access, and personal and fire safety.

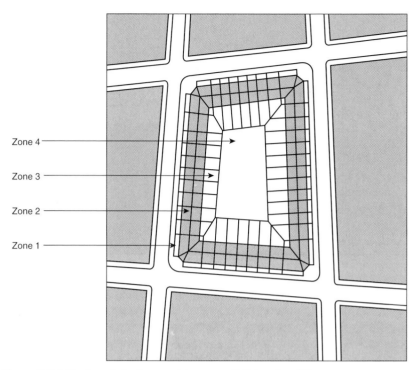

Figure 5.2.1 The four distinct concentric zones. © University of Liege

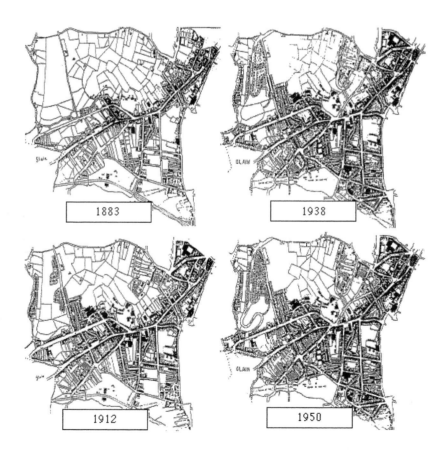

Figure 5.2.2 Urban evolution 1883–1912–1938–1950: Sainte Marguerite in Liege.
© University of Liege

Solution A: renewal of the core of an existing urban cluster

In a few cases clearing urban clusters is a possible solution to this problem.
This involves removing underused and decaying buildings from the interior of
the cluster. Besides the obvious benefits of improved solar access and privacy
in the surrounding buildings, the cluster's core can then be reallocated to
other functions as follows.

● *Public area:* a park or garden for the whole community
● *Semi-public area:* provision of a leisure area for the inhabitants or users of the buildings on the block
● *Private area:* the whole cluster's core is occupied by private gardens

Clearing urban clusters, however, brings with it a series of problems: who will manage and finance the works? how to acquire the buildings? and where to rehouse the people? The impact of such an operation on existing social networks can be very damaging.

Solution B: the new open cluster

Christian de Portzamparc has proposed opening out city blocks (Figure 5.2.3) by having:

● only 60–65% of the street frontage occupied by buildings (40% of the block being open space),
● opposite a building, an open space,
● always a free angle in the cluster,
● changes in the heights of buildings at the corners of the block,
● a limit to the physical built length, but not to the visual length of public–private spaces,
● because the blocks are open, only narrow streets (10–15 m) are needed.

The goal is thus to open the interior of the block to the light and for it to be linked to the street. Sunlight can also reach the street because of the discontinuity of the frontages. The interiors of the clusters can contain sunlit gardens, with a range of nearby and distant views.

This strategy mostly applies to new buildings on vacant urban land areas. It does not address the social problems of rehabilitating existing city blocks.

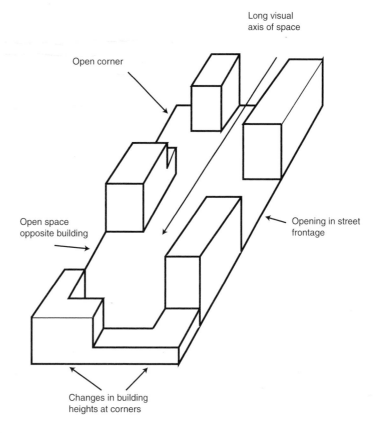

Figure 5.2.3 Illustrations of the rules of the open cluster

Solution C: the adapted response

An alternative approach for existing urban blocks is a 'soft' solution, which considers both the physical environment and the social network. This involves making minimal, but effective changes in the local urban layout.

Solar radiation access

Courtyards, completely enclosed on all four sides, will have less than ideal natural lighting. Rooms lit by windows near the corners of the courtyard may appear gloomy and heavily obstructed. For all but the widest courtyards sunlight will, at most, reach only a quarter of the courtyard in winter (Figure 5.2.4).

Such problems can be overcome in a number of ways[5.2.1] as follows.

● *Redefining the site layout planning of buildings*
  Example:
  Including gaps between buildings, especially on the south side of the courtyard, will improve access to sunlight and daylight. If the gaps are not too large the space will still appear reasonably enclosed.

● *Changing the window design*
  A number of different issues have to be addressed: daylighting, visual comfort, overheating risks, building standards and of course energy consumption both for heating and artificial lighting.
  Example:
  Smaller spacings could be compensated for by increasing window size, especially window head height, and decreasing room depth.

● *Reorganizing the whole housing layout*
  Example:
  In some circumstances the need for daylight at ground-floor level may not be great, for example where shops occupy the ground floor.

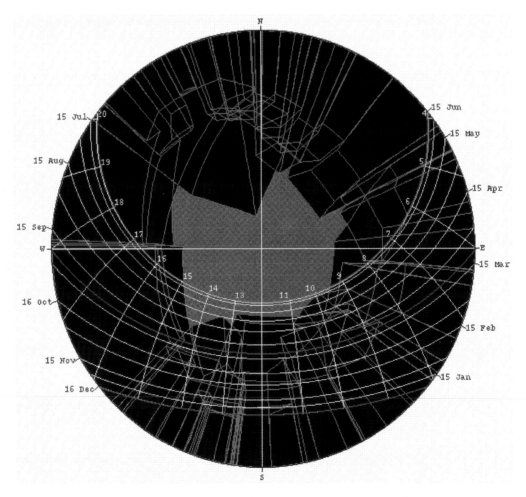

Figure 5.2.4 Solar radiation (direct, diffuse, reflected) in the courtyard (ground floor). © University of Liege

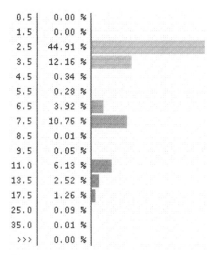

0.5	0.00 %
1.5	0.00 %
2.5	44.91 %
3.5	12.16 %
4.5	0.34 %
5.5	0.28 %
6.5	3.92 %
7.5	10.76 %
8.5	0.01 %
9.5	0.05 %
11.0	6.13 %
13.5	2.52 %
17.5	1.26 %
25.0	0.09 %
35.0	0.01 %
>>>	0.00 %

Figure 5.2.5 View length and sky opening in a typical North European courtyard.
© University of Liege

Privacy (see also section 6.3)

Overlooking, from other buildings or from the courtyard, can be a major problem in buildings of this type. The way in which privacy is achieved will have a major impact on the natural lighting of a layout.

In general, the use of remoteness (by arranging for enough distance between buildings) is impossible; Figure 5.2.5 shows the lengths of view for a point near a building in a typical North European courtyard. Another way of achieving privacy is by design. But in a high density courtyard, high walls or projecting wings cannot be constructed.

There is no practicable way to achieve complete privacy in courtyards, and each high density courtyard differs. Nevertheless, the following strategies may be helpful.

● *Modifying the site layout planning of buildings*
  Examples:
  The choice of building occupation and the subdivision of the grounds of a development so that as few families as possible share a common entry.
  Placing of amenities – recreation, parking, planting – within the areas defined for the use of particular inhabitants.
● *Organizing the whole housing layout*
  Example:
  The choice of building types and their positioning so as to develop close physical associations between the interior areas of buildings and the adjacent outdoor spaces.

Accessibility

Buildings in dense urban clusters can have multiple access levels from the public space outside. The outer ring of buildings is directly connected to the street; this then gives access to some other areas which may themselves form the access routes to areas further within, and so on.

It is important to know how building occupants reach each part of the cluster, what is its level of privacy, how many people have access there, and what is its status (passage, private garden, etc). An access graph (Figure 5.2.6), which has a tree-like form, can show the sequences required to reach each area. Often there may be several different ways to reach the same place.

In rehabilitation, the most critical situations occur when these access graphs show status conflicts: when there is no simple connection between a house and its private garden, or when a semi-public passage affords direct views into private rooms. In these cases, the traditional balance between public rooms (the living room and hall) directed towards the public open space and private rooms facing the private cluster's core, cannot always be realized. Access routes through the cluster may need to be modified.

Reference to section 5.2

[5.2.1] **Littlefair P J.** Site layout planning for daylight and sunlight. Building Research Establishment Report, Garston, 1991.

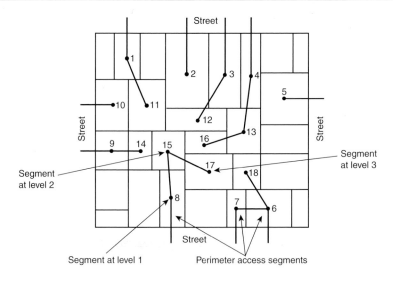

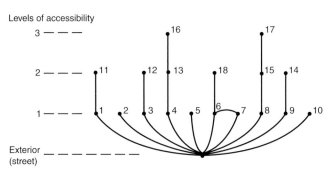

Figure 5.2.6 Access graph for a hypothetical access pattern. © University of Liege

5.3 Courtyards: ventilation and cooling

Strategy: In warm climates deep enclosed courtyards can provide a cool area next to the building, especially if they are shaded by trees or awnings, or have water features

Courtyards maximize the thermal interaction between the building and the outdoor environment, introducing the outdoors into the building's core. It is commonly assumed that this helps maintain cool indoor temperatures. However, the actual climatic effects of a courtyard depend greatly on its detailed design.

Characteristics of the thermal performance of a courtyard
Air flow

The air temperature in a courtyard is a result of the surface temperature of all its elements (ground, surrounding walls, fountains and pools in the courtyard, etc) and mixing with the outside ambient air.

The fact that a courtyard is confined means it can have its own thermal environment. The air temperature in the courtyard can be markedly different from that of the outside air, since the mixing action between both is impeded by the surrounding walls.

This depends mainly on the aspect ratio of the courtyard (depth/width) and the wind speed and direction. Other issues involved are the location (whether the building is isolated or not) and the surface temperatures in the courtyard.

Wind-driven flow

We can define a dimensionless temperature within the courtyard which is:

$$\theta = \frac{\rho\, C_p\, (T - T_{ref})\, U_{ref}\, W^2}{G}$$

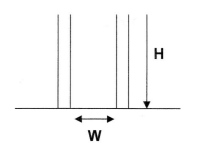

Figure 5.3.1 Courtyard representation
© University of Seville

H/W < 0.3

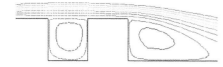

Figure 5.3.2 Streamlines for low aspect ratio courtyards. © University of Seville

0.3 < H/W > 1

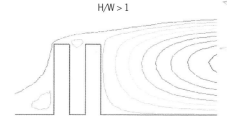

Figure 5.3.3 Streamlines for medium aspect ratio courtyards. © University of Seville

H/W > 1

Figure 5.3.4 Streamlines for high aspect ratio courtyards. © University of Seville

where:
ρ = air density (kg/m^3)
C_p = air specific heat $(J/kg\,K)$
T = temperature in the courtyard (K)
T_{ref} = external or reference temperature (K)
U_{ref} = reference wind velocity (m/s)
W = courtyard width (m)
G = heat flow released in the courtyard (W)

A low θ shows the courtyard is good at dissipating the energy generated inside it. θ depends on the rate of external air entrance, and the pattern of air flow in the courtyard. A vortex or swirl of air can form which can encourage air movement in the volume.

Figure 5.3.1 shows a representation of the courtyard, simulated with CFD tools. The main parameters are height and width of the courtyard, since aspect ratio (height/width) is an important characteristic to classify all of the cases. With different aspect ratios, outdoor air access and indoor air recirculation will vary.

For low aspect ratios, ie wide courtyards, a great deal of outdoor air entrance takes place. Figure 5.3.2 shows streamlines for this case, which show a very effective access to outdoor air. The geometry of this situation means the air does not recirculate very much. This behaviour is valid for aspect ratios H/W < 0.3.

When courtyards get narrower, outdoor air access becomes less efficient. Figure 5.3.3 shows a drop in the outdoor air mass flux getting into the enclosure. By contrast recirculation is now very important, with the appearance of a swirl or vortex which efficiently mixes the air in the whole internal volume. Therefore, heat dissipation is better for medium aspect ratios, 0.3 < H/W < 1, since mixing efficiency has a powerful effect in spite of the reduced incoming outdoor air.

For high aspect ratio courtyards, H/W > 1, both the recirculation and the outdoor air entrance drop dramatically. This fact can be appreciated from Figure 5.3.4. It can be seen that the swirl, which appeared in the centre of medium-sized courtyards, has moved up, and is now confined to the top of the volume. In addition, outdoor air does not get inside the courtyard because of the large aspect ratio. Both effects reduce the heat dissipation, raising the temperature within the courtyard if there are heat sources inside it.

Figure 5.3.5 shows the dimensionless temperature θ as a function of the aspect ratio. For low aspect ratios (H/W < 0.3), narrowing the courtyard tends to increase the temperature inside the volume, as a result of a drop in the

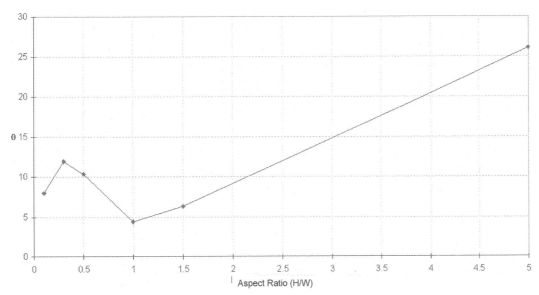

Figure 5.3.5 Dimensionless temperature on the ground as a function of the aspect ratio H/W. © University of Seville

outdoor air getting into the enclosure. When aspect ratio increases (0.3 < H/W < 1), dimensionless temperature gets reduced as a result of a recirculation growth, caused by the vortex within the courtyard. Though outdoor air entrance drops as well, the global effect is a temperature reduction. Finally, for large values of aspect ratio (H/W < 1) outdoor incoming air is further reduced, with little air movement deep in the courtyard. There is a temperature increase for large aspect ratios, mainly produced by inefficient ventilation.

All the above analysis assumes heat is generated in the courtyard. If there are no heat sources, then cool air can be trapped in a deep courtyard. If the courtyard air temperature is lower than that of the outside air, this situation is thermally stable. No buoyancy effects cause additional mixing of the air.

Thermally driven flow

At night, the air in the courtyard is usually much warmer than the outdoor air. Since the walls and the ground of the courtyard have been receiving solar radiation throughout the entire day, their temperature increases and enclosed air gets warm. The walls and floor of the courtyard have relatively poor exchange of radiation to the cold night sky, so they stay warm for most of the night. Wind tends to stop at night, and this creates natural convection situations where flows are thermally driven.

In these cases, cold air from outdoors gets into the volume by the centre of the enclosure. This cold air descends until it reaches the bottom of the courtyard, then changes its direction by moving upwards. Thus, a natural convection pattern appears, with cold air going down by the centre line and warm air ascending close to the walls. This behaviour is similar for any aspect ratio, with an identical flow pattern but a different temperature. The temperature goes up for larger aspect ratios, as a result of less effective heat removal which is more important for the bottom of the courtyard.

Shading

The walls of a courtyard shade themselves in hours with low solar altitudes, which improves the solar control of glazing and reduces external surface temperatures. To stay cool around the middle of the day, the courtyard must incorporate additional elements such as trees or canvas awnings. This is the basis of the Spanish 'patio'. The trees and awnings not only help control solar gain into the building, but also shade the site, which reduces the surface temperatures. A pergola with climbing vines can provide this shade early in the life of the courtyard. Later, tall trees with a wide canopy, rising above the roof, can provide the shade. It is desirable that the shading vegetation creates a semi-barrier between the courtyard air space and the ambient air above which reduces air exchange on windy days.

Trees not only promote cooling during daytime, but also prevent overheating during late evening and at night. The upper part of the tree's leaf canopy loses heat to the sky by transpiration[5.3.1]. The leaves cool the air around them, which becomes heavier and sinks into the courtyard. Figure 5.3.6 shows average values of the temperature at the urban reference station and in a courtyard with dense and tall trees (Figure 5.3.7). The values are averages over the months from July to September.

If a canvas awning is used, it should be retractable; closed during daytime and open at night to help night radiative cooling of the space and make the courtyard more comfortable. Provided that the site is shaded, the colour of the paved areas has little effect on its surface temperature.

Water features

An effective reduction of the air temperature in a courtyard can be achieved with the use of water features. These have a reduced temperature during daytime due to the high thermal capacity of the water. However, little heat is transferred from the air into plain horizontal water. Better conditions are

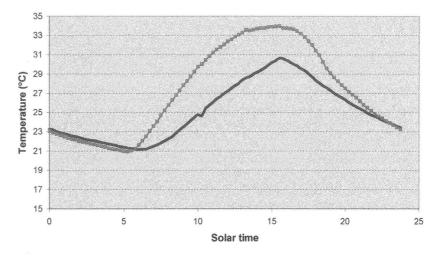

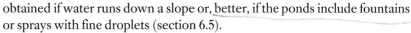

Figure **5.3.6** Average temperatures inside a courtyard with tall trees (solid line) and at a reference, unshaded site (squares). © University of Seville

Figure **5.3.7** Courtyard with trees

obtained if water runs down a slope or, better, if the ponds include fountains or sprays with fine droplets (section 6.5).

Hall et al[5.3.2] have investigated the dispersion of pollutants in courtyards. As the above analysis has shown, they are generally quite poorly ventilated spaces even down to quite shallow forms of height to width of 0.2. Figure 5.3.8 shows results from small-scale wind tunnel measurements of concentrations at the base of courtyards of varying depth, set in thick-walled building forms (see the inset diagram). The contaminant discharges are from within the courtyard. The scale of concentration on the left side of the graph is a dimensionless concentration, K, of the form,

$$K = \frac{CUL^2}{Q}$$

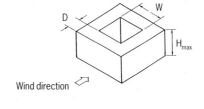

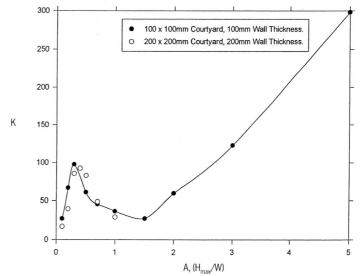

Figure **5.3.8** Contaminant concentrations at the base of courtyards of varying depth, from discharges within the courtyard

where:
C = contaminant concentration,
U = external windspeed,
L = physical scale of the courtyard (in the present case its width), and
Q = rate of discharge of the contaminant.

K automatically accounts for the effects of windspeed, physical scale and the discharge rate of the contaminant on its concentrations. The values of K vary considerably depending on the depth of the courtyard, but are generally very high. The value of K on the outside downwind wall of the courtyard block (where the discharged contaminant is eventually entrained) is about 1, while inside the courtyard values of K are much higher, of around 100 or more. Thus, contaminant concentrations are much higher inside these enclosed spaces than outside and this helps to keep high concentrations of pollutants within the urban canopy.

The ventilation of courtyards is markedly affected by other factors besides their relative depth. Their shape, the presence of openings and of ground clutter, wind direction and aerodynamic effects due to the surrounding buildings are also important. Figure 5.3.9 shows the effect of ground clutter, both porous (trees and bushes) and solid (small buildings and urban furniture), which is to increase internal contaminant concentrations. The effects of openings in the walls of courtyards are more complex. Figure 5.3.10 shows the effects of ground level tunnels and of open corners on contaminant levels, which can be both higher and lower than with a closed courtyard, depending on the wind direction.

Heating and cooling within courtyards can also modify ventilation rates. Contaminant levels are increased in stable stratification (from ground surface cooling) and decreased in unstable stratification (from ground surface heating). However stratification is very sensitive to windspeed and is rapidly destroyed in stronger winds. Stable stratification is sometimes generated by the evaporation of water as a part of local climate modification techniques.

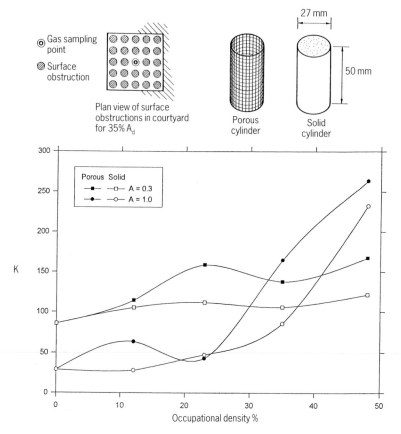

Figure 5.3.9 Effects of ground clutter on contaminant concentrations in courtyards, from discharges within the courtyard

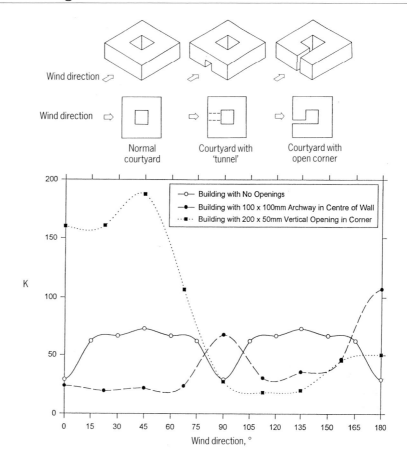

Figure 5.3.10 Effects of openings on contaminant concentrations in courtyards, from discharges within the courtyard

In summary, in hot climates a well-designed courtyard improves solar control, reduces heat transfer through the walls and glazing and can be used to provide natural ventilation cooling taking advantage of the cool air of the courtyards. As an unfavourable effect, there can be a loss of cross-ventilation potential for the rooms on the leeward side of the courtyard, compared with a building where inlet and outlet openings direct the airflow across the whole building. Polluting discharges within the courtyard need to be minimized.

References to section 5.3

[5.3.1] **Givoni B.** *Urban design in different climates.* WMO/TD No. 346. Geneva, World Meteorological Organization. 1989.

[5.3.2] **Hall D J, Walker S & Spanton A M.** Dispersion from courtyards and other enclosed spaces. *Atmospheric Environment* 1999: 33: 1187–1203.

5.4 Colonnades

Strategy: use colonnades as circulation to provide adaptive solar shading and rain protection

Colonnades are probably one of the oldest urban built forms, known and used by Mediterranean civilizations in antiquity. They serve a number of purposes, both climatic and visual; they provide natural solar shading in summer, snow and rain protection in winter, and relative visual screening throughout the year. This multi-purpose nature probably accounts for their widespread use all around Europe, despite important cultural and climatic differences. However, it makes their design quite complex because of the number of constraints, sometimes conflicting, to be considered.

Colonnades and urban pattern

There are three main ways colonnades relate to the urban fabric.

1 The colonnade is shared between public open space and private buildings

In this case, the colonnade acts as a buffer between public and private areas. Both the private buildings and public open space will constrain the design. A unified design may be especially difficult to achieve when the colonnade links several buildings, and must fit in with each of them. Royal palaces and modern shopping centres can be good examples of this kind of development. (Figures 5.4.1, 5.4.2)

Local planning guidelines or regulations can help in this process. For instance, in Arras, France, colonnade design was fixed through a 1692 ordinance. This bylaw required the colonnade design of refurbished houses to conform to a single locally defined type. The uniformity of the whole is usually less than if a single designer is responsible, but the visual richness may prove to be more attractive.

2 The colonnade belongs to the private building itself

Colonnades may also be used as a means of solar control in private courtyards. In southern latitudes (Islamic architecture, Italy and Spain), the central courtyard, around which the whole of the house is grouped, is often bordered

Figure 5.4.1 Colonnade and fountain in the Alcazar palace, Seville

Figure 5.4.2 Colonnade at Trinity College, Cambridge

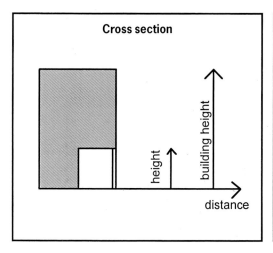
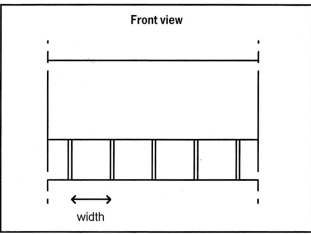

Figure 5.4.3 Geometry of colonnade. © University of Liege

by a colonnade. In this case the relation between open space and building is less of a problem since it is under the sole control of a single designer.

3 The colonnade belongs to the public open space
Finally, the colonnade may also be considered as an element by itself in a public space. St Peter's Square in Rome is one of the most outstanding examples of this kind of layout, where the colonnade is completely detached from buildings and mainly forms a visual boundary between the central space and peripheral areas.

Colonnades and solar control
Although the geometry of a colonnade seems simple, there are a number of parameters (Figure 5.4.3) which determine its impact on solar radiation:

The depth of the colonnade (variation of the solar radiation along distance axis)
Obviously, the deeper the colonnade, the less direct solar energy will reach the ground. However, the rate of solar radiation decrease is much faster in June than in December or even March, because of the higher solar altitude in June. Thus, at certain areas within the colonnade the solar radiation can be greater in March than in June. This is therefore a valuable technique for intermediate latitudes because excessive summer radiation is blocked and profitable spring and autumn radiation maintained. Consider a colonnade running alongside a south-facing wall (Figure 5.4.4). For the latitude of Brussels (50° N), the optimal distance from the edge of the colonnade would be between 0.6 and 1.4 times its height (assuming it had a width/height ratio of 1).

For diffuse radiation (Figure 5.4.5), the colonnade's impact increases gradually with its depth. By contrast with direct radiation, the building itself has a very important impact on open space diffuse radiation (50% loss at the limit between colonnades and open space). Diffuse radiation is reduced by 75% at 0.4 times and by 90% at 1.2 to 1.4 times the height of the colonnade.

Orientation
When the colonnade is next to an east-facing wall (Figure 5.4.6), the solar reduction is more regular over the year, given the lower altitudes when the sun is opposite: the direct radiation in June never drops below its value in March or December. Also, the building has an important impact on direct solar radiation in front of the colonnade: at the divide between colonnade and open space, the building blocks the sun for half of the day.

The impact of orientation on diffuse radiation is much more limited because it comes from the whole of the sky.

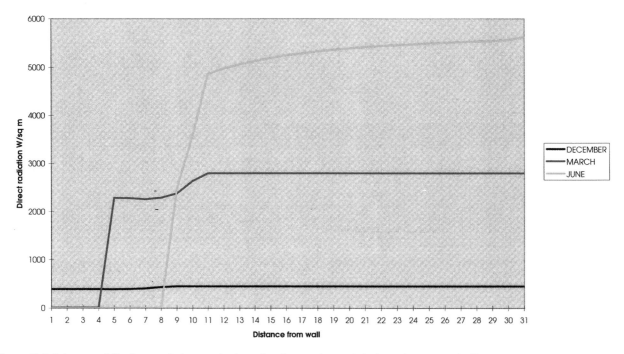

Figure 5.4.4 Average daily direct radiation on a horizontal surface under south-facing colonnades of different depths (latitude of Brussels). © University of Liege

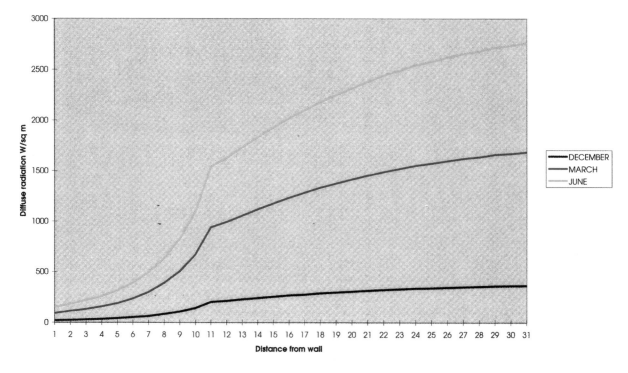

Figure 5.4.5 Diffuse radiation on a horizontal surface under colonnades of different depths. © University of Liege

Height of the building (adjoining the colonnade)

The overall building height has no impact on solar radiation within the colonnade adjoining it. It can reduce the radiation which would have been received without the colonnade, but not enough to negate the value of the colonnade for solar shading.

Latitude

At low latitudes the benefits of colonnades are greater because of the higher solar altitudes. For the latitude of Seville (37° N), the distance from the edge at which direct radiation is almost completely blocked in June is 0.4 times the

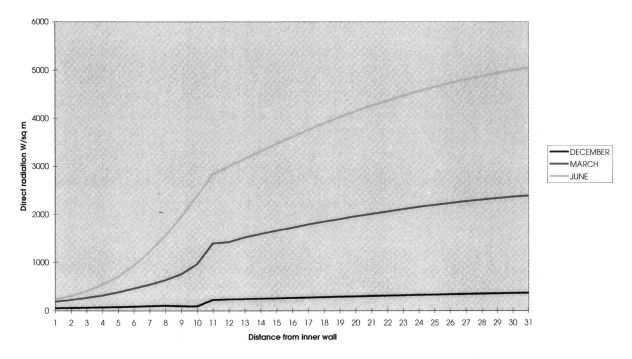

Figure 5.4.6 Average daily direct radiation on a horizontal surface under east-facing colonnades of different depths (latitude of Brussels). © University of Liege

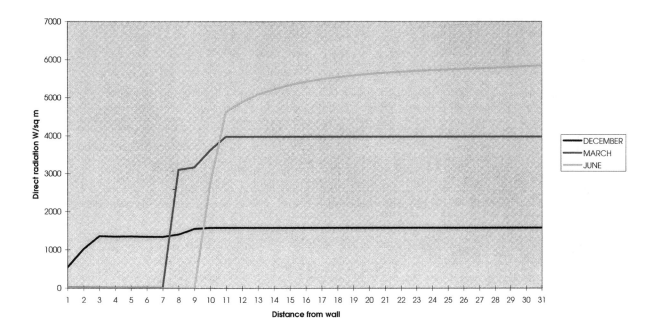

Figure 5.4.7 Average daily direct radiation on a horizontal surface under south facing colonnades of different depths (latitude of Sevilla). © University of Liege

height of the colonnade. This is for a colonnade adjacent to a south-facing wall (Figure 5.4.7). March radiation is blocked at 0.8 times the height, December radiation at 1.6 times. Thus, the optimal distance from the colonnade edge would probably be between 0.8 and 1.6 times the colonnade height if both spring and summer radiation are to be controlled.

Width/height ratio of the colonnade
The distance from the edge of the colonnade at which good solar shading is provided depends largely on its height. The width/height ratio of the colonnade has little impact on this dimension. However a wider colonnade will have a larger area with good solar protection.

5.5 Earth sheltering

Strategy: use earth sheltered forms to reduce temperature swings and reduce the building's impact on its local environment

During the summer the ground has a lower temperature than ambient. Thus, the excess heat of a building can be dissipated to it, providing passive cooling of the spaces. The opposite heat flow can occur during the winter period as ground may be warmer than the ambient air and thus may supply heat to the building or contribute to decrease its thermal losses.

Heat can be dissipated to the ground either by direct contact or by means of earth-to-air heat exchangers. In the first configuration a high part of the building envelope is in contact with the ground. In the second, air is cooled by circulating through underground pipes that play the role of earth-to-air heat exchangers.

An estimation of earth-sheltering potential requires a full knowledge of the soil characteristics. The main parameters influencing the thermal behaviour of the soil are thermal conductivity and heat capacity. It should be noted that most minerals have a similar density and specific heat. The thermal conductivity, k, and heat capacity, ρ_c, can be combined to give thermal diffusivity, a, defined as the ratio of the thermal conductivity to the heat capacity:

$$a = k / \rho_c$$

The thermal diffusivity influences the temperature variation of the soil as do the average annual temperature of the soil, Tm, and the amplitude of surface temperature variation, As. According to Labs[5.5.1], for a homogeneous soil having a constant thermal diffusivity a, the ground temperature at any depth z and time t (expressed in days), is given by the following expression:

$$T(z,t) = T_m - As \exp[-z \, (\pi/(365a)0.5] \cos[(2\pi/365)(t - t_o - z/2 \, (365/(\pi a)^{0.5})]$$

where:
t = time elapsed from the beginning of the calendar year (days),
t_o = phase constant in days and corresponds to that day of the year presenting the lowest average ground surface temperature (Figure 5.5.1).

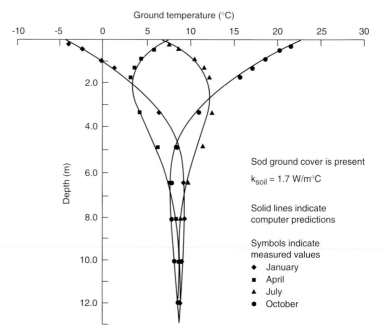

Figure 5.5.1 Ground temperature variation as a function of depth

Advantages of earth-sheltered buildings. Carmody et al[5.5.2]

Visual impact — aesthetics
Since these buildings are below ground level and their envelope is covered by earth, they are better integrated into the landscape, compared with common buildings.

Preservation of surface open spaces
The roof of an underground building can be used as a garden or other type of open space.

Environmental benefits
As well as the reduced visual impact of the buildings and the low disruption of the landscape, there are various benefits like the absorption of carbon dioxide by the planted roofs, reduced energy consumption, etc.

Noise and vibration control
The heavy mass of the buildings absorbs ambient noise and vibration.

Maintenance
Earth-buried buildings require, in general, less maintenance than normal surface buildings since the major part of their envelope is sheltered and therefore not degraded by the weather.

Other benefits
Fire protection, protection against earthquakes, suitability for civil defence, protection against storms and tornadoes and higher security against outside intrusions.

Major limitations of earth-contact buildings. Carmody et al[5.5.2]

Structural and economic limitations
Earth-contact buildings require more expensive structures since the roofs must bear the great weight of the soil.

Daylight aspects
Earth-contact buildings may experience poor daylight conditions.

Slow thermal response
Slow response due to the high thermal inertia of the ground is one of the major advantages of these buildings. This advantage might become a disadvantage in cases where energy conservation strategies such as night thermostat setback would be applied.

Condensation — Indoor air quality
Condensation might occur on the internal surfaces of the building, if their temperature drops below the dew point temperature. Low infiltration and ventilation rates may create major air quality problems.

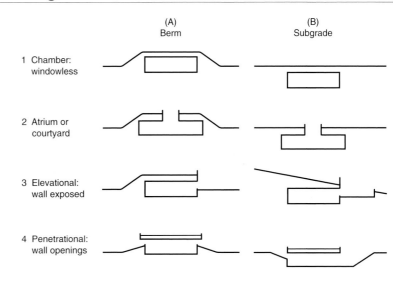

Figure 5.5.2 Classification of earth-contact buildings according to Labs[5.5.1]

Underground buildings give good thermal behaviour during the summer period. By being in contact with the ground, their indoor environment is protected from the extreme variation of the outdoor conditions, while conductive heat losses are increased and the thermal inertia of the building increases.

Labs[5.5.1] has classified earth-sheltered buildings in various categories (Figure 5.5.2). Two main categories, 'berm' and 'subgrade' buildings have been defined. Then for each category, four types are found:
● Windowless chamber,
● Atrium or courtyard,
● Elevational: wall exposed, and
● Penetrational: wall openings.

Carmody et al[5.5.2] have summarized the main advantages and disadvantages of earth-sheltered buildings which are given in the box, left.

Various examples of buried or semi-buried buildings can be found[5.5.3]. On the island of Santorini, in the Aegean sea in Greece, there are many semi-buried dwellings built during various historical periods.

Figure 5.5.3 shows an earth-sheltered experimental house in Milton Keynes, UK. Another interesting example is the Llavaneres semi-buried house, located close to Barcelona, on the Costa Brava in Spain (Figure 5.5.4). This house is built near the top of a sloping site, the slope descending towards the south. This gives the advantage of contact with the ground at the north facade, thus increasing the heat losses during summer and giving the building an important thermal inertia.

References to section 5.5

[5.5.1] **Labs K.** Earth coupling. In: Cook J (ed) *Passive cooling*. Cambridge, Massachusetts, MIT Press, 1989.

[5.5.2] **Carmody J C, Meixel G D, Labs K B & Shen LS.** Earth contact buildings: applications, thermal analysis and energy benefits. In: Boer K W & Duffie J (eds) *Advances in solar energy*. Vol 2. New York, Plenum Press, 1985.

[5.5.3] **Santamouris M & Asimakopoulos D (eds).** *Passive cooling of buildings*. London, James & James Science Publishers, 1996.

Figure 5.5.3 Earth-sheltered house in Milton Keynes, UK

Figure 5.5.4 Roof of the Llavaneres building integrated with the surrounding landscape.
© University of Athens

5.6 Location of passive cooling systems

Strategy: Passive cooling includes ventilation, solar control and evaporative and radiative cooling. However, such systems have to be planned and located with care

A reduction in summertime temperatures in buildings can be achieved by:

- reducing solar and heat gains: shading devices, insulation, appropriate color and materials, and decrease of internal gains, eg using lighting controls,
- use of the building's heat capacity to modulate heat gains,
- dissipating excess heat from the building to an environmental sink of lower temperature. This could be via convection to the ambient air, evaporative cooling of water, radiation to the sky and conduction to the ground.

Reducing heat gains

Appropriate location of the solar control devices in a building is of vital importance[5.6.1]. Shading devices should stop the direct solar radiation reaching the window surface during the summer period but may allow some solar penetration during the winter months. At the same time they will ideally provide a clear view to the outdoor environment and permit sufficient daylight to enter. External shading devices are more efficient than internal ones as they do not allow solar radiation to enter the building. Shading of the external opaque walls of the building may reduce the incident solar radiation but also decrease the infrared radiation emitted by the walls especially during the night. Solar control to protect the building roof during the daytime and removed during the night period, may significantly improve indoor comfort especially in poorly insulated buildings.

Insulation of the external envelope reduces conductive heat gains during the summer period and reduces losses during the winter months. The location of the insulation determines the thermal mass of the building available for heat store and dissipation. Insulation on the inside of the fabric reduces the building's potential to soak up the excess heat and may cause important overheating problems. On the contrary, positioning the insulation on the external facade of the building maximizes the potential for heat dissipation and can decrease the building's peak temperature.

The colour and the nature of the external materials in the building envelope play an important role in the thermal balance of walls and roofs. Light colours associated with low solar absorptivity and high albedo decrease the absorbed solar radiation, while high emissivity coefficients increase losses through infrared radiation to the sky. The impact of the optical characteristics of external materials on the external surface temperature is very high. Surface temperature differences of up to 15 °C can occur between similar walls having different external finishes.

The direct impact of high external temperatures on indoor air may be low if the building is sufficiently insulated. However, high external surface temperatures increase considerably the air temperature close to the building. This air then enters the building through its openings and causes an increase of the indoor temperature.

Heat storage

Appropriate location of the thermal mass of the building may significantly help to reduce indoor temperature and improve thermal comfort. When the building is night ventilated, coupling of the building's thermal mass with the circulating air is especially important. The amount and location of the building's mass can be optimized using dynamic simulation techniques.

Rejecting excess heat

Natural ventilation of buildings and especially night ventilation is one of the more efficient passive cooling techniques. Air flow rates through the building depend on the relative position and the area of the openings, as well as the wind pressure and any temperature differences between the indoor and outdoor environment. To optimize the air flow through the building openings, windows have to be placed in facades in such a way that the maximum pressure difference is achieved. At the same time, the maximum possible area of the building should be ventilated and short circuits of air and high indoor speeds should be avoided. Optimization of the building openings as well as appropriate positioning may be achieved by using natural ventilation prediction tools like AIOLOS[5.6.2]. The distribution of the air speed inside the building may be calculated by using computational fluid dynamic models (CFD) provided that the boundary conditions are well defined and known.

The use of evaporative systems may significantly reduce indoor temperature. Vegetation around the building can, through evapotranspiration, decrease considerably the ambient temperature and thus improve the building's thermal balance. Trees planted nearby can also provide shading to decrease ambient and surface temperature; however, they may decrease the net radiative losses of the walls. Hybrid evaporative systems integrated in the roof of the buildings have been proposed in the last few years. A complete review of these systems is given in ref.[5.6.3]. These systems reduce the temperature of the roof through evaporation and thus decrease indoor temperature and improve indoor comfort. The specific contribution of roof hybrid evaporative systems is directly related to the degree of insulation of the building, and less insulated buildings may benefit more from such systems.

The direct use of the ground to improve the indoor building environment has been discussed in section 5.5. The use of indirect systems like earth-to-air heat exchangers coupled to the buildings may be a very efficient way to dissipate the excess building heat to the ground. Earth-to-air heat exchangers are plastic, metallic or concrete pipes buried at a depths between 1.5 m and 4 m below the building or below the surrounding space. Air is circulated through them and because of the low ground temperature it exits with much lower temperature and then is circulated in the building. Indoor or fresh air may be circulated through the pipes. Care should be taken to avoid smell and indoor air quality problems. Sizing of the earth-to-air heat exchangers is a complex procedure, but simpler methods have been developed and are presented with some very successful examples in ref.[5.6.4].

The use of the sky as a sink to dissipate the excess heat of the building can be interesting especially in locations of low radiative potential. Unfortunately, urban environments generally have higher pollution levels that decrease the radiative cooling potential of surfaces. Hybrid radiative cooling techniques based on the use of metallic radiators have been extensively studied during the last few years. These radiators have high emissivity coefficients and may or may not be covered by a polyethylene film to decrease convection from the cool surface to the ambient air. The temperature of the surface of the radiators is below the ambient temperature because of its negative thermal balance. Air is circulated through the radiators during the night time, where it is cooled from the low temperature surface of the radiator. The cooled air may be circulated directly inside the building or may be used to decrease the temperature of a storage medium like water or concrete.

The cooling potential of hybrid radiative systems has been studied for various European locations and presented in ref.[5.6.5]. In cities, the cooling potential rarely exceeds 60–70 W/m^2. Much higher values have been measured in rural and arid areas. Methodologies to design and predict the performance of hybrid radiative systems are also presented in ref.[5.6.5]. However, it should be pointed out that these techniques are more of research interest.

References to section 5.6

[5.6.1] **Littlefair P J.** *Solar shading of buildings*. Garston, CRC, 1999.

[5.6.2] **Allard F, Alvarez S, Dascalaki E, Guarracino G, Maldonado E, Santamouris M, Sciuto S & Vandaele L (eds).** *Handbook of natural ventilation of buildings*. London, James & James Science Publishers, 1997.

[5.6.3] **Argiriou A.** Evaporative cooling. In: Santamouris M & Asimakopoulos D N (eds). *Passive cooling of buildings*. London, James & James Science Publishers, 1995.

[5.6.4] **Argiriou A.** Ground cooling. In: Santamouris M & Asimakopoulos D N (eds). *Passive cooling of buildings*. London, James & James Science Publishers, 1995.

[5.6.5] **Argiriou A.** Radiative cooling. In: Santamouris M & Asimakopoulos D N (eds). *Passive cooling of buildings*. London, James & James Science Publishers, 1995.

5.7 Solar dazzle

Strategy: Avoid unwanted glare reflected from shiny building surfaces

Figure 5.7.1 Solar dazzle reflected from a sloping facade (Aylesbury, UK)

Glare or dazzle can occur when sunlight is reflected from a glazed facade (Figure 5.7.1). This can affect road users outside and the occupants of adjoining buildings. The problem can occur either when there are large areas of reflective tinted glass or metal cladding on the facade, or when there are areas of glass which slope back at up to 35° from the vertical so that high altitude sunlight can be reflected along the ground (Figures 5.7.2, 5.7.3). Thus solar dazzle is only a long-term problem for some heavily glazed (or mirror clad) non-domestic buildings. A glazed facade also needs to face within 90° of due south for significant amounts of sunlight to be reflected.

If it is likely that a building may cause solar dazzle the exact scale of the problem should be evaluated. This is done by identifying key locations such as road junctions and windows of nearby buildings, and working out the number of hours of the year that sunlight can be reflected to these points. Ref.[5.7.1] gives full details.

At the design stage solar dazzle can be remedied by reducing areas of glazing, substituting clear or absorbing glass for reflective glass, reorienting the building, or replacing areas of tilted glass by either vertical or nearly horizontal glazing. Alternatively, some form of opaque screening may be acceptable, although this usually needs to be larger than the glazing area.

Reference to section 5.7

[5.7.1] Littlefair P J. Solar dazzle reflected from sloping glazed facades. BRE Information Paper *IP3/87*. Garston, CRC, 1987.

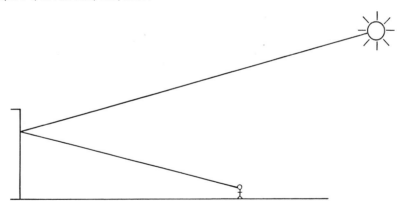

Figure 5.7.2 With a vertical facade, solar reflection is usually only a problem if the sun is high in the sky

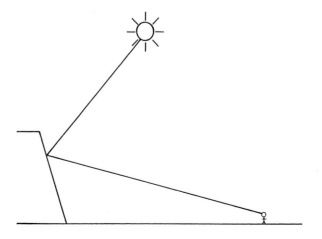

Figure 5.7.3 A sloping facade can reflect high-angle summer sun along the ground

5.8 Conclusions

Environmentally sensitive building design needs to consider the interaction between the built form and the spaces surrounding it. In cool to intermediate climates the emphasis is on forms which avoid adverse effects on their surroundings, eg:

● overbearing visual impact,
● wind effects on the ground, especially where there are tall buildings (section 5.1),
● areas in permanent shade (section 4.4) [eg courtyards should be opened out if possible to catch sunlight and daylight (section 5.2)],
● glare or dazzle from reflective building faces (section 5.7).

The linking of appropriate built forms can form part of an urban renewal strategy (section 5.2).

In warmer climates the strategy is the creative use of built forms to generate climatically comfortable areas bordering the building. These can include:

● shaded courtyards (section 5.3),
● colonnades (section 5.4),
● earth-sheltered structures (section 5.5),
● self-shading buildings (section 5.6),
● buildings with radiative or evaporative cooling (section 5.6).

Such areas can be used as semi-outdoor 'rooms' in summer as well as providing a cool buffer zone around the building.

6 Landscaping

Landscaping can have a big impact on the overall climatic quality of a site, and the performance of buildings within it. Plants can provide wind shelter, shade and evaporative cooling on hot days. Water features can give additional cooling, while use of high reflectance materials can reduce heat absorption.

6.1 Vegetation and hard landscaping: wind shelter

Strategy: Provide shelterbelts and windbreaks to reduce site wind exposure

Trees, bushes, walls, fences and ground profiling (eg mounds and banks) can all contribute to wind shelter, in addition to their value in providing summer shade (section 6.2). For maximum benefit, landscape elements need to be designed in conjunction with the arrangement of buildings, following many of the same principles, eg avoiding channelling or funnelling of ground-level winds. Vegetation, being permeable to the wind, is less inclined to generate downdraughts than buildings, solid fences or earth banks; tall trees, suitably placed, can therefore offer substantial wind protection.

Uses of vegetation divide into:
- major shelter belts to protect the edges of built-up areas, or placed at regular intervals within large developments,
- smaller-scale planting of trees and bushes to give local protection to buildings or open spaces, and to enhance ground roughness generally.

Shelterbelt design

The use of major shelter belts to protect building developments are rare at present, although they have a long history in agriculture and forestry. When fully grown they have the potential to provide wind protection over the entire height of low-rise buildings. However, their effectiveness in early years is more limited, since even quick-growing tree species take up to 10 years before giving useful protection. Their establishment therefore calls for a long-term landscape planning strategy which extends to the development and maintenance of the plants over the lifetime of the buildings. The belt may be designed to grow in several successive stages, with quicker-growing species offering early wind protection and acting as 'nursery' stock to protect slower-growing trees that will form the eventual belt. As the trees grow taller, infilling at their base with bushes becomes important; this prevents gaps that would channel the wind at low level.

Artificial windbreaks can be used to create 'instant' shelter, either as a permanent solution or as an expedient until plants grow sufficiently to become effective. Solid walls, banking and close fences can reduce mean windspeeds locally, but they are inclined to increase the unsteady, turbulent, component of the wind, which produces more gusts. Permeable walls or fences (Figure 6.1.1) tend to be more effective as they reduce mean windspeeds without increasing gusts. This mimics the behaviour of planted

Figure 6.1.1 Permeable walling as windbreak and decorative screen

shelter, which also should not be too dense if a large protected area is required. The optimum permeability for wind shelter is generally about 40–50%[6.1.1]. If the design enables permeability to be varied, it should decrease from top to bottom, ie the windbreak should be more solid at the base, more open at the top. This is likely to be best for wind control in the 'human' zone, 0–2 m; agricultural windbreaks often have a gap at the base, to avoid possible frost damage to plants if cold air is trapped. The windward depth of windbreaks is also important as a belt of trees or several fences carefully spaced can be more effective than a single fence or a narrow band of trees. The heights of trees or multiple fences can be built up towards the sheltered area to provide a greater overall reduction in windspeed.

A porous barrier will obviously allow some daylight and solar radiation through as well as being permeable to air. However, the visual (and radiant) porosity is usually less than the air porosity. According to Fry[6.1.2] an air porosity of 50% corresponds to a visual porosity of 30%. Table 6.1.1, taken from ref.[6.1.3], gives the solar radiation transmission factors of a range of deciduous trees, both in full leaf and with bare branches. Figure 6.1.2 gives the foliation periods (in England) for these trees. Further data on tree transparency are given by Wilkinson et al[6.1.4].

The height of the shelterbelt or windbreak is a compromise between both wind shelter and solar access. Finbow[6.1.5] quotes a recommendation that wind protection is effective for a height up to half the height of the shelterbelt. Thus for a two storey house a shelterbelt 10 metres high would provide shelter up to the eaves, and a 15 metre high shelterbelt would provide shelter to the ridge. However other authors (refs[6.1.6-6.1.7]) suggest that a shelterbelt reduces wind flow both up to, and even beyond, its own height (Figure 6.1.3). This would mean that only a 5 metre high belt would be needed to protect a two storey house to the eaves. Shelterbelt depth along the wind can also be used as a substitute for height as a deeper shelterbelt generates reductions in windspeed at greater heights.

The distance of the shelterbelt from the building or external space it protects is also very important. The greatest protection[6.1.1] occurs at a distance 2 H from the belt, where H is the shelterbelt height; for medium porosity shelter, Finbow[6.1.5] quotes a distance of 4 H (Figure 6.1.4) with good protection between 2 H and 6 H. Where there is a system of parallel

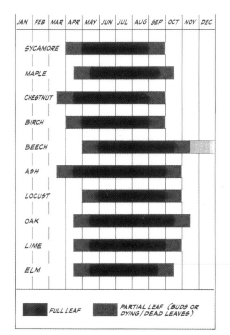

Figure 6.1.2 Range of foliation periods of common tree species. Reproduced from BRE Digest 350[6.1.3]

Table 6.1.1 Transparencies of tree crowns to solar radiation. Reproduced from BRE Digest 350[6.1.3]			
		Transparency (% radiation passing)	
Botanical name	**Common name**	**Full leaf**	**Bare branch**
Acer pseudoplatanus	Sycamore	25	65
Acer saccharinum	Silver maple	15	65
Aesculus hippocastanum	Horse chestnut	10	60
Betula pendula	European birch	20	60
Fagus sylvatica	European beech	10	80*
Fraxinus exelsior	European ash	15	55
Gleditsia	Locust	30	80
Quercus roba	English oak	20	70
Tilia cordata	Lime	10	60
Ulmus	Elm	15	65

* The beech tends to retain dead leaves for much of the winter, reaching bare branch condition only briefly before new leaf growth in the spring.

Notes:

These data apply to individual tree crowns; multi-row belts or blocks let virtually no radiation through when in leaf, and very little when in 'bare-branch' condition.

Most of the data are based on measurement of light, but may be used for solar radiation generally.

The values are averages from a range of sources, which show large differences for some of the values. They must therefore be treated with caution, noting that in any case there will be considerable divergence in the transparencies of individual trees, especially in summer.

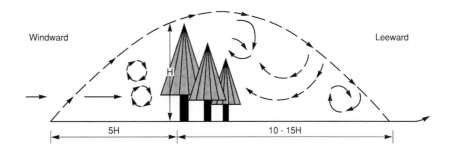

Figure 6.1.3 Basic flow characteristics of a shelter belt. Reproduced from WMO[6.1.6]

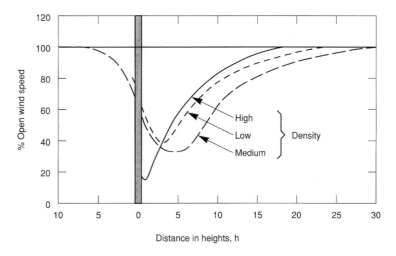

Figure 6.1.4 Wind speed reduction near shelterbelts with different densities. Reproduced from Oke[6.1.9]

shelterbelts, Bache & MacAskill[6.1.1] recommend a spacing between 10 H and 30 H.

For a passive solar building facing due south, with planted shelter to the south and west, good access to winter sunlight will be maintained if the shelter is at least 4 H distant in up to 55 °N, and 5 H distant up to 60 °N (see section 4.3). Here H is the height of the shelterbelt as before. These distances should achieve adequate shelter according to the guidance above. However, further north there may be problems achieving adequate shelter with winter solar access. For reasonable daylighting, for example to the north of passive solar buildings, a shelter distance of 2 H or more is suitable.

For most of Europe it therefore appears possible to combine the demands of solar access and wind shelter. However in practice it may not be so easy to do this. There may not be enough space available between the building and the proposed shelter. The shelterbelt may be sheltering not one building but many, for example in a housing estate. For these reasons it may be necessary to have a building nearer to the shelterbelt or windbreak. A spacing of 2 H, while losing winter solar gain, will offer adequate daylighting (section 4.1) and protection from tree root growth[6.1.8]. Buildings further from the shelterbelt can have the full range of passive solar features.

In a housing estate in an exposed area, a reasonable approach is to rely on a sizeable shelterbelt to protect the dwellings on the edge. Houses further within the estate can be sheltered by other homes and by smaller scale planting. Figure 6.1.5 shows what such an estate might look like on plan. Buildings are staggered, and roads are curved and tree-lined.

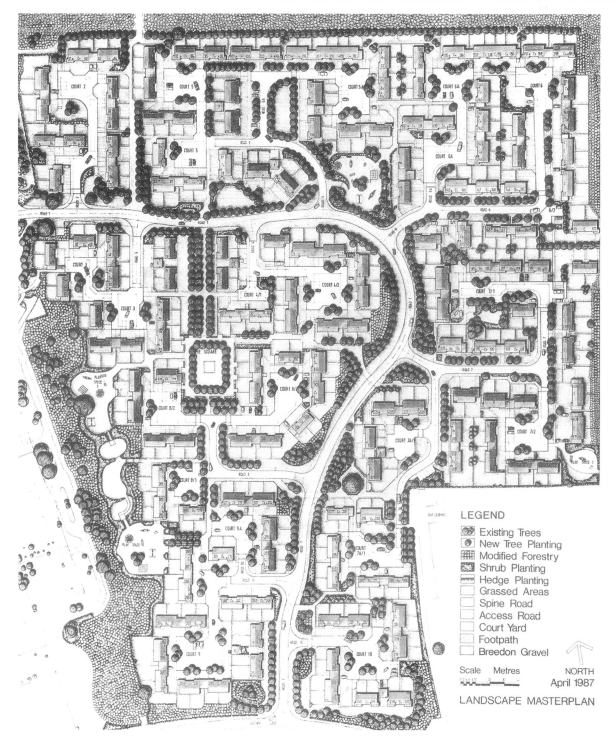

Figure 6.1.5 Multi-scale shelter. A scheme of 326 dwellings with macro-scale shelter around the site, meso-scale subdivision within it and at micro-scale clumps of trees to reduce wind speed through surface roughness. Reproduced from Dodd et al[6.1.10]

Snow

In northern climates, and at high altitudes in lower latitudes, a significant amount of precipitation may fall as snow. Snow, compared with rain:

● has greater bulk (10 cm depth of fallen snow is equivalent to about 1 cm depth of rain),
● falls more slowly, which allows it to be carried readily by the wind and to deposit preferentially into uneven drifts (Figure 6.1.6),
● tends to remain in bulk where it falls (rather than to flow away as rainfall does),
● produces low friction surfaces,
● has high albedo.

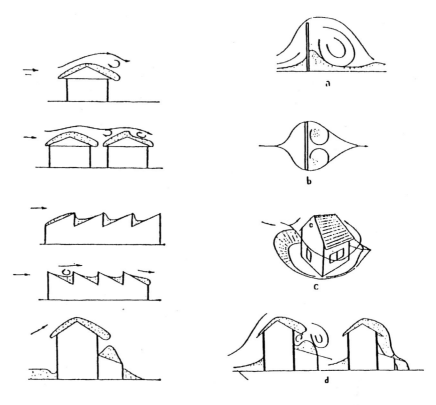

Figure 6.1.6 Snow on roofs and deposition patterns around buildings and fences. Reproduced from Izumi[6.1.11]

Because of these differences from rainfall, snowfall in urban areas produces specific problems which must be dealt with as a matter of course in areas commonly subject to it. Where snowfall is uncommon and not planned for, it can cause severe local difficulties for short periods. Izumi et al[6.1.11] quote the case of Washington, USA, which received 60 cm of snowfall in a blizzard in 1996 (its first since 1922) which effectively closed down US government activities there for one week.

The high surface albedo and low conductivity of snow minimize absorption of solar radiation, usually resulting in slow melting so that snow can linger for long periods and successive snowfalls can then accumulate. The accumulated bulk of snowfall on buildings generates high roof loadings and encourages water penetration. Falling snow from sloping roofs can also be a hazard to pedestrians. Snowfall on the ground blocks roads and pedestrian pathways and partial surface melting generates hazardous slippery surfaces. The aerodynamic disturbances around buildings and other surface obstacles in urban areas markedly modify snow deposition patterns and it is common for both substantial snow drifts and areas quite clear of snow to appear around buildings. The nature of snow flakes, usually fragile agglomerates of fine crystalline ice particles, also allows ready penetration of snow crystals or fractured crystal particles through fine cracks and cavities in buildings and other enclosures in ways analogous to (but often more severe than) that of driving rain.

These important practical consequences of snowfall have led to a substantial base of scientific investigation[6.1.11–6.1.13] and the development of practical techniques for dealing with snow in urban areas. The loading of building roofs and control of snow falling from sloping roofs ('mini-avalanches') have been considered of sufficient importance to generate specific codes of practice. UK practice has recently been reviewed by Currie[6.1.14] and new European Codes for snow loading are presently in preparation[6.1.15]. The control of snow drifting in urban areas is also a matter of importance and it is possible to do this within limits by the judicious design and positioning of snow fences, buildings and landscaping. The general principles of application of snow fences and building layout are analogous to the problems of wind shelter and landscaping described above. Regions of wind shelter encourage even snow deposition and the use of porous fences especially can encourage preferential deposition around the fence.

References to section 6.1

[6.1.1] Bache D H & MacAskill I A. *Vegetation in civil and landscape engineering*. London, Granada, 1984.

[6.1.2] Fry M. *Potential savings in building heating requirements through the use of shelterbelts*. University of Exeter briefing paper for Department of the Environment (UK), 1991.

[6.1.3] BRE. Climate and site development. *Digest 350*: Parts 1–3. Garston, CRC, 1990.

[6.1.4] Wilkinson D M, Yates D, McKennan G T. *Light attenuation characteristics of seven common British trees*. RR/89/3. Manchester (UK), Manchester Polytechnic, 1989.

[6.1.5] Finbow M. *Energy saving through landscape planning*. Volume 3: The contribution of shelter planning. Croydon, PSA, 1988.

[6.1.6] World Meteorological Organization. *Meteorological aspects of the utilization of wind as an energy source*. Technical Note 175. Geneva, WMO, 1981.

[6.1.7] Goulding J R, Lewis J O & Steemers T C (eds). Energy in architecture. *The European passive solar handbook*. London, Batsford for CEC, 1992.

[6.1.8] BRE. The influence of trees on house foundations in clay soils. *Digest 298*. Garston, CRC, 1985

[6.1.9] Oke T R. *Boundary layer climates*. London, Methuen, 1987.

[6.1.10] Dodd J S, Gerry G K & Harvey G. *Energy saving through landscape planning*. Volume 1: The background. Croydon, PSA, 1988.

[6.1.11] Izumi M, Nakamura T, Sack R L (eds). *Snow engineering: recent advances*. Rotterdam, Balkema, 1997.

[6.1.12] Sack R L (ed). *Proceedings 1st International Conference on Snow Engineering*, Santa Barbara, California, July 1988. US Army Corps of Engineers, CRREL Special Report 89-6. Hanover (New Hampshire, USA), Cold Regions Research and Engineering Laboratory, 1998.

[6.1.13] Sack R L (ed). *Proceedings 2nd International Conference on Snow Engineering*, Santa Barbara, California, June 1992. CRREL Special Report 92-27. Hanover (New Hampshire, USA), Cold Regions Research and Engineering Laboratory, 1992).

[6.1.14] Currie D M. *Handbook of imposed roof loads: a commentary on British Standard BS 6399 'Loading for Buildings': Part 3*. Building Research Establishment Report (BR247). CRC, Garston, 1994.

[6.1.15] Del Corso R et al. *New European Code for Snow Loads: background document*. Proceedings of Department of Structural Engineering, University of Pisa, No 264. 1995.

6.2 Vegetation and hard landscaping: solar shading and cooling

Strategy: Use planting to provide shade and cooling

Energy balance
'Green' areas, covered by plants, have different thermal properties compared with built-up and hard-surfaced unplanted areas. The main differences are listed below.
- Plants have lower heat capacity and thermal conductivity than building materials and hard surfaces.
- Solar radiation is mostly absorbed in the leaves, so that the reflected radiation is very small (low albedo).
- Rainwater is absorbed in the soil. Water is later evaporated from the soil and mainly from the leaves. The evaporation rate is much higher in green areas than in unplanted, hard covered areas.
- Plants reduce the wind speed and its fluctuations near the ground.

As a result, the micro-climate within and near to green areas differs from unplanted, built-up areas. The main differences are in the temperature, wind velocity and turbulence, air and radiant temperatures, humidity, and air cleanliness.

The leaves of plants absorb most of the solar radiation which strikes them.

They transform a very small part of the radiant energy by photosynthesis into chemical energy, and in this way reduce the rate of heating of the urban space slightly. But quantitatively, the plant's efficiency in transforming energy is very small (1–2%) and therefore this effect can be practically discounted.

On the other hand, evaporation of water from the leaves (evapotranspiration) causes significant cooling of the leaves and the air in contact with them, and at the same time increases the humidity of the air. How important and desirable this is depends on the prevailing humidity and temperature conditions.

Effect of vegetation on wind patterns

Different types of vegetation and planting patterns can produce wind catchers and wind screens. In general terms the following applies.
- Grassy areas give maximum ventilation conditions.
- Bushes impede the wind flow near the ground surface and some way above it.
- Trees, especially high trees with large canopies, significantly reduce wind speed in the area of the group of trees and downwind.
- A single tree with high trunk and wide canopy can concentrate the wind near the ground, thus increasing the wind speed.
- A large tree placed beside a window on the windward side of a building can improve the indoor ventilation.

Wind channelling for ventilation cooling does not just affect a single building. Usually, on typically sized residential sites, effective wind channelling plantings would have to be located in neighbouring gardens.

Solar control of buildings by landscaping

Vegetation is a natural solar control device with significant potential for improving the thermal performance of a building. The leaves of trees intercept solar radiation before it strikes the building, do not produce undesirable reflection of this radiation because of their dark colour (high absorptivity) and are always at a controlled temperature as they dissipate the heat absorbed by evapotranspiration.

The compromise[6.2.1] between landscaping to allow useful winter solar heat gains and landscaping to block undesirable summer solar heat gains is not too difficult to achieve. Essentially, all the useful winter gains reach the building through a zone that extends about 45° to the east and west from the southern corners of the building. In summer, solar heat gain will come from a much wider range of directions. Leaving the zone to the south relatively unobstructed can allow the majority of the useful winter heat to reach the building but summer heat gain can still be reduced by extensive planting in other areas. Alternatively, the use of deciduous planting can restrict summer heat gain without too much reduction in winter.

The west and east sides of a building are the most important concern for shading during summer. In a warm climate, the temperature of a west-facing exterior wall surface could be reduced by as much as 22 °C by protecting the wall with vines planted on a trellis.

Although shading of opaque surfaces is beneficial, glazing areas are the first priority for shading by landscaping. Solar gains of more than 600 W/m² are common through glazing areas; solar gains through an opaque insulated wall are an order of magnitude lower.

Deciduous plants offer a further benefit with their natural co-ordination of leaf growth with shading requirements. Plants are generally much more closely co-ordinated with building heating and cooling needs than sun angles. Although the sun's position is identical in September and March, cooling is often required in September and heating is required in March. Deciduous plants provide a very effective dynamic response because they shed and regrow their leaves in co-ordination with air temperature.

References to section 6.2

   [6.2.1] Abrams D W. *Low-energy cooling.* New York, Van Nostrand Reinhold, 1986.

   [6.2.2] Alessandro S, Barbera G. & Silvestrini G. *State of the art of the research concerning the energy interaction between the vegetation and the built environment.* Palermo (Italy), CNR-IEREN, 1987.

6.3 Vegetation and hard landscaping: privacy

Strategy: Use site layout to ensure privacy for buildings and open spaces where it is required

In the city, privacy is a major concern. People like to have privacy inside their homes, and ideally in a private external space like a rear garden or courtyard. Privacy requirements can vary with culture. In commercial buildings, too, privacy can be important, especially if confidential information is being dealt with.

   Various types of privacy can be identified:

● visual privacy, so others cannot see in,
● aural privacy, eg avoiding overhearing of conversations,
● electromagnetic privacy, against computer hacking, telephone bugging, etc,
● privacy against unwanted ingress, eg strangers wandering into the home or garden.

In the design of the external environment, visual privacy and privacy against unwanted visitors are most important. Aural privacy is best dealt with by good sound insulation of buildings, although the design of the external environment plays a part.

   Various design techniques help promote privacy:

● distance,
● external screening,
● screening of windows,
● use of private or semi-private spaces,
● visual cues to deter intruders.

Privacy distances

In some countries privacy distances have been a traditional method. The Scottish Building Regulations for example[6.3.1] used to contain a requirement for a spacing of up to 60 feet (18 m) between windows that face each other. Other design guides[6.3.2] suggest greater distances up to 35 metres or more (Figure 6.3.1). These can act as a major constraint on layout design.

   Distance helps promote visual privacy but does not guarantee it. An early study[6.3.3] suggests complete visual privacy indoors is only achieved at distances of 90 metres or more. For outdoor activities like sunbathing the required distances will be even greater. However, if a building is a long way from public areas the view is more likely to be screened by trees. Distance is also likely to give a feeling of privacy and it enhances aural privacy significantly. The effects on unwanted ingress are less clear. It may be harder for an intruder to reach the building without being seen, but also harder to supervise the far side of a garden.

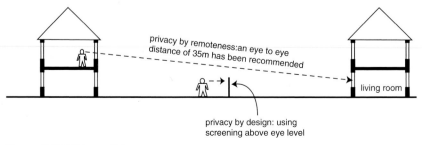

Figure 6.3.1 Privacy distance

Figure 6.3.2 At Pennyland, Milton Keynes, UK, raised planting provides privacy but causes some winter overshadowing

External screening
Trees, hedges, fences and walls can all provide screening and enhance privacy. However they can also block daylight, sunlight and solar gain (Figure 6.3.2). Various factors, including height and porosity, affect the privacy achieved.

Height
For visual privacy, screens need to be above standing eye height. But higher screens will block more sunlight and daylight with little extra privacy benefit.

Porosity
Completely opaque barriers (Figure 6.3.3) give the best privacy but block most light and solar gain. Porous fences and hedges give a degree of privacy which is enhanced if:
● the holes are neither too large, nor very small and regular[6.3.4],
● people outside cannot go right up to the barrier to peer through,
● the barrier is light coloured, superimposing a bright distracting pattern on the view in[6.3.5],
● the barrier has depth, restricting viewing angles into the property.

For shielding of gardens in cooler climates, deciduous hedges and shrubs may be an acceptable compromise. They let through solar gain in winter, but provide effective shielding in summer when most outdoor activities take place. External screening of any type, even suspended chains between posts, will restrict casual access.

Figure 6.3.3 A hedge can be effectively opaque

Screening on windows
Where external protection cannot provide visual privacy, windows may need to be screened in some way.
● Diffusing glass lets through light but ruins view out.
● Reflective glass (Figure 6.3.4) or light-coloured net curtains allow a view, but are ineffective at night[6.3.5].
● Narrow windows with deep reveals restrict viewing into property.
● Adjustable curtains or shutters allow the occupants to control the degree of privacy.

Private or semi-private outdoor spaces
A feature of some traditional Mediterranean housing is a private courtyard (section 5.3) onto which the main windows look (Figure 6.3.5). Only tiny, barred or shuttered windows may face the street[6.3.6].

Figure 6.3.4 Reflective glass restricts view in

Figure 6.3.5 A private courtyard in Seville, Spain. © University of Seville

Visual cues to deter intruders

Private and semi-private spaces can be delineated using visual cues[6.3.7]:

- gates (Figure 6.3.6),
- archways (Figure 6.3.7),
- walls,
- thresholds — changes in paving,
- enclosed view.

References to section 6.3

[6.3.1] **Scottish Development Department.** *Building Standards (Scotland) Regulations 1963. Explanatory Memorandum 11: Daylighting and space about houses.* London, HMSO, 1964. Quoted in: Brierly ES. Exploratory study of the sunlight, daylight, visual privacy and view factors that affect the design of low rise high density housing. Glasgow, University of Glasgow, 1970.

[6.3.2] **Essex County Council.** *A design guide for residential areas.* Chelmsford, Essex County Council, 1973.

[6.3.3] **Manthore W.** Machinery of sprawl. *Architectural Review* 1956: **120**: 409–422. Quoted in: Finighan W R. Privacy in suburbia: a study of four Melbourne areas. Melbourne, CSIRO, 1979.

Figure 6.3.6 The gate, the change of paving, the enclosed view and the sign all deter entry to this garden in Innsbruck, Austria

Figure 6.3.7 Archway in Delft, Holland. The pathway sign, and the view through to the next archway, help pedestrians overcome their natural reluctance to enter.

[6.3.4] Hill A R & Markus T A. Some factors influencing vision through meshes. *Proceedings of the Royal Society A* 1969: **312**: 13–29.

[6.3.5] Treado S J & Bean J W. *Optical performance of commercial windows.* NISTIR 4711. Gaithersburg (Maryland, USA), National Institute of Standards and Technology (NIST), 1992.

[6.3.6] Bindal M. Privacy requirements and its effect on housing design. *International Journal of Housing Science and its Application* 1982: **6**(4): 301–312.

[6.3.7] Greater London Council. *An introduction to housing layout.* London, Architectural Press, 1978.

6.4 Ponds and fountains

Strategy: Use water features to cool enclosed outdoor spaces

Ponds and fountains can be effective air-conditioning systems in open spaces because of their ability to keep water temperatures lower than air temperature and their low reflectivity. Ponds have a reflectivity of approximately 3% at times of maximum solar radiation, and therefore reflect little solar radiation towards occupied zones. They absorb a lot of solar radiation: up to 80% depending on the depth of pond. All this solar radiation does not however produce a significant increase of water temperature because of the pond's thermal inertia and evaporation at its surface. The water pond inertia is directly proportional to water mass and therefore to its depth. With increasing water pond inertia, the water temperature decreases. The daily range of water temperature (difference between maximum and minimum) is reduced and there is a phase shift between air and water temperatures.

When the pond is in shadow, the incoming solar radiation is reduced, with a reduction in water temperature. This temperature reduction increases with increased shading of the pond.

As water evaporates from a drop its temperature decreases. Evaporation is proportional to the air-water contact surface area, so incorporating fountains and sprayers (drops with a diameter of the order of several mm) or nozzles (drops of the order of 1 mm or less), produces a large decrease in water temperature. The smaller drops are, the greater the air–water contact surface is, increasing evaporation. With a constant flow rate, the contact surface produced by a nozzle is 100 times greater than from a sprayer.

Energy flows of water droplets

A single water drop moving through still air experiences the following processes.

● Heat flows from the air to the drop (if the air is hotter than the drop).
● Water evaporates from the drop to the surrounding air. The hotter the drop is, the more water will be evaporated.
● The drop slows down as it moves through the air.

The first two processes affect the temperature of the drop in different ways. Inward heat transfer will warm it up but evaporation will cool it down. As a result of these two opposite tendencies, an equilibrium drop temperature is reached (the wet bulb temperature of the air). Once the drop has reached the wet bulb temperature, the extra energy needed to evaporate more water has to come from the surrounding air. This means the surrounding air is cooled, unless the air becomes saturated after which no more evaporation takes place.

So there are two different periods in the evaporation of a single water drop in air:

● the drop temperature is changing from its initial temperature to its equilibrium temperature (the air wet bulb temperature),
● the drop reaches equilibrium temperature and its radius decreases with evaporation.

The relative length of each period within the airborne life of the drop depends mainly on the initial drop size and so this will be the most important design variable for cooling by fountains and sprays.

Cooling by water drops can be achieved by two different ways.

● Water drops directly cool the air of the space being conditioned. Total evaporation of the water droplets is preferred so that their air-cooling capacity is maximized while preventing people from getting wet.

● Indirect cooling of the air by using cool water as an intermediate medium. In this case, water drops cool the water in a pond and the aim is to obtain the maximum reduction of the temperature of the drops with the minimum water loss.

In short, water pond temperature depends on the existence of sprays, their number and kind, when they operate, if the pond is shaded, and pond depth.

A large set of experiments[6.4.1] were performed in a pond (Figure 6.4.1), 30 cm depth, in the EXPO '92 grounds. Figure 6.4.2 shows water pond temperature and air temperature in a nearby meteorological station over four consecutive days. The sprayer system worked during the first two days. There were typical ranges of 17 °C in air temperature but only 3 °C in water temperature with sprayers working and 6 °C on the other days. When the sun is shining, the water temperature is always less than the air temperature. On days with the sprayer system working, the water temperature is less than 24 °C whilst the maximum air temperature is almost 40 °C.

For the same days, the surface temperatures of sun-facing pavements at the same area were typically above 50 °C during central hours[6.4.2].

Figure 6.4.1 Pond with fountains at EXPO '92 site in Seville. © University of Seville

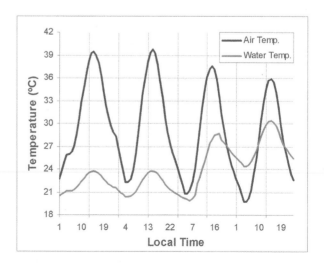

Figure 6.4.2 Variation in pond temperature with air temperature. © University of Seville

Figure 6.4.3 Cooling towers on the EXPO site, Seville

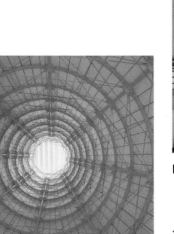

Figure 6.4.4 Looking up inside the tower

The EXPO site also contained large 'cooling towers' (Figures 6.4.3, 6.4.4). Water droplets are released inside the tower, cooling the air through evaporation. The cold air sinks out of the base of the tower, cooling the surrounding open space.

References to section 6.4
[6.4.1] Alvarez S et al. *Climatic control of outdoor spaces*. The EXPO '92 Project (in Spanish). Seville (Spain), University of Seville, 1994.

[6.4.2] Guerra J et al. *Design guidelines for the climatic conditioning of open areas* (in Spanish). Seville (Spain), University of Seville, 1994.

6.5 Albedo

Strategy: Use light-coloured materials to reduce the absorption of solar heat and keep the site cool

The optical characteristics of materials used in city environments have a very important impact on the urban energy balance. Two key parameters are the albedo to solar radiation, and emissivity of long-wave radiation.

The albedo of a surface is defined as the reflected solar radiation divided by the incident solar radiation. This is integrated over all directions and wavelengths. High albedo materials (Figure 6.5.1) reduce the amount of solar radiation absorbed through building envelopes and urban structures and keep their surfaces cooler. Materials with high emissivities are good emitters of long-wave energy and readily release the energy that has been absorbed as short-wave radiation. Lower surface temperatures contribute to a decrease in

Figure 6.5.1 High albedo surfaces in a Greek island village

the temperature of the ambient air as the heat convected from a cooler surface is lower. Such temperature reductions can have significant impacts on cooling energy consumption in urban areas, a fact of particular importance in hot climate cities.

In summer, the surface temperature, heat storage and its subsequent emission to the atmosphere are significantly greater for asphalt than for concrete and bare soil. At most, asphalt pavement can emit an additional 150 W/m² in infrared radiation and 200 W/m² in overall heat flow compared with a bare soil surface. The rate of infrared absorption by the lower atmosphere over an asphalt pavement is up to 60 W/m² greater than that over the soil surface or concrete pavement. Other research studies have found an influence of road construction on road surface temperature. A test road with a bed of blast furnace slag had a night-time temperature up to 1.5 °C higher than another road based on gravel.

Table 6.5.1 gives the albedo of various typical urban materials and areas, while Table 6.5.2 gives the emissivity as well as the reflectivity albedo for selected materials.

Taha[6.5.1] has compiled data for snow-free urban albedos for several cities and where possible has given the difference between the urban and rural albedo (Table 6.5.3).

An increase in the surface albedo has a direct impact on the energy balance of a building. Large-scale changes in urban albedo may have important indirect effects on the city scale. Numerous studies have been performed to evaluate direct effects from albedo change. Using computer simulations and actual measurements, Bretz et al[6.5.2] report that the increase in the roof albedo of a house in Sacramento, USA, from 0.2 to 0.78 reduced the cooling energy consumption by 78%. Parker & Barkaszi[6.5.3] have measured the impact of reflective roof coatings on air-conditioning energy use in occupied buildings by whitening the roofs in mid summer. For similar weather conditions, measured air-conditioning electrical savings in the buildings averaged 19%, ranging from a low of 2% to a high of 43%, with a slightly larger reduction in consumption at peak times of day.

Simpson & McPherson[6.5.4] used scale model residences in Arizona to show that white roofs (~ 0.75 albedo) were up to 20 °C cooler than grey (~ 0.30 albedo) or silver (~ 0.50 albedo), and up to 30 °C cooler than brown (~ 0.10 albedo) roofs. However, measurements also showed that simply increasing the albedo of a building surface may not be effective in reducing its

Table 6.5.1 Albedo of typical urban materials and areas

Surface	Albedo
Streets	
Asphalt (fresh 0.05, aged 0.2)	0.05–0.2
Walls	
Concrete	0.10–0.35
Brick/stone	0.20–0.40
Whitewashed stone	0.80
White marble chips	0.55
Light colored brick	0.30–0.50
Red brick	0.20–0.30
Dark brick and slate	0.20
Limestone	0.30–0.45
Roofs	
Smooth-surface asphalt (weathered)	0.07
Asphalt	0.10–0.15
Tar and gravel	0.08–0.18
Tile	0.10–0.35
Slate	0.10
Thatch	0.15–0.20
Corrugated iron	0.10–0.16
Highly reflective roof after weathering	0.6–0.7
Paints	
White, whitewash	0.50–0.90
Red, brown, green	0.20–0.35
Black	0.02–0.15
Urban areas	
Range	0.10–0.27
Average	0.15
Other	
Light-coloured sand	0.40–0.60
Dry grass	0.30
Average soil	0.30
Dry sand	0.20–0.30
Deciduous plants	0.20–0.30
Deciduous forests	0.15–0.20
Cultivated soil	0.20
Wet sand	0.10–0.20
Coniferous forests	0.10–0.15
Wood (oak)	0.10
Dark cultivated soils	0.07–0.10
Artificial turf	0.05–0.10
Grass and leaf mulch	0.05

Table 6.5.2 Albedo and emissivity for selected surfaces

Material	Albedo	Emissivity
Concrete	0.3	0.94
Red brick	0.3	0.90
Building brick	—	0.45
Concrete tiles	—	0.63
Wood (freshly planed)	0.4	0.90
White paper	0.75	0.95
Tar paper	0.05	0.93
White plaster	0.93	0.91
Bright galvanized iron	0.35	0.13
Bright aluminum foil	0.85	0.04
White pigment	0.85	0.96
Grey pigment	0.03	0.87
Green pigment	0.73	0.95
White paint on aluminium	0.80	0.91
Black paint on aluminium	0.04	0.88
Aluminium paint	0.80	0.27–0.67
Gravel	0.72	0.28
Sand	0.24	0.76

Table 6.5.3 Selected urban albedo values		
Urban area	Albedo	Difference in albedo (urban–rural)
Los Angeles, CA (city core)	0.20	0.09
Madison, WI (urban)	0.15–0.18	0.02
St Louis, MI (urban)	0.12–0.14	—
St Louis, MI (center)	0.19–0.16	0.03
Hartford, CT (urban)	0.09–0.14	—
Adelaide, AUS (commercial)	0.27 (mean)	0.09
Hamilton, Ontario	0.12–0.13	—
Munich, West Germany	0.16 (mean)	–0.08
Vancouver, BC	0.13–0.15	—
Tokyo	0.10 (mean)	–0.02
Ibadan, Nigeria	0.12 (mean)	0.03
Lagos, Nigeria	0.45	0.25

temperature and heat gain if emissivity is reduced simultaneously. Reductions in total and peak air-conditioning load of approximately 5% were measured for otherwise identical white compared with grey and silver: roofed scale model buildings with roof insulation. When ceiling insulation was removed, air-conditioning reductions were much larger for white compared with brown roofs, averaging about 28% and 18.5% for total and peak loads, respectively.

Measurements of the indirect energy savings from large-scale changes in urban albedo are almost impossible. However, using computer simulations the possible change of urban climate conditions can be evaluated. Taha et al[6.5.5], using one-dimensional meteorological simulations, have shown that localized afternoon air temperatures on summer days can be lowered by as much as 4 °C by changing the surface albedo from 0.25 to 0.40 in a typical mid-latitude warm climate. Taha[6.5.6] using three-dimensional mesoscale simulations of the effects of large-scale albedo increases in Los Angeles has shown that an average decrease of 2 °C and up to 4 °C may be possible by increasing the albedo by 0.13 in urbanized areas. Further studies by Akbari et al[6.5.7] have shown that a temperature decrease of this magnitude could reduce electricity load from air-conditioning by 10%. Recent measurements in White Sands, New Mexico, have indicated a similar relationship between naturally occurring albedo variations and measured ambient air temperatures.

Taha et al[6.5.1] have analysed the atmospheric impacts of regional scale changes in building properties, paved surface characteristics and their microclimates and they discuss the possible meteorological and ozone air-quality impacts of increases in surface albedo and urban trees in California's South Coast Air Basin. By using photochemical simulations it is found that implementing high albedo materials would have the net effect of reducing ozone concentrations. Over the whole population, excessive exposure to ozone above local standards would be decreased by up to 12% during peak afternoon hours.

The above results are valid for southern climates with important cooling problems. For heating-dominated northern climates the situation is less clear. The radiation reflected from the ground or from external obstructions forms a small but significant part of the solar heat gain to a vertical or sloping passive collector. For example, consider an unobstructed south-facing window, surrounded by asphalt pavement (solar reflectance = 0.07). Reflection off the pavement increases the solar radiation entering the window by roughly 4%. This contribution goes up to 18% if the window is surrounded by concrete (reflectance = 0.30), and 20% if it is surrounded by grass (reflectance = 0.33). The daylight entering the window will also increase, although visible reflectances are not necessarily the same as radiant reflectances. Goulding et al[6.5.8] and Iqbal[6.5.9] tabulate solar reflectance of ground and building

Table 6.5.4 Reflectances of external surface materials

	Reflectance	
	Visible	Solar
Grass	0.06	0.26–0.33
Asphalt pavement	0.07	0.07
Soil	0.07	0.05–0.25
Red clay brick	0.15	0.23
Concrete	0.20–0.30	0.30
Snow, fresh	0.80	0.87

materials; Hopkinson et al[6.5.10] and Robbins[6.5.11] do the same for daylight reflectances. Table 6.5.4, selected from these sources, gives typical values.

The radiation and light reflected by external obstructions depends on the size, position and orientation of the obstruction as well as its reflectance. In lightwells and enclosed courtyards the externally reflected component is particularly important and light-coloured surfaces are desirable.

In cold climates there may be an advantage in having dark surfaces like soil or asphalt to store and release solar warmth. However, these surfaces can get uncomfortably hot in summer. Vegetation, which stays cool due to evaporation and transpiration, can act as a buffer, reducing maximum surface temperatures.

In practice, surface types and colours may already be fixed for aesthetic or practical reasons. Where there is a choice, it seems best to opt for light colours on surfaces which face a passive solar facade, and darker finishes on the wall areas of the facade itself, with plenty of planting to moderate extreme surface temperatures and provide roughness to restrict wind flow.

References to section 6.5

[6.5.1] **Taha H, Douglas S & Haney J.** Mesoscale meteorological and air quality impacts of increased urban albedo and vegetation. *Energy and Buildings* 1997: **25**: 169–177.

[6.5.2] **Bretz S, Akbari H, Rosenfeld A & Taha H.** *Implementation of solar reflective surfaces: materials and utility programs.* LBL Report – 32467, University of California, 1992.

[6.5.3] **Parker D S & Barkaszi S F.** Roof solar reflectance and cooling energy use: field research results from Florida. *Energy and Buildings* 1997: **25**: 105–115.

[6.5.4] **Simpson J R & McPherson E G.** The effects of roof albedo modification on cooling loads of scale model residences in Tucson, Arizona. *Energy and Buildings* 1997: **25**: 127–137.

[6.5.5] **Taha H, Akbari H & Rosenfeld A.** Residential cooling and the urban heat heat island: the effects of albedo. *Building and Environment* 1988: **23**: 271.

[6.5.6] **Taha H.** Meteorological and photochemical simulations of the south coast air basin. In: Taha H (ed) *Analysis of energy efficiency of air quality in the south coast air basin — Phase II.* Report No. LBL-35728. Berkeley (CA, USA), Lawrence Berkeley Laboratory. Ch. 6, pp 161–218, 1994.

[6.5.7] **Akbari H, Rosenfeld A & Taha H.** Recent developments in heat island studies: technical and policy. *Proceedings Workshop on Saving Energy and Reducing Atmospheric Pollution by Controlling Summer Heat Islands*, Berkeley (CA), 23–24 February 1989. pp 14–20.

[6.5.8] **Goulding J R, Lewis J O, Steemers T C (eds).** Energy in architecture. *The European passive solar handbook.* London, Batsford for CEC, 1992.

[6.5.9] **Iqbal M.** *An introduction to solar radiation.* London, Academic Press, 1983.

[6.5.10] **Hopkinson R G, Petherbridge P & Longmore J.** *Daylighting.* Heinemann, London, 1966.

[6.5.11] **Robbins C L.** *Daylighting design and analysis.* New York, Van Nostrand, 1986.

6.6 Conclusions

As well as providing an attractive, pleasant site, landscaping can also benefit site climate and help provide privacy. In cool to intermediate climates vegetation and hard landscaping provide wind shelter. This can range from small-scale bushes to provide surface roughness, to full-sized shelterbelts. Porous obstacles like tree belts and permeable fences give the largest sheltered areas, to a distance up to six times the obstruction height.

In warm and intermediate climates appropriate landscaping can keep a site cool on hot days. Techniques include:
● use of plants, particularly deciduous trees, to provide shading,
● large areas of vegetation to lower temperatures nearby,
● ponds to keep relatively small, enclosed areas cool,
● fountains and sprays to cool the air: a very fine spray provides good cooling without wetting site users,
● highly reflective materials, particularly on walls and roofs exposed to the sun.

Privacy is particularly important in cities. In densely populated areas it may not be possible to achieve privacy distances. Instead privacy can be obtained by:
- external screening with walls and fences,
- internal screening using curtains,
- private or semi-private outdoor spaces like courtyards,
- visual cues like gates or changes in level to deter intruders.

7 Conclusions

The advice in this guide is intended for a wide range of audiences. These include:
- local authorities developing environmental plans for their cities and towns,
- designers and their clients aiming to emphasize the 'green' nature of their buildings,
- consultants in environmental design,
- individual building owners threatened with overshadowing by a new development,
- landscape architects wanting to improve the environmental quality of sites,
- policy makers setting out guidance for future urban design,
- manufacturers and suppliers of building coating materials.

The potential applications are broad and include the design of the following.
- Any major building development within a city centre. These are certain to have an environmental impact on their surroundings.
- New estates of housing or commercial buildings.
- Parkland and outdoor leisure facilities, where an improved microclimate can significantly increase amenity.
- Pollution sources in or near urban areas.
- Buildings, and in particular groups of buildings, which rely on solar energy.

The case studies and the monitoring work from the project have shown that urban layout does have a big impact on the environment generally. As an example, the Santa Cruz district of Seville has traditional architecture with narrow streets and small squares, with high mass walls, mainly white in colour, and solar protection with trees and water fountains. On very hot days the Santa Cruz district is up to 6–8 °C cooler than the airport at Seville; an apparent reversal of the heat island effect. This shows that it is possible to achieve significant improvements in outdoor thermal comfort using traditional urban layout techniques.

The loss of daylight, sunlight and solar gain due to obstructions is an important feature of the city. Tall buildings and other obstructions close by can affect the distribution of daylight in a building as well as reducing the total amount received. Sunlight too is blocked, particularly winter sunlight. This has important implications for the viability of passive solar buildings.

This book includes Europe-wide guidance on site layout for daylight, sunlight and solar gain. The general approach incorporates simple obstruction angle techniques to determine if there is likely to be a problem, coupled with more complicated calculation methods where neighbouring obstructions are unusually tall or close. The guidance also deals with the complex but important question of overshadowing of existing buildings by a new development.

In southern Europe, shade can be welcome. A study of the EXPO '98 Exhibition in Lisbon evaluated the impact of canopies on the solar protection

of a walkway. In the design of a solar protection covering the following conclusions were reached.
- The amount and location of shadow produced depends on the shape, size, height and position of the covering.
- The quality of the shadow (solar radiation blocked) depends on the type of material used.
- The temperature reached by the shade depends on the type of covering, and its shape and colour.

In cities there can be localized concentrations of pollutants caused by individual sources of pollution like roads, industrial plant and air-conditioning equipment. Site layout can have an important impact on the dispersion of these pollutants. Some layout types, for example narrow streets at right angles to the prevailing wind, can have poor ventilation characteristics, trapping pollutants within them. Sometimes simple modifications to the layout, creating openings or varying the heights of buildings, can promote dispersion. Alternatively, the location of pollution sources can be changed to improve the local environment.

The heat island effect means that city centres can be considerably warmer than their surroundings. This can cause significant problems in warm climates. To investigate the effect, automatic meteorological stations measuring temperature and humidity were installed in the major Athens area. The heat island intensity in Athens is close to 15 °C, and causes a very important increase in the cooling load of buildings. Simulations show that because of the temperature increase in the city centre the cooling load of a reference office building increases by up to 80% compared with the same building located in suburban areas. At the same time, the peak electricity load for cooling purposes is found to increase by about 120%. The higher temperatures decrease the efficiency of air-conditioning equipment by about 25%.

Tall buildings lining a street turn it into an 'urban canyon' with its own microclimate. This can further enhance the heat island effect and reduce the dispersal of pollutants. Monitoring of canyons in Athens has shown how modifying street geometry, and the presence or absence of traffic influence temperatures and air flow.

Urban heat sinks such as forests, urban parks, sea, lakes or rivers are important. Vegetation and water cool the air. The amount of cooling depends on:
- upwind air conditions: temperature, humidity and velocity,
- characteristics of the urban heat sink: surface temperature and humidity, roughness, exchange area,
- length of the urban heat sink (measured in the wind direction).

This cooler area provides a reduction in the air temperature that depends on the position (distance and height) downwind. Using boundary layer theory the University of Seville has developed a way of expressing the effect of forests and lakes on the air temperature of an urban environment. In open areas the impact of a lake on the surrounding area is small unless the lake is very large. Smaller ponds can have more impact in enclosed spaces, though, especially if coupled with fountains or sprays.

CFD modelling and measurement of courtyards, backed by wind tunnel tests, have shown that the ventilation characteristics of courtyards depend on the height-to-width ratio, H/W. At high H/W there can be very poor ventilation during the day. This can be an advantage in hot climates as cool air can be trapped in the courtyard. Water features or vegetative shading can reduce the temperature further. However it is important to keep sources of pollution out of the courtyard.

Until now a key issue has been the lack of suitable design tools to enable designers and planners to assess the impact of new developments on the urban environment. TOWNSCOPE II, developed by the University of Liege, is an integrated computer software package to support environmentally aware urban design. It combines a user-friendly graphical interface with powerful analysis tools. Thermal comfort, critical wind discomfort risk and the visual qualities of urban open spaces can be assessed very quickly using TOWNSCOPE. The software can also rank alternative design proposals with its multi-criterion decision module.

It includes fast and easy-to-use simulation tools for a range of environmental parameters:

- the thermal comfort of open spaces,
- the solar obstruction at a point,
- daylight to building facades,
- wind pattern analysis to identify critical wind situations within the urban layout,
- a morphological analysis package to predict the visual quality of urban open spaces.

BRE has produced a simple manual tool that designers can use to evaluate solar access and daylight in obstructed urban areas. The full design tool including indicators for locations throughout Europe, and explanatory text, is available[7.1].

Reference

[7.1]   **Littlefair P J & Aizlewood M E.** *Calculating access to skylight, sunlight and solar radiation on obstructed sites in Europe.* BRE Report BR 379. Garston, CRC, 1999.

Appendix A. Calculation methods

Appendix A1. TOWNSCOPE

TOWNSCOPE II is an integrated computer software package to support urban design decision-making within the perspective of a responsive environment. The software was designed to make it easier to apply the recommendations of this design guide to real-world situations. It combines a user-friendly graphical interface with powerful analysis tools (Figure A1.1).

Thermal comfort, critical wind discomfort risk and the perceptual qualities of urban open spaces can be assessed very quickly using TOWNSCOPE. In addition, the software provides an integrated multi-criterion decision module to rank various alternative design proposals.

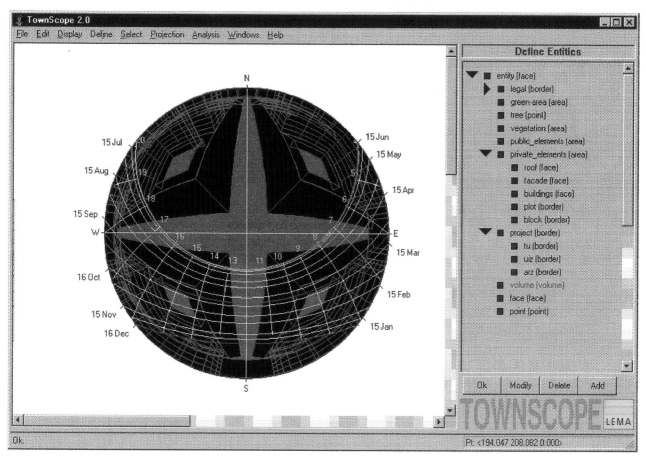

Figure A1.1 The TOWNSCOPE interface. © University of Liege

Specific functions were developed to facilitate the data acquisition and handling:

- data importation and exportation facilities for exchange with commercial software (DXF format);
- a user-friendly graphical interface for 3D information encoding and manipulation;
- triangulation algorithms for easy modelling of ground and other irregular surfaces;
- user-defined entities to tailor the urban database structure to the requirements of the project and its surroundings;
- a spatial and alphanumeric query interface.

Solar radiation and thermal comfort

TOWNSCOPE II integrates fast and easy-to-use simulation tools for solar radiation and thermal comfort predictions.

- A project's overall impact on the thermal comfort of open spaces can be estimated rapidly by the software. These numerical methods were applied to the design of the EXPO '98 Lisbon exhibition site to determine the best geometry for future solar shading. The lower the shading is placed, the better it obstructs the sun, but there is also more long-wave radiation from their material to the human body. The optimal geometry had thus to balance these conflicting effects (Figure A1.2).
- Visual tools within the software can be used to represent the solar obstruction at a point in a comprehensive way. For instance, stereographic projections were used to visualize the solar obstruction caused by the shading devices described above on a major pedestrian walkway of the EXPO '98 site (Figure A1.3).

Wind patterns

TOWNSCOPE II incorporates a multimedia interface, based on experimental results from laboratory tests, for wind pattern analysis. It helps the designers to identify critical wind situations (Venturi effect, WISE effect, bar effect) within the urban pattern. Additional information about any discomfort risks that may be predicted are included within an on-line tutorial.

Urban morphology

TOWNSCOPE includes a morphological analysis package to predict the visual quality of urban open spaces. It is based on spherical projections to integrate the full 3D visual environment of an observer. A number of indicators and/or qualitative instruments were developed to do this. They include equal area projections, sky opening factor, view length indicator, and equidistant and cylindrical projections of an outdoor space.

Figure A1.4 is a stereographic representation (view from the sky) of the Piazza del Parlemento in Rome. It was used to analyse:

- the visual connections (landmarks, views) between one outdoor space and its neighbours,
- the relationship between the ground and the vertical faces of the square (axiality, enclosure, discontinuities).

System requirements and software availability

Operating system: Windows NT 4.0 or Windows 95
Processor: Pentium 200, Pentium Pro 233 or greater recommended
Disk space: 15MB minimum
Memory requirements: 32MB RAM minimum, 64MB recommended
Display requirements: resolution 800 x 600 or greater color palette 64K colors (16bits) minimum

The software and its user manual is available as a CD-ROM from LEMA - ULg for the price of 100 Euros which mainly covers the electronic handling

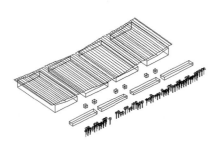

Figure A1.2 View of the EXPO '98 site modelled using TOWNSCOPE.
© University of Liege

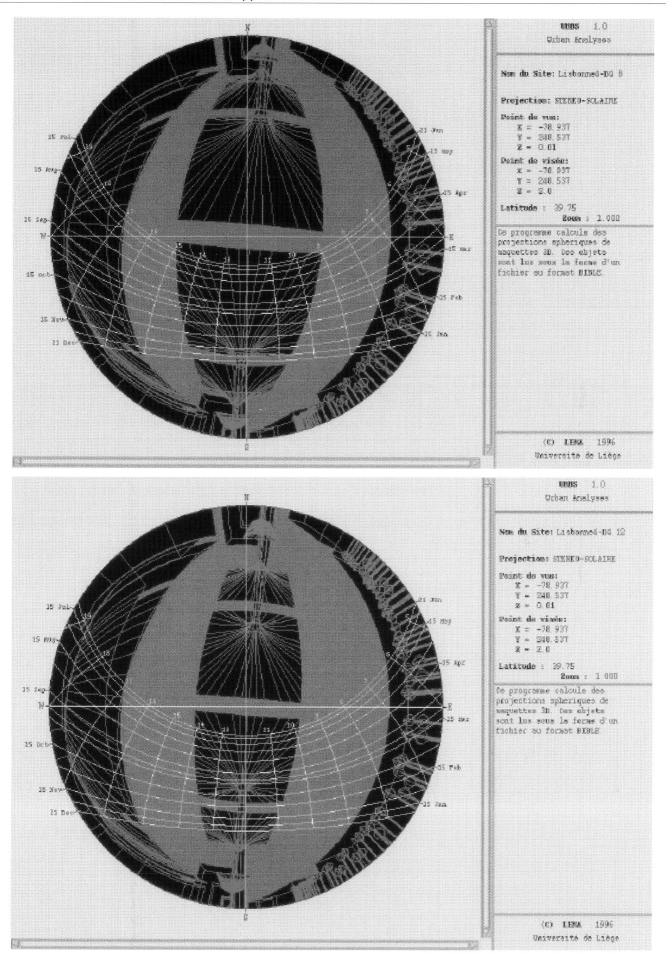

Figure A1.3 Solar obstruction caused by shading. © University of Liege

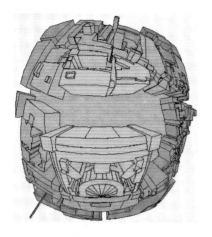

Figure A1.4 Stereographic representation (view from the sky) of the Piazza del Parlemento in Rome. © University of Liege

and shipping costs. No additional technical support or debugging is included within this offer.

The software can be ordered by surface- or electronic- mail at the following address:

Albert Dupagne
LEMA – University of Liege
15, avenue des Tilleuls, D1
4000 Liege
Belgium
Fax: 32 4 366 94 99
E-mail: lema@lema.ulg.ac.be

Appendix A2. Manual tools for solar access

This appendix describes manual tools ('indicators') to predict daylight, sunlight and heating season solar gain in obstructed situations[A2.1, A2.2]. They can be used to assess the solar potential of new sites, and also to evaluate overshadowing of an existing building following a new development nearby. Even complex sets of obstructions can be modelled: the method is not limited to long parallel obstructions.

The indicators comprise the following.

The skylight indicator (Figure A2.1)

This is to find the vertical sky component (in %) on the outside of a window wall. This is the ratio of the direct sky illuminance falling on the vertical wall at a reference point, to the simultaneous horizontal illuminance under an unobstructed sky (section 4.1). The maximum value is almost 40% for a completely unobstructed vertical wall. The skylight indicator has 80 crosses marked on it. Each of these corresponds to 0.5% vertical sky component.

The sunlight availability indicators (Figure A2.2)

These are to find the probable sunlight hours received by a window wall or at any other point in a building layout. 'Probable sunlight hours' means the total number of hours per year the sun would shine on unobstructed ground given average amounts of cloud. UK Standards[A2.3] recommend that interiors where the occupants expect sunlight should receive at least a quarter of annual probable sunlight hours, including in the winter between

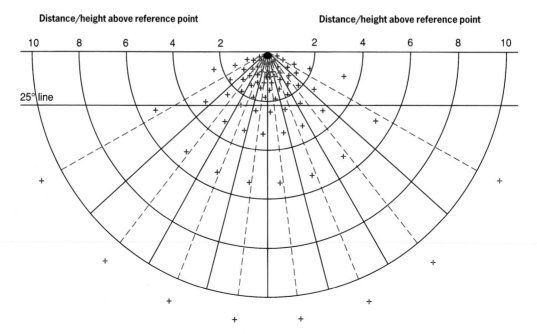

Figure A2.1 The skylight indicator

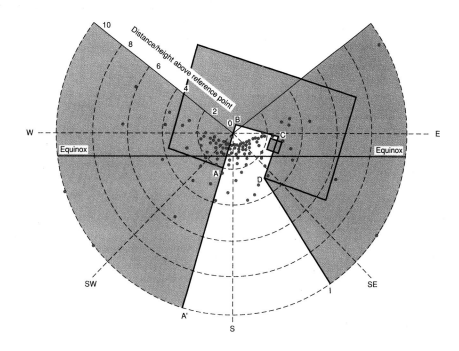

Figure A2.2 Sunlight availability indicator for London showing site plan drawn to the correct scale on it (*Note:* Figure has been reduced)

21 September and 21 March at least 5% of annual probable sunlight hours. Each spot on the indicator represents 1% of annual probable sunlight hours.

The sunpath indicators (Figure A2.3)

These are to find the times of day and year for which sunlight is available on a window wall or point in a layout. The bold curved lines which run across the indicator are sunpaths for the 21st of each month. Each sunpath is divided into hours by the thinner straight solid hour lines which radiate outwards. These are labelled with solar time.

The solar gain indicators (Figure A2.4)

These are to find the incident solar radiation on a vertical window wall during the heating season (October–April). The wall should face within 30° of due south. Each spot on the indicator represents 1% of heating season solar gain.

Indicators have been developed for a wide range of latitudes covering nearly all the EC (Table A2.1). The skylight indicator is independent of latitude and may be used anywhere.

The skylight and solar gain indicators are semi-circular; the sunlight availability and sunpath indicators are shaped like a circle with a segment removed. In each case the centre of the circular arc corresponds to the reference point at which the calculation is carried out. Radial distances from this point correspond to the ratio of the distance of the obstruction on plan divided by its height above the reference point. So if the reference point was 2 metres above ground, and the ground was flat, this height would be the obstruction height above ground, minus two metres. The indicators are all drawn to the same scale so that it is easy to calculate a number of different quantities at the same time. Note, however, that Figures A2.1–A2.4 are not reproduced to scale and cannot be used directly.

Directions on the indicator from the central point correspond to directions on the site plan. The skylight indicator is used with its straight base parallel to the window wall. The sunlight availability, sunpath, and solar gain indicators, however, are always used with the south point of the indicator pointing in the

Table A2.1 Reference locations for indicators	
Latitude °N	Reference location
60	Bergen
56	Edinburgh
53.5	Manchester
51	London
48	Weihenstephan
45	Lyon
42	Rome
38	Athens

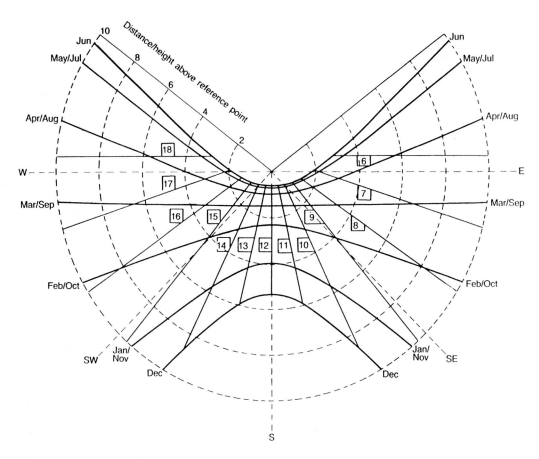

Figure A2.3 Sunpath indicator for Edinburgh

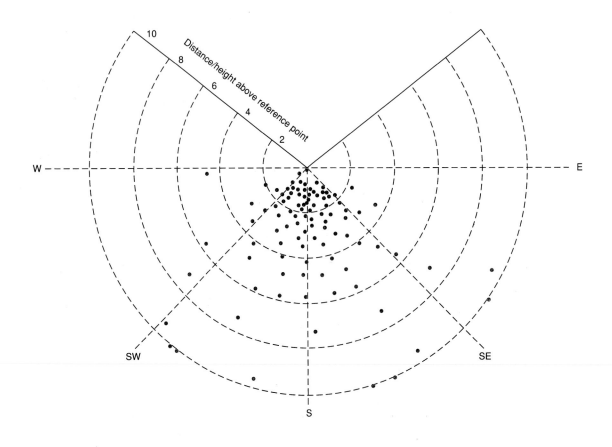

Figure A2.4 Solar gain indicator for Edinburgh

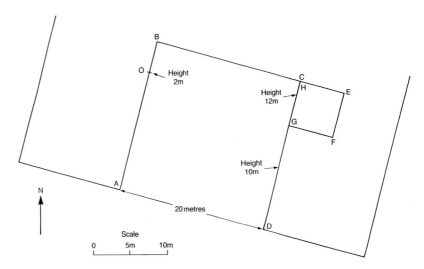

Figure A2.5 Site plan of an example situation

south direction on plan, whatever the orientation of the window wall.

The indicators are not intended to be laid over standard scale site plans because the distance scale on the indicator is unlikely to correspond to the scale of the plan. To plot a layout on the indicator a transparent direction finder may be used[A2.1, A2.2]. This looks similar to the skylight indicator. Alternatively a plan may be specially drawn on tracing paper or acetate to the exact scale of the indicator. This depends on the height of the obstruction h (metres) above the reference point for the calculation. The plan should be drawn to a scale of 1:100h. Figure A2.5 shows a typical site layout; Figure A2.2 shows it plotted to the right scale and laid over the sunlight availability indicator. The small obstruction at a different height is drawn to a different scale distance.

The plan or direction finder is then laid over the relevant indicator. If a cross or spot or sunpath arc lies nearer to the centre of the indicator than any obstruction in that direction (as marked on the direction finder or special site plan) then it is unobstructed and counts towards the total. If it lies beyond the obstruction then it will be obstructed and does not count. In Figure A2.5, the total sunlight availability at O is 48% of annual probable hours, 16% of these being in the winter months (spots beyond the equinox line).

These indicators form a relatively quick manual method to assess the impact of obstructions on daylight, sunlight and solar gain in a layout. The obstructions need special plotting but the same plot can be used with all four sets of indicators. Indicators have been developed for a wide range of latitudes covering nearly all the EC.

References to Appendix A2

[A2.1] **Littlefair P J & Aizlewood M E.** *Calculating access to sunlight and daylight in obstructed sites in Europe.* BRE Report BR 379. Garston, CRC, 1999.

[A2.2] **Littlefair P J.** *Site layout planning for daylight, and sunlight: a guide to good practice.* BRE Report BR 209. Garston, CRC, 1991.

[A2.3] **British Standards Institution.** *BS 8206: Lighting for buildings. Part 2: Code of practice for daylighting.* London, BSI, 1992.

Appendix A3. Building thermal simulation

Thermal simulation tools

Building thermal simulation tools study various aspects of performance:
- temperatures in the different zones of a building,
- air movement between the different indoor zones and infiltration from outside,

- air quality, humidity and pollutant levels inside the building,
- performance, design and energy consumption of the heating, air-conditioning and ventilation systems in the buildings.

Generally, the thermal simulation covers all aspects related to the human comfort inside the building. Historically, thermal simulation tools have evolved in parallel with the computer science tools available. Current thermal simulation tools can be divided into four different generations[A3.1].

1st Generation
Very simple software based on analytic calculations with a lot of simplifying assumptions. These codes did not include hourly simulations. Their main objective was the design and sizing of HVAC systems. A typical example of this kind of development is the use of the global heat transfer steady state coefficient for the whole building.

2nd Generation
During the 1970s, at the time of the energy crisis, new codes appeared. These included hourly simulation, but using very simple methods for the calculations of the different constructive elements. They were very limited in the amount of memory that could be used, and in calculation speed.

3rd Generation
During the 1980s, and due to improvement in computers, the thermal simulation could be treated as a classic field problem, where all the variables depend on space and time. Thermal phenomena can be treated using numerical methods that are very memory and speed consuming.

4th Generation
Now, in the 1990s, Object Oriented Programming (OOP)[A3.2] and visual design systems (CAD systems) improve the flexibility and complexity of thermal simulation tools.

Problems with predicting the impact of site layout on building performance
It is widely recognized that the outdoor environment near a building may modify the thermal performance of the indoor spaces of the building. One way to simulate this is to include these nearby spaces in the thermal simulation. All the spaces and elements (outdoor or indoor) which are thermally linked to each other must be simulated.

There are many examples where the difference between internal and external spaces is not well defined, for example urban canyons, squares, courtyards and other buffer zones.

To simulate the thermal performance of outdoor spaces at the same level as indoor zones, current tools assume that the thermal phenomena present in external zones are the same as those in internal zones, and that they can be treated at the same level of accuracy. However, the behaviour of some heat transfer phenomena in outdoor spaces is completely different from the behaviour in indoor zones.

The main differences are given in the three sections which follow.

Absorption of solar radiation
Indoors, direct and diffuse solar radiation largely penetrates through perfectly defined semitransparent elements, such as windows and doors, so the total amount of solar radiation coming into the zone can be easily calculated. For outdoor zones the primary incidence of direct solar radiation and the consequent multi-reflection process is a very complex three-dimensional problem.

Long-wave radiant exchange
The different surfaces present in the indoor environment of a building commonly have low temperature differences, so the long-wave radiant exchange between them is small. Outdoor surfaces may exchange heat with very hot surfaces (high impact of solar radiation) and with the sky. This difference means long-wave radiant exchange is not negligible for external surfaces.

Air movement
For external open spaces the air movements are more complicated than for indoor zones, due to the more complicated three-dimensional configurations and also air entering through large gaps between buildings. More complicated methods must be used to simulate the air movement, for example CFD codes (Appendix A6) or wind tunnel experiments (Appendix B1). There are also problems related to the heat island or the oasis effect.

References to Appendix A3

[A3.1] Rodriguez E A. Sistematizacion de Acoplamientos Termicos y Termoaeraulicos en la Simulacion de Edificios. Tesis doctoral, Escuela Superior de Ingenieros Industriales, Universidad de Sevilla. 1990.

[A3.2] Rumbauch J, Blaha M, Premerlani W, Eddy F & Lorensen W. *Object-oriented modeling and design.* Englewood Cliffs (New Jersey, USA), Prentice Hall, 1991.

Appendix A4. Comfort calculations

Thermal balance of the human body
The thermal balance equation for the human body is:

$$E_{sw} = M(1 - \eta) + (R + C) - C_{res} - E_{res} - E_{dif}$$

where:

$M(1 - \eta)$ =	net metabolic heat production,
R =	heat transmitted to the body through radiation,
C =	heat transmitted to the body through convection,
C_{res} =	sensible heat due to respiration,
E_{res} =	latent heat due to respiration,
E_{dif} =	heat diffused out through the skin.

The regulatory sweating term (E_{sw}) closes the thermal balance and gives a measure of the requirement for the person to adapt to their surroundings and in consequence the level of comfort.

The right-hand term of the equation can be calculated using different assumptions and correlations. The expressions used to quantify the different terms assume steady-state conditions and derive from widely accepted models. The exception is the effect of solar radiation which is calculated from the incident values using a simultaneous balance over clothing and skin considering their short-wave radiant properties.

Use of the equations
Evaluation of a specific action
The thermal balance of the human body can be used to analyse the variation occurring in a situation when action is taken to improve climatic conditions. As an example, Figure A4.1 shows the values for the reference situation and those obtained following the inclusion of a covering of vegetation overhead with zero transmissivity and whose surface temperature is equal to the ambient temperature.

This analysis provides information about the degree of conditioning still required to obtain a given level of comfort, and the relative order in which actions to improve comfort should be taken.

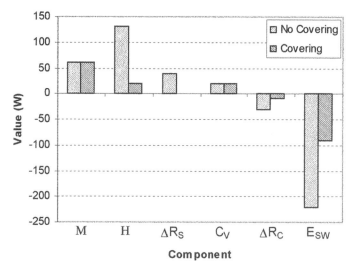

Figure A4.1 Comparison between heat flows with and without vegetation cover. © University of Seville

Comparative performance of components

This is usually done using the concept of sensation temperature and, more precisely, increase in sensation temperature. The sensation temperature is analogous to the effective temperature and can be defined as the temperature of an environment (air and surfaces) at 50% relative humidity, no solar radiation and still air that results in the same total sweating rate as in the actual environment.

Changes in the sensation temperature are usually derived by comparison with a reference situation. The reason for using the increase rather than absolute values is to keep the analysis independent of other factors in the balance, which are not affected by the components under study. Calculations of the increase in sensation temperature help decide which of a number of design solutions is the most effective at improving comfort.

The example below compares various types of shading with different transmissivities and different surface temperatures. The base case chosen was a covering with zero transmissivity and no overheating (surface temperature = ambient temperature). Figure A4.2 shows the results for 8 shading types.

Design (isocomfort graphs)

In order to achieve the required comfort conditions in a given zone, there are a number of possible ways to alter the heat flows. However, in practice, due to prior design decisions or functional or aesthetic constraints, the number of variables which can be manipulated is at most 3. If this is the case, it is possible to construct an isocomfort graph of the area under study which contains all the possible combinations of the variables which can be manipulated and which lead to the same level of comfort. This enables a decision regarding the best option.

Figure A4.3 shows a specific case of an isocomfort graph for a sweating rate of 60 g/h obtained for a rotunda with outdoor design conditions. The variables which appear are the surface temperature of the covering (X-axis), the temperature of the air (Y-axis) and the velocity of the air (variable parameter).

It may be seen, for example, that for zero air velocity, the same sensation of comfort is obtained with the values given in Table A4.1.

Or that, for a given temperature of the covering (say, 34 °C), the combinations given in Table A4.2 are equivalent.

It is apparent that irrigation of the covering is essential (in its absence the temperature of the covering would exceed 45 °C) and that there are great benefits from movement of the air, however slight.

Table A4.1 Temperatures of air and covering that give the same sensation temperature (with no wind)

Air temperature (°C)	Covering temperature (°C)
30	27
26	35
20	44

Table A4.2 Air temperatures and velocities that give the same sensation temperature (covering at 34 °C)

Air temperature (°C)	Air velocity (m/s)
26	0
30	0,5
32.5	1

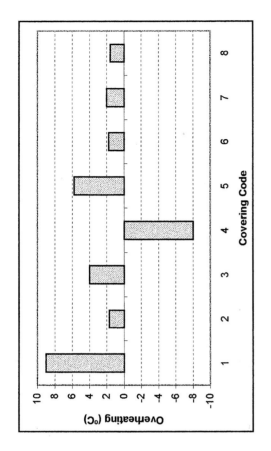

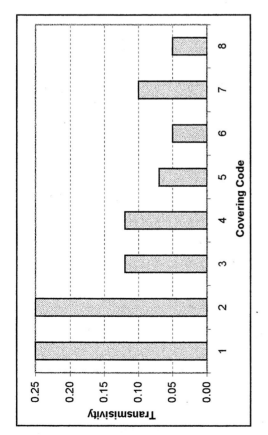

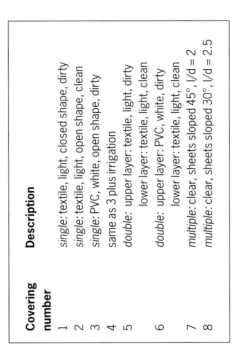

Covering number	Description
1	*single:* textile, light, closed shape, dirty
2	*single:* textile, light, open shape, clean
3	*single:* PVC, white, open shape, dirty
4	same as 3 plus irrigation
5	*double:* upper layer: textile, light, dirty lower layer: textile, light, clean
6	*double:* upper layer: PVC, white, dirty lower layer: textile, light, clean
7	*multiple:* clear, sheets sloped 45°, l/d = 2
8	*multiple:* clear, sheets sloped 30°, l/d = 2.5

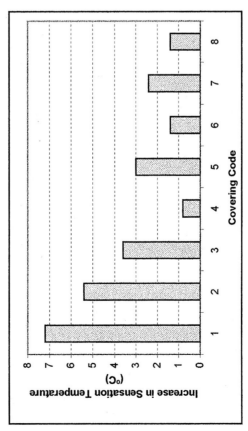

Figure A4.2 Effects of different shading types on sensation temperatures. © University of Seville

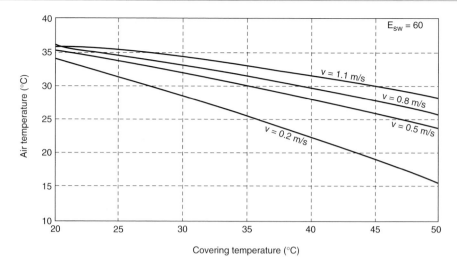

Figure A4.3 Isocomfort graph. © University of Seville

Appendix A5. Pollution prediction methods

Predicting the levels of pollutants in urban areas is important as these areas usually have the highest density of pollution sources and therefore pollutant concentration. Prediction may be for regulatory purposes, for example to find if concentrations of particular pollutants are (or are likely to be) exceeded and if so over what areas and times. Alternatively, there may be a planning need for predicting the effects of long-term changes in polluting discharges, of the effects of new discharges (from industrial sources or from combustion plant, for example) or of the effects of new buildings or changed road layouts.

The more common pollutants (sulphur and nitrogen oxides, particles, carbon monoxide, etc) are often monitored in urban areas. There is a requirement that this should be done in EC countries in order to assess whether the various regulatory limits for different pollutants are being exceeded. In the UK, for example, there are 85 monitoring sites operating in the national network, the majority of which are in urban areas, and the data from these is available on the internet. These data can be used to find typical pollution levels in urban areas, the probable long-term trends and the shorter term (down to about an hour) variation in levels that can be expected due to changes in pollutant discharge patterns and to the weather pattern or diurnal changes. However, it is usually much more difficult to use monitoring data to assess the contribution of specific pollution sources or the more detailed spatial patterns of pollution levels. Also it is of limited use in predicting the effects of changes of the sort noted above.

To satisfy these needs for predicting pollution levels, dispersion modelling is used. It is the only practical way in which the pollutant concentrations at a given site can be attributed to particular sources. A major feature of urban pollution modelling is the wide range of problems that have to be addressed. They may vary from very short-term exposure problems over distances of a few tens of metres or less, to the effects of multiple source discharges reacting chemically in the atmosphere over distances of tens of kilometres. The disparity between this wide variety of modelling needs cannot be met with any single model, or type of model. Thus a range of approaches to predicting urban pollution has to be considered. The main concern here is with the shorter ranges, up to a few kilometres distance.

Unfortunately, few of the commonly available models are well tuned to urban problems. As outlined in section 2.6, model requirements have been divided into three regimes, depending on the size of the dispersing plume cross-section compared with the sizes of buildings and obstructions within the urban canopy.

The far field regime

This regime is, in principle, well provided with suitable models. Apart from conventional models in current use, the recent meeting at Mol, Belgium[A5.1] reviewed many of the more recent developments.

The main point of concern with models for urban areas in this regime is to ensure that they deal adequately with the surface roughness and its effects on dispersion. This is not difficult to do in principle, but in practice many of the current models, especially the older or simpler types, do not handle the effects of surface roughness (due to buildings, other surface obstacles and topography) very well. Both the vertical and lateral rates of dispersion are modifed by the surface roughness, an increase in which increases the rate of dispersion. The most commonly used long-range dispersion model, the USEPA ISC model in fact only allows for two types of surface: 'rural' and 'urban'. The UK standard model for many years, the NRPB model[A5.2], corrects the rate of vertical dispersion for any surface roughness but not the rate of lateral dispersion, which is fixed. More recent models, such as the UKADMS model and the US AERMOD model, provide a full correction for surface roughness effects on dispersion.

The intermediate field regime

Since dispersion in this regime appears to generate Gaussian plumes, the dispersion of contaminants in this regime could be predicted using a conventional Gaussian model, but with dispersion rates and windspeeds modified to account for the other effects of the surface roughness. Most conventional Gaussian models, of the types noted above, contain procedures for dealing with the effects of buildings and other structures. However, these use quite simple models which do not account for many of the known effects of arrays of buildings over large areas, which is the condition of the intermediate regime.

Until recently, published experimental data (from field experiments and from small-scale wind tunnel experiments) on the more complex dispersion characteristics of arrays of buildings and other obstructions has been too limited to improve much on these models. However, this situation is changing as more data is presently appearing and a number of experimental programmes are under way. Within the next few years the required modifications to dispersion rates will be available in forms which can be used in conventional Gaussian dispersion models.

The near field regime

Dispersion in this regime gives rise to individualistic, highly variable concentration fields which are difficult to model with a high degree of accuracy (section 2.6). This is especially so if rapid short-term fluctuations in concentrations are of interest, as they are with odours or the consequences of accidents, where there may be a discharge of toxic contaminants at high concentration over short periods. There are three major options for predicting dispersion patterns. These are listed below.

The use of simple 'rules of thumb'

These give ball-park estimates of likely upper and lower levels of concentration that may occur. Chapter 12 of the ASHRAE handbook[A5.3] is a good example of this approach.

Detailed investigation using small-scale wind tunnel models

These are very effective at investigating this type of dispersion problem and most of the experimental data on which computer models are based comes from this source. They can reproduce both the mean and fluctuating concentrations in dispersion at short ranges. Wind tunnel models are discussed in more detail in Appendix B1.

Computational fluid dynamics (CFD) (section A6)
There is a growing use of these computer tools and many commercial models
are available. However, dispersion is one of the most difficult features of a fluid
flow to model numerically. One of the main difficulties lies in the turbulence
models presently used and their poor ability at handling the large eddies in
the flow. These are critical to predicting dispersion. Another practical
difficulty is the large number of grid points needed to define an urban area
with more than a few buildings, which greatly increases computational times.

The use of field experiments
These are quite rare due to the difficulty and expense involved. It is also often
difficult to interpret the data due to the high variability in the experimental
conditions that is usually experienced. They are, however, invaluable as a
basis for testing all other types of model.

References to Appendix A5
   [A5.1] *Proceedings of Workshop on Operational Short Range Atmospheric Dispersion
Models for Environmental Impact Assessment in Europe*, Mol, Belgium, 21–24 November 1994.
International Journal of Environment and Pollution 1995: 5(4–6).
   [A5.2] **Clark R H.** *A model for short and medium range dispersion of radionuclides
released to the atmosphere*. National Radiological Protection Board Report No. R91.
Oxfordshire, NRPB, 1979.
   [A5.3] **American Society of Heating, Refrigerating and Air Conditioning Engineers.**
Handbook of fundamentals. Atlanta, ASHRAE, 1997.

Appendix A6. CFD modelling

Wind is one of the main climatic factors influencing the urban environment
and that of the buildings within it. The flow of wind around buildings can be
uncomfortable and hazardous for pedestrians, and also influences energy use,
ventilation, rain penetration, air pollution and noise.

Wind tunnel studies (Appendix B1) can be used to analyse the impact of
wind, minimizing the negative effects and enhancing the positive influences of
airflow around the built environment. These studies provide valuable
information concerning the escape of smoke from fires inside the building,
concentration of pollutants around building complexes, behaviour of exhaust
fumes and surface pressure distributions.

Numerical modelling, based on computational fluid dynamics (CFD)
techniques, allows detailed analysis of building airflow and hence temperature
and pressure distribution, and contaminant concentration. These are obtained
by solving equations for mass, momentum, thermal energy and chemical
species, together with a model that best describes the turbulence
characteristics of the flow. The results of the simulation then may be used for
analysing the wind environment around the buildings and related issues such
as identifying uncomfortable and hazardous areas for pedestrians, airflow rate
through openings on a building (ie for natural ventilation design), etc.

The main advantage of CFD over the physical wind tunnel is that there is
no need to reduce the scale, thus eliminating uncertainties in scaling factors
and errors in representing complex geometrical features. A further benefit of
CFD is the visual representation for analysis and appreciation of otherwise
invisible circumstances. However, in common with physical wind tunnel
modelling, care must be taken to identify how appropriate the model is for a
given problem, the accuracy of boundary conditions (ie wind profile, ground
friction, nearby buildings and obstructions), and last but not least the expertise
of the modeller. The main parameters that may limit the application of CFD
are outlined below.

Geometrical aspects of buildings

Architectural features of buildings could create a complex flow domain. This may make dividing up the area into a grid, for numerical solution, a real challenge. For this reason some compromises may be necessary depending on the scale of geometrical complexity in practice. Further, due to the large flow domains and the existence of small, but important features, the number of computational grid nodes may become enormously large in some applications. For example, openings on the building may need to be represented for airflow rate calculations. It is therefore important to represent these features accurately, but this requires local mesh refinement and a large number of grid cells. When these features are represented only roughly, the reliability of simulated airflow rates is questionable.

Boundary conditions

The time-dependence of external conditions means that the domain boundary conditions may vary with time. Since CFD models require extensive iterative solution on very small timescales, often some compromises have to be made on the scale of transient interaction. Indeed boundary conditions are often assumed to be steady-state, based on analytical or experimental results, except when CFD is used to predict the dispersion time of gases or smoke.

Turbulence

The airflow around buildings is usually complex turbulent flow. There is currently no universal turbulent model available that can reflect the behaviour of the full range of complex turbulent flows observed around buildings. This has been reflected in a number of comparative studies of turbulence models for predicting wind conditions on and around a building. The aim has been to improve the accuracy with which CFD models approximate the actual outdoor conditions in the vicinity of a building.

Murakami et al[A6.1] have studied the airflow around a building through CFD simulations using four different well-known turbulence models in order to assess their accuracy. The relative performance of the turbulence models was examined by comparing numerical simulation results with those derived from a wind tunnel experiment. Selvam[A6.2] has studied the application of two-layer methods for the evaluation of wind effects on a cubic building and compared predictions with experimental results from a wind tunnel experiment. Zhou[A6.3] reports that a better approximation of the convection term reports in an improvement of the accuracy of numerical simulation predictions when the k–e turbulence model is used. In all of the above studies, the building is regarded as a cubic closed box standing as an obstacle in the free stream flowpath of the wind. Therefore, the pressure distribution at the surface of an opening in a natural ventilation configuration has not been studied.

User expertise

Finally, CFD modelling of the built environment is complex, time-consuming and usually requires considerable resources and expertise to obtain meaningful results. There are many factors that can influence the predicted results from CFD, and the knowledge and expertise of the user play a significant part in the accuracy of the predicted results. Indeed, different users may produce different results even from the same CFD software. In any case, for complex building airflow problems the resources of skilful CFD modellers and researchers are necessary, working together with architects, building services and environmental designers.

References to Appendix A6

[A6.1] **Murakami S, Mochida A, Ooka R, Kato S & Iizuka S.** Numerical prediction of flow around a building with various turbulence models: comparison of k–e EVM, ASM, DSM and LES with wind tunnel tests. *ASHRAE Transactions* 1996: **96**: 741–753.

[A6.2] Selvam P R. Numerical simulation of flow and pressure around a building. *ASHRAE Transactions* 1996: **96**: 765–772.

[A6.3] Zhou Y & Stathopoulos T. Application of two-layer methods for the evaluation of wind effects on a cubic building. *ASHRAE Transactions* 1996: **96**: 754–764.

Appendix A7. Passive cooling tools

Tools to evaluate the impact of passive cooling of buildings can be classified in two main categories as follows.

● Those estimating the performance of specific passive cooling systems and techniques like solar control, natural ventilation, evaporative coolers, etc. This type of tool can help optimize the design of these systems or the way that passive cooling techniques operate in practice. A number of tools permitting calculation of specific passive cooling techniques have been developed through the PASCOOL research program of the European Commission and are available (A7.1).

● Those estimating the global performance of the building when passive cooling systems or techniques are used. These tools can evaluate the contribution of passive techniques (A7.2–A7.4).

There are many tools to evaluate the performance of shading devices. Most of them consider shading of the beam solar radiation and neglect diffuse and reflected radiation. Some of the tools provide a graphical interface to view the objects as well as the shadows. More accurate tools are available and are usually integrated with existing detailed building simulation tools.

Models to evaluate natural ventilation phenomena are classified in three main categories:

● empirical models,
● network models, and
● computational fluid dynamic (CFD) models.

Empirical models provide analytical formulae to calculate the airflow rate through single-zone buildings. These models are based on experimental data and are accurate within the limits of the experiments used to develop the code. Network models are based on the mass balance equation and are the most widely used algorithms for natural ventilation calculations. The models are quite accurate and do not require input data, which are in any case difficult to measure or predict. These models can calculate the airflow through an opening or in a zone, but do not permit evaluation of the air-speed distribution in the building. Finally, the CFD modelling approach, discussed in the previous section, can be applied to a wide range of airflow and related phenomena. However, it requires appropriate boundary conditions, extensive computer resources and user expertise.

There are relatively few models for calculating the performance of heat dissipation techniques. Some of these tools have been grouped together and are available through the SAVE program of the European Commission[A7.5]. Ground cooling models simulate the performance of earth-to-air heat exchangers and thus can help design these systems and select the necessary parameters like depth, length, diameter, air speed, etc. Similar tools are available to evaluate the performance of direct, indirect and two-stage evaporative coolers. Finally, various tools to evaluate the performance of radiative coolers coupled with water, rock bed storage or direct use of the cooled air have been developed and are available through the SAVE and ALTENER programs of the European Commission.

References to Appendix A7

[A7.1] European Commission. *PASCOOL: Final reports and CD of computerized tools.* Research Program of the European Commission, Directorate General for Science, Research and Development. Santamouris M (Co-ordinator). 1995.

[A7.2] *AIOLOS: A computerized tool to evaluate natural ventilation and passive cooling in buildings.* London, James and James Science Publishers. 1998

[A7.3] *SUMMER: A computer tool to calculate the performance of passively cooled buildings.* University of Athens, ALTENER Program, European Commission, Directorate General for Energy. 1996.

[A7.4] **LESO.** *LESOCOOL.* Developed by LESO, Ecole Polytechnique Federal de Lausanne, Switzerland. 1997.

[A7.5] **European Commission.** Final report of the SAVE program: Creation of an educational structure to provide information on the use of passive cooling systems and techniques for buildings. European Commission, Directorate General for Energy. Santamouris M (Co-ordinator). 1996.

Appendix A8. Daylight computer modelling

Many computer programs are now available which will carry out daylighting calculations, and surveys have been carried out which list their features[A8.1–A8.3]. Programs can often be quick to use and helpful; but the modelling of the external environment is a weakness in most currently available programs, which tend to concentrate on what happens to the daylight indoors.

The simplest programs assume a horizontal obstruction outdoors, parallel to the window wall. This is only suitable for the most straightforward site layouts. Other programs allow more complex obstructions to be entered, but they may contain other simplifications. Often the obstruction is itself assumed to be unobstructed; or the ground reflected light is unaffected by obstructions. This can result in daylight levels being overestimated in tight urban sites. Sometimes obstruction reflectance, or ground reflectance, cannot be varied; and it is often impossible to model sloping obstructions like pitched roofs.

More complex programs are available which can do this. They divide each external obstruction and internal room surface, into a number of elements. Reflections between each element, and every other element which can receive light from it, are then modelled, often on the basis that each surface is perfectly diffusing. Although potentially accurate, this can be time-consuming if the program models potential reflections between all the surfaces, even the tiny amounts of light which reach an external surface from an internal one.

Passport-Light is an example of this more complex type of program. It uses a ray tracing procedure: rays are emitted from each measurement point using a Monte Carlo random process. Each ray is followed as it is reflected from surface to surface, until the ray hits the hemisphere which describes the sky. Some rays are absorbed in this process. An additional function is the calculation of daylight coefficients. This can save computation time because once the file of daylight coefficients exists the calculations can be repeated for different skies without the time-consuming calculation of inter-reflections.

Direct light from the sky often forms the major contribution to daylight, and some programs are surprisingly poor at modelling it. Sometimes only a standard overcast sky can be chosen, and sunny conditions cannot be modelled. Some programs divide the sky into relatively large finite elements. Significant errors can occur if an obstruction covers only part of one of these elements. The best programs subdivide the sky very finely and can allow for irregular obstructions.

In conclusion, if considering computer modelling it is important to find out:
- what obstructions the program can model,
- how easy it is to input the obstructions,
- if it models obstruction reflectance explicitly or if it makes simplifying assumptions about how much light the obstruction and ground receive,
- if complex external obstructions require a lot of extra computer memory or result in long run times,
- how direct light is modelled and if there are errors for irregular obstructions,
- whether sunlight and non-overcast skies can be modelled.

References to Appendix A8

[A8.1] **Baker N, Fanchiotti A & Steemers K.** *Daylighting in architecture.* London, James and James, 1993.

[A8.2] **IESNA.** 1994 IESNA software survey. *Lighting Design & Application* 1994: **24**(7): 24–32.

[A8.3] **Engelsholm K O.** FRI-test af lysteknisk edb (in Danish). *Lys* 1994: **2/94**: 86–107.

Appendix B. Experimental prediction methods

Appendix B1. Wind tunnel tests

Wind tunnel testing of small-scale models remains a favoured technique for investigating local wind effects on individual buildings or groups of buildings. It is used for investigating:

- wind loading on structures,
- local wind patterns for ventilation, thermal comfort and wind exposure studies,
- the dispersion of contaminants.

The technique is very versatile and usually allows a large number of variables to be investigated quickly and easily. Water channels and water tunnels are also used for these purposes, the general principles of use remain the same despite the different working fluid.

Wind tunnel testing is of greatest use at short ranges, its practical upper limit of application being over distances of about 10 km. There is almost no lower limit of range. Within these distances it is a versatile technique and provides reliable data, both visual and numeric, which have been subject to intercomparison between facilities and effective validation studies over many decades. The basic technique is that, firstly, the windflow approaching the site is simulated at the required scale (typically around 1/200 to 1/500). If a model of the building of interest and its surroundings, or of the site or areas of interest, are placed in the airflow then the wind patterns in the area, both mean and unsteady, are correctly reproduced. From this, the scaled loads on any structures, variations in windspeed and the spreading and dispersion of contaminants around the model will follow identical behaviour to the full-scale buildings.

Wind loadings on structures can be measured directly on a model as forces, or the distribution of wind pressure on the structure's surfaces can be measured and both the overall loading and its distribution over the surface determined. This can be done for both the steady and the unsteady loads on the structure. In the latter case the effects of oscillatory loading and both the aerodynamic and structural damping can be assessed.

Wind pressures on the surfaces of buildings are also important in assessing ventilation behaviour, both for the infiltration of external air and for designed ventilation whether forced or natural. For ventilation purposes they are determined in the same way as with building loading.

Wind effects around buildings are an important feature of architectural design since they directly affect human thermal comfort and irritation due to intermittent exposure to locally strong winds. External wind-flow patterns can be visualized by smoke, or by dye in water tunnels. Also, both the mean and unsteady components of the windspeed can be measured directly at places of interest. In addition, the wind-flow patterns on the surface can be both visualized and measured directly.

Figure B1.1 Model in a wind tunnel

Figure B1.2 Smoke photograph of a dispersing plume over a building

The dispersion of contaminants on a small scale can be both highly variable and unsteady, but can be simulated readily in small-scale wind tunnel models. Normally the contaminant of interest is replaced by a tracer gas whose concentration is measured around the site at places of interest. The use of appropriate scaling laws then allows equivalent concentrations of the full-scale contaminant to be calculated. It is also readily possible to visualize the dispersion of contaminants using smoke. Wind tunnel dispersion experiments are used to investigate a great variety of air pollution problems, including the effects of buildings on local pollution discharges, determining the correct height of chimney stacks, the effects of hills and other topography on longer range dispersion, and accident scenarios involving fire plumes or the accidental escape of toxic or flammable gases.

Bibliography for Appendix B1

The references below contain descriptions of wind tunnel studies carried out for a variety of purposes and show the sort of results that can be obtained.

Rae W H & Pope A. *Low speed wind tunnel testing.* New York, Wiley. 1984.

Cook N J. *The designer's guide to wind loading of building structures.* Parts 1. London, Butterworths. 1985.

Cook N J. *The designer's guide to wind loading of building structures.* Part 2. London, Butterworths. 1990.

Cermak J E et al. *Wind climate in cities.* Proceedings NATO Advanced Study Institute, Waldbronn, Germany. Dordrecht, Kluwer Academic. 1995.

Hall D J (ed). *Proceedings 5th International Wind and Water Tunnel Dispersion Modelling Workshop,* 30 Oct–1 Nov 1991, Warren Spring Laboratory, UK. Atmospheric Environment 1994: 28(11).

ASO. *Proceedings 6th International Wind and Water Tunnel Dispersion Modelling Workshop,* 25–27th August 1993, Japan. Atmospheric Environment 1996: 30(16).

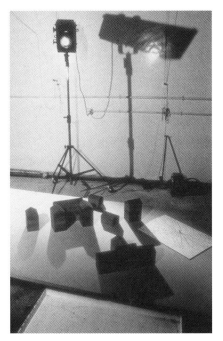

Figure B2.1 Using a spotlight to represent the sun

Appendix B2. The use of models in sunlighting studies

To assess the access to sunlight of a particular site, one option is to make a scale model of it[B2.1]. The sunlighting of the site can then be assessed with either a lamp or the real sun.

Using a lamp to represent the sun means the study can be carried out under any sky condition or even after dark, and it is possible to move the 'sun' relatively easily to simulate different times of day and year. Although specialist heliodons are available[B2.2–B2.4], any small, powerful lamp can represent the sun (a theatre spotlight is ideal). By moving the lamp up and down and rotating the model (Figure B2.1) it is possible to generate different sun positions[B2.5–B2.6]. A small sundial[B2.7–B2.8], mounted on the model, will indicate when the right time of day and year has been reached.

The main disadvantage of an artificial sun is that its rays are not parallel. If the 'sun' is too close to the model, it may apparently be a different time of day and year in different areas of the site. For best results the lamp should be at a distance of at least five times the model dimensions.

If the real sun is used, the model must be tilted and rotated to represent different times of day and year (a sundial fixed to the model, is essential here[B2.5–B2.9]). This limits the size of the model (Figure B2.2) and everything on the model must be securely fixed.

The model itself should include all the different obstructing buildings, including those adjoining the site. If photographs are used to record shadow patterns, each one should be carefully documented. This can be on a label placed inside the model so it appears on the photograph.

References to Appendix B2

[B2.1] **Littlefair P J.** Measuring daylight. *BRE Information Paper IP23/93*. Garston, CRC, 1993.

[B2.2] **Hopkinson R G, Petherbridge P & Longmore J.** *Daylighting*. London, Heinemann, 1966.

[B2.3] **Van Santen C & Hansen A J**. *Simuleren van daglicht* (simulation of daylight). Delft, Faculteit der Bouwkunde, Technische Universiteit Delft, 1991.

[B2.4] **Tregenza P R.** Daylight measurement in models: new type of equipment. *Lighting Research & Technology* 1989: **21**(4): 193–194.

[B2.5] **Baker N, Fanchiotti A & Steemers K.** *Daylighting in architecture*. London, James and James, 1993.

[B2.6] **Bell J & Burt W.** *Designing buildings for daylight*. Garston, CRC, 1995.

[B2.7] **Lynes J A.** Natural lighting: use of models. *Architect's Journal* 1968: **148**(43): 963–968.

[B2.8] **Moore F**. *Concepts and practice of architectural daylighting*. New York, Van Nostrand Reinhold, 1985.

[B2.9] **Schiler M (ed).** *Simulating daylight with architectural models*. Los Angeles, DNNA/University Southern California, 1991.

Figure B2.2 Using the real sun. This very large model had to be tilted and rotated using a dumper truck

Appendix C. Glossary

Absorptivity
The fraction of incoming solar radiation absorbed by a surface (usually used for solar radiation).

Albedo
Ratio of radiation reflected from a surface to the incoming radiation onto that surface.

Aspect ratio
Height-to-width ratio in urban configurations (streets, courtyards, etc).

Average daylight factor
Ratio of total daylight flux incident on the working plane to the area of the working plane, expressed as a percentage of the outdoor illuminance on a horizontal plane due to an unobstructed CIE Standard Overcast Sky.

Block
The smallest urban built form that could be defined by the adjacent streets. In general, the block is the simple result of the surrounding streets.

CIE Standard Overcast Sky
A completely overcast sky for which the ratio of its luminance L at an angle of elevation γ above the horizontal to the luminance L_z at the zenith is given by $L = L_z (1 + 2 \sin \gamma)$.

Daylight, natural light
Combined skylight and sunlight.

Emissivity
The ratio of the intensity of the radiation emitted by a surface at temperature T to the radiation emitted by a theoretical black-body at the same value of T.

Evapotranspiration
Process by which vegetation loses water through its leaves (transpiration) which then evaporates (evaporation) cooling the surrounding air.

Exceptional buildings
Major structures, quite different from common buildings either in their proportions, their dimensions, or their complexity. Exceptional buildings often stand out from the usual built environment as visual and/or socio-economic landmarks (for instance churches or public buildings). They help people find their way around the city.

Focal points (landmarks)

In an urban space, focal points (landmarks) are outstanding elements (built or natural) belonging to the space (or seen from the observation point). They have the strongest visual attraction for the observer. They may include built elements, monuments or parts of monuments, urban structures, squares, bridges, or views down a street. Observers select the focal points on a space in a way which depends on their individual characteristics and intentions at the time (way-finding, orientation, identification, etc).

No sky line

The outline on the working plane of the area from which no sky can be seen.

Obstruction angle

The angular altitude of the top of an obstruction above the horizontal, measured from a reference point in a vertical plane in a section perpendicular to the vertical plane.

Orthogonal projection

see Spherical projections (*Orthogonal*).

Probable sunlight hours

The long-term average of the total number of hours during a year in which direct sunlight reaches the unobstructed ground (when clouds are taken into account).

Semi-cylindrical illuminance

see section 3.1.

Sensible heat

Heat associated with the dry bulb temperature changes in moist air.

Sky opening

The sky opening is defined as ratio of the solid angle of the sky visible from a point divided by 2π, the solid angle of a complete unobstructed hemisphere. In practice, sky opening percentage is used as an indicator of the perceived confinement felt by an observer in the open space. It is a purely geometrical indicator which doesn't take into account the daylight and sunlight in the space. Sky opening indicator highlights a number of features of an urban open space, especially its level of enclosure and its legibility.

Sky view factor

Fraction of radiation from a uniformly diffusing surface in an urban configuration, which would go directly to the sky. It is proportional to the radiation reaching the surface from a uniform sky.

Spherical projections

Spherical projections are computed in two different steps: (1) projection from the 3D space to the surface of a sphere, and (2) projection from the sphere to a plane. It is the second step of the projection, from the sphere to a plane, that characterizes the properties of the different projections, since a spherical surface cannot be 'unrolled' onto a plane surface without some deformation. Three main constructions are commonly used:
- projection to a plane,
- projection to a cylinder that is unrolled on a plane,
- projection to a conical surface that is unrolled on a plane.

Five different transformations are used in morphological analysis: gnomonic, stereographic, equidistant, isoaire and cylindrical projections. Once projected onto a sphere, all objects are sized relative to their distance from the observer:

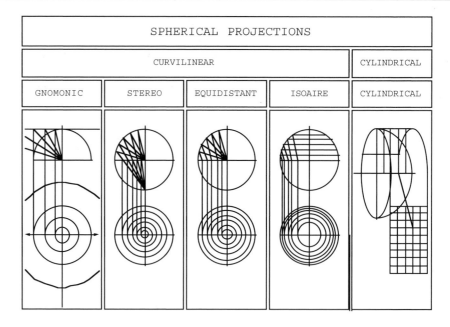

Figure C1 Construction method of 5 spherical projections

a small, nearby object can be as important in projection as a large, more distant one.

Cylindrical
A distinctive feature of cylindrical projections is that vertical lines in the 3D world remain vertical once projected onto the plane. Cylindrical projections are used as qualitative instruments that naturally put forward vertical landmarks within urban open space. It is closest to the panoramic view of an observer inspecting an open space for visual cues of orientation and landmarks.

Equidistant
Equidistant projections respect vertical angles, which means that the radial dimensions within the circle are directly proportional to the visual heights in the 3D world. Equidistant projections are needed for vertical angle visualizations and comparisons.

Gnomonic
Perspective drawings can be considered as gnomonic projections. Gnomonic projections transform great circle arcs of the sphere into lines in the projection plane. The main weakness of this projection is that, mathematically, the representation is not bounded: points can be at any distance from the projection centre.

Isoaire
In isoaire projections, areas projected onto the plane are proportional to solid angles on the sphere. This means that they can be used to compare the visual obstruction of two different elements from specific viewpoints on the site.

Orthogonal
Orthogonal projections respect the view factor between an elementary horizontal surface located at the origin of the axes and any face of the 3D model. This view factor can be directly measured as the ratio between the projected polygon representing the face and the reference circle area. As the isotropic diffuse sky component of radiation reaching a point is directly proportional to the sky view factor, it can be immediately visualized in orthogonal projections from the area of visible sky.

Stereographic

In stereographic projections the angles of tangents are conserved after projection. A circle drawn on the sphere will thus be projected as a circle in the plane. Lines crossing at right angles will be represented as curves crossing at right angles in the plane. Thus the visual aspects of 3D shapes are quite well respected by the projection.

Upside-down stereographic

Upside-down stereographic projections are stereographic projections from above the open space with their pole oriented towards ground. It is a kind of bird's eye view, only spherical: dimensions decrease with distance from the open space.

Urban air canopy

The space bounded by the city buildings up to their roofs.

Urban air dome

That portion of the planetary boundary layer whose characteristics are affected by the presence of an urban area at its lower boundary. The 'urban air dome' extends above the roof tops, to about 2–3 times the building height.

Urban form

Any identifiable geometrical shape of the urban environment can be considered as an urban form. In traditional European cities, urban form was characterized by two types of component: built elements on the one hand (blocks, monuments and so on) and, on the other hand, public open spaces or urban spaces.

Vertical sky component

Ratio of that part of illuminance, at a point on a given vertical plane, that is received directly from a CIE Standard Overcast Sky, to illuminance on a horizontal plane due to an unobstructed hemisphere of this sky.

View length (mean)

Let $F_1, F_2, ..., F_i, ..., F_n$, be the visible faces of an urban environment observed from a specific point P. The solid angles subtended by these faces are $S_1, S_2, ..., S_i, ..., S_n$ and their distances from the point P are $L_1, L_2, ..., L_i, ..., L_n$. The mean view length in the point P is equal to the mean value of the distances of these faces from the observer (L_i), weighted according to their visual obstruction (S_i). The mean view length is thus equal to:

$$L_m = \Sigma_{i=1,n}\, S_i \times L_i \,/\, \Sigma_{i=1,n}\, S_i \quad \text{metres.}$$

The mean view length is representative of the mean distance from the observer to surrounding faces. It is an absolute value, directly proportional to the dimensions of the open space. In most simple configurations, this value would thus be equal to half the dimension of the space, but in complex urban environments this is generally not true.

Working plane

The horizontal, vertical or inclined plane inside a building in which a visual task lies. Normally the working plane may be taken to be horizontal, 0.85 m above the floor in houses and factories, 0.7 m above the floor in offices.